JOHN FRÉMONT'S 100 DAYS

CLASHES AND CONVICTIONS IN CIVIL★WAR MISSOURI

GREGORY WOLK

MISSOURI HISTORICAL SOCIETY PRESS

ST. LOUIS

DISTRIBUTED BY UNIVERSITY OF CHICAGO PRESS

TO MY GRANDCHILDREN, WITH LOVE
Paige, Jack, Ashton, Beckett, and Eliza

© 2025 by Missouri Historical Society Press
ISBN 979-8-9855716-5-3

Library of Congress Cataloging-in-Publication Data

Names: Wolk, Gregory author
Title: John Frémont's 100 days : clashes and convictions in Civil War Missouri /
    Gregory Wolk.
Other titles: John Frémont's one hundred days
Description: St. Louis : Missouri Historical Society Press, [2025] |
Includes bibliographical references and index | Summary: "The first book-length study
    of John Frémont's time in Missouri written since the Civil War, revealing the story
    of the first enslaved person ever set free by military order of the United States and
    exploring six campaigns in the Trans-Mississippi theater"—Provided by publisher.
Identifiers: LCCN 2025019793 | ISBN 9798985571653 paperback
Subjects: LCSH: Frémont, John Charles, 1813-1890 | Wilson's Creek, Battle of,
    Mo., 1861 | Lexington, Battle of, Lexington, Mo., 1861 | Fredericktown, Battle
    of, Fredericktown, Mo., 1861 | Enslaved persons—Emancipation--Missouri |
    Generals—United States—Biography | Missouri—History—Civil War, 1861-1865 |
    BISAC: HISTORY / Military / Civil Wars (see also United States / Civil War Period
    (1850-1877)) | HISTORY / United States / Civil War Period (1850-1877) | LCGFT:
    Biographies
Classification: LCC E472.2 W65 2025
LC record available at
    https://url.avanan.click/v2/r01/___https://lccn.loc.gov/2025019793___.
    YXAzOm1vaGlzdG9yeTphOm86YTE3MWYxYTFmNTIzN2I1NmNm
    MWI1MTg4MTg4MWExODk6Nzpj OTZlOjg2ZmUxZjc0OWU1Yjlm
    MzFhZWJhNmY0MDkyNjgxZWQ0NjllNzAxMDdhYWViOTZh
    M2NmNmE3NmQzN2NjOGE3NDg6dDpUOk4

Distributed by University of Chicago Press
Designed by Debbie Schuller
Printed and bound in the United States by Holland Litho Printing Service
Cover image: General John C. Frémont.
Photograph by Emil Boehl, 1862. Missouri Historical Society Collections.

CONTENTS

PROLOGUE

On May 23, 1861, three enslaved men rowed a small boat to a Union bastion in Virginia called Fort Monroe. The fort was, and is still, situated on a spit of land where the James River enters the Chesapeake Bay. Lately, the men had been constructing shoreline fortifications for the fledgling Confederacy, but not of their own volition. Six weeks earlier, secessionist troops had surrounded a federal defensive installation in Charleston Harbor, which led to the Union's surrender of Fort Sumter. It would be different this time.

Benjamin Franklin Butler of Massachusetts—who became known as a famously inept military commander as the Civil War progressed—was nonetheless an astute attorney and politician. He was the first major general of volunteers appointed by President Abraham Lincoln. General Butler, along with several thousand Union troops, arrived at Fort Monroe on May 22. One of his first tasks was to entertain the demands of a Confederate officer under flag of truce. A rebel colonel claimed ownership of the three enslaved men—Frank Baker, Shepard Mallory, and James Townsend—and demanded that Butler return them to him. Applying a lawyer's logic, Butler declined: Virginia *claimed* to be a sovereign nation, and it *claimed* that these men were property of another. According to the laws of war, Butler reasoned, once the men had been used to commit acts of war directed against the United States, they could be seized as if they were arms or ammunition. In Butler's words, Baker, Mallory, and Townsend were "contrabands of war."

The US Congress was not in session in May 1861. But in July, Congress considered and passed what came to be known as the First Confiscation Act, which authorized the government to seize property, including enslaved persons, used to further the Confederate insurrection. When President Lincoln signed the act, Gen. Butler's impromptu formulation became the law of the land. The language of the act itself reveals that this step toward the abolition of slavery, small as it was, flowed naturally and logically from a doctrine of maritime law known as the right of prize and capture. This early in the Civil War, Gen. Butler and the US Congress had reached conclusions that were dictated by property law, not by any notion of human rights. Most important, Baker, Mallory, and Townsend were not freed on account of Butler's decision. Simply stated, the Union army was now the men's new employer, and that was that.

Just after midnight on May 9, 1861, a different drama had unfolded 900 miles west, when the steamboat *J. C. Swon* landed at the St. Louis levee following a run from New Orleans. The city was tense. Three days before, about 1,000 men of the Missouri Volunteer Militia assembled 6 miles west of the riverfront, in an open space called Lindell's Grove. Missouri's secessionist governor Claiborne Fox Jackson called the militia out for its annual encampment and deliberately located it in St. Louis to provoke the city's largely unionist elements. The camp was named Camp Jackson in honor of the governor; its two main streets were Davis and Beauregard. This was part of a pattern: For months, secessionists in the Deep South threatened US arsenals and took control of several of them, including those at Little Rock and Baton Rouge. The St. Louis Arsenal was the best-stocked federal arsenal in the southern and western United States.

The man charged with defending the St. Louis Arsenal was Nathaniel Lyon, a Connecticut-born abolitionist captain in the Regular Army, the nation's standing army. After Lyon arrived in St. Louis in February, he moved rapidly to take control of the local situation. He was aided immeasurably by an alliance he forged with the Blair brothers of St. Louis and Washington City, as the nation's capital was then known: Francis (Frank) Preston Blair Jr., a United States congressman, and Montgomery Blair, Lincoln's postmaster general. As pressure mounted in April, open hostility developed between the Blairs and Brigadier General William S. Harney, commander of the US Army's Department of the West. Harney, one of only four general officers in the nation's peacetime army, was a Tennessean who'd married into a wealthy, slave-owning St. Louis family. The Blairs thought that Harney was too susceptible to Southern influence to handle the evolving crisis in St. Louis. One point of contention was the enlistment of a home guard to protect Union interests, a group of men Frank Blair and Capt. Lyon were surreptitiously organizing, particularly among the immigrant population in south St. Louis. On April 21, 1861, the Blairs and their allies managed to have Gen. Harney recalled to Washington City, clearing the way for Lyon's ascent to command.

In an order endorsed by Abraham Lincoln, on April 30, Secretary of War Simon Cameron directed Lyon to ramp up his efforts to enlist pro-Union armed forces.

When the *J. C. Swon* docked in St. Louis in the dark, early-morning hours of May 9, it ignited a very short fuse. An explosion was imminent. The *Swon* had stopped in Baton Rouge on its way north, where men carried aboard tons of ordnance, arms, and ammunition from the Baton Rouge Arsenal. This act was approved by Jefferson Davis, president of the Confederacy, who was aware of the plan to force the surrender of the St. Louis Arsenal. Agents of the militia carted this load to Camp Jackson, believing they had successfully evaded detection. Capt. Lyon knew all about the scheme—and might have interrupted the conveyance—but instead he merely tracked its delivery. It was a sting: By this means, Lyon could establish intent to use stolen US property to attack the arsenal at St. Louis.

Lyon had also just learned that Gen. Harney had been reinstated and would arrive to resume command of the Western Department on May 11. So on May 10, 1861, Lyon marched 7,000 men to Camp Jackson, surrounded it, and exacted the surrender of the militiamen encamped there. But while the captured men were under guard, a terrible incident occurred. A company of one of the German regiments fired into the amassed prisoners and into a crowd of onlookers, leaving 28 civilians and 3 militiamen dead; many more were injured. Arguments persist about the extent of provocation, or the absence of it, but this is certain: The massacre at Camp Jackson started a hot war for control of the Trans-Mississippi West.

Step forward two weeks to the arrival of the enslaved Baker, Mallory, and Townsend at Virginia's Fort Monroe. On May 22, just hours before Gen. Butler arrived with his troops to take control of that fortress, the *J. C. Swon* was resting in a quiet cove of the Mississippi, 30 miles south of St. Louis. There is no telling where the renegade vessel had been since it took part in the Camp Jackson affair, but by then, it had to be obvious to the steamer's crew—as well as to army authorities in St. Louis—that it would not escape the wrath of Nathaniel Lyon. Civilian steamboat traffic north of Memphis had been shut down days earlier. The *Swon* had no place to go.

Manned only by a watchman, a first mate, and several deckhands, the *Swon* bobbed in the predawn hours on the Missouri side of the river, near the hamlet of Herculaneum. At 4am on May 22, the side-wheeler *Iatan* slipped into the channel from the wharf at the St. Louis Arsenal with 100 soldiers of the 4th Regiment Missouri Volunteers onboard. These veterans of the capture of Camp Jackson were on the hunt for the infamous *J. C. Swon*. When the *Iatan* reached Herculaneum at 7am, the *Swon*'s crew offered no resistance. This was a more conventional case of the right of prize and capture. For its part in aiding Missouri insurrectionists, Lyon saw to it that the *J. C. Swon* was condemned and pressed into service for the Union.

★ ★ ★

Thomas Hart Benton.
Unknown photographer, ca. 1855.
Missouri Historical Society Collections.

Thomas Hart Benton, Missouri's first full-term United States senator, was the first senator in American history to serve five consecutive terms, from 1821 to 1851. His 30 years in office, as well as his skills as an orator, brought him into a league of senator-statesmen that also included Henry Clay, Daniel Webster, and John Calhoun.[1] Benton staked out a unique position on the critical question of slavery's future in the United States. He would become the Senate's leading "Free Soil" Democrat, a movement that tolerated slavery in the South but opposed its spread into new Western territories. Many politicians in the "border states"—Maryland, Kentucky, and Missouri—held the same view. But the arguments posed by Free Soil Democrats, as well as those who argued for slavery's immediate and total abolition, reached a new level of intensity late in 1848, when news of the California gold strike reached the

East Coast. It was then clear that the compromises of old wouldn't be sustained as the nation pushed west to the Pacific.

During President Andrew Jackson's administration, Thomas Benton had forged an alliance with Francis Preston Blair of Maryland. Benton and Blair were members of Jackson's so-called Kitchen Cabinet, a group of men who informally advised him on policy. What's more, Senator Benton had married into the Preston family in 1821, when he wed Elizabeth Preston McDowell, a Virginian who shared a common ancestor with Francis Preston Blair.

The Bentons did not fit squarely within mid-19th-century stereotypes. Although Senator Benton declared in 1849 that "[his] sentiments are against the institution of slavery, and against its introduction into places in which it does not exist," it is also true that he owned enslaved persons throughout his entire adult life. His wife, who grew up near Lexington, Virginia, was the daughter of a slave owner, but her brother (a former Virginia governor), as a member of Congress in 1850, voted to admit California to the Union as a free state.

Seven children were born to Thomas Hart Benton and Elizabeth Preston McDowell, including a middle daughter named Jessie Ann. In 1841, Jessie married John Charles Frémont.

John C. Frémont initially worked as a topographical engineer. Through the influence of his mentor, prominent South Carolina politician Joel Roberts Poinsett, he was soon commissioned second lieutenant in the US Army Corps of Topographical Engineers. Just as quickly, Frémont was assigned to assist geographer, astronomer, and mathematician Joseph Nicollet on a two-year expedition to the Northern Plains, which departed in June 1838. In the meantime, Poinsett joined President Martin Van Buren's cabinet as secretary of war. After the expedition, Frémont moved to Washington.

At the same time, Jessie Benton and her older sister, Sarah, were attending a finishing school called Miss English's Seminary for Young Ladies in Georgetown. The sisters boarded there, even though the school was just a few miles from the family's home on C Street in Washington City, close to the US Capitol.

John Frémont and Thomas Benton had much in common. With his passion for westward expansion, Senator Benton was certainly intrigued to meet the accomplished topographical engineer. Frémont visited the Benton home many times after he was first introduced to the senator, but Sarah and Jessie were always away at school. Frémont finally met Jessie when he escorted Sarah to a concert at Miss English's Seminary. One could say that Frémont was awe-struck by the encounter. Jessie was 15 years old. John was 27. Jessie's concerned parents watched closely; they could see that romance was in the offing. To squelch the relationship, Senator Benton went so far as to pull strings so the army would send Frémont on another Western expedition, this time to Iowa. Frémont returned to Washington from that journey during the summer of 1841, and in October of that year, John and Jessie eloped.

The Bentons were angry when they learned of the elopement, of course, but they eventually warmed to Frémont. The father and son-in-law's shared interest in Western exploration would win out. Meanwhile, Frémont had concluded that the life of an explorer and adventurer was the life for him. With Senator Benton's active support and patronage throughout the 1840s, Frémont organized and led four separate expeditions to the lands west of the American frontier (in 1842, 1843–1844, 1845–1847, and 1848–1849). As Jessie spent most of the decade in Washington without his company, she lent her talents as a writer to produce detailed reports from his notes. These reports became bestsellers.

The 1840s in the United States were punctuated by the Mexican-American War, which lasted from 1846 to 1848. While away on his third expedition beginning in 1845, Frémont, now a major in the US Army, brought his band of explorers into California. War clouds were gathering along the Rio Grande in Texas, but fighting had not yet broken out. Frémont stumbled and bumbled his way into becoming—in the public eye, at least—the conqueror of California by supporting a group of American settlers who had declared California an independent republic.

But Frémont ran into serious trouble when Gen. Stephen Watts Kearny arrived in January 1847. By this time, the war with Mexico was in full swing, and Kearny was prepared to take possession of California. Maj. Frémont did not immediately acknowledge Kearny's authority over him, an act of insubordination for which he was court-martialed in Washington and convicted of in January 1848. President Polk offered Frémont clemency if he returned to his military duties, but instead Frémont resigned his commission: To him, accepting clemency was to admit that he had been wrong.

Frémont's third expedition had another lasting impact on the family's future. By 1845, Frémont had become enamored with California, so much so that he contemplated relocating there. He arranged for a man to acquire property for him near San Francisco Bay. Against Frémont's wishes, the man purchased some 44,000 acres high in the foothills of the Sierra Nevada, nowhere near the settlements of American newcomers. This acquisition was largely forgotten, but by the time Frémont arrived in California as a civilian for his fourth expedition, gold had been found at Sutter's Mill. The Frémonts' 44,000 acres, known as Rancho Las Mariposas, was the site of a major discovery of the yellow metal. Overnight, the Frémonts had become rich, to a degree almost beyond comprehension.

John Frémont traveled extensively throughout the 1850s, including a final cross-country trek in 1854. John and Jessie traveled together back and forth to San Francisco, and to England and Europe, on several occasions. John became one of the first US senators from California, and in 1856, he was the new Republican Party's candidate for president. He lost the general election to James Buchanan.

Whenever luck visited John Frémont's life, loss invariably followed. In the case of his Mariposa holdings, which had evolved into an industrial-grade mining venture, the good times lasted nearly a decade. Nevertheless, by the time the Civil War broke out, the mines were more of a burden than an asset. They were hit by the bust that followed the California boom, but more to the point, Frémont had put too much trust in the people he'd hired to manage his affairs during his many absences. It seems his aptitude for judging people was surpassed in the negative only by his poor business sense.

ENDNOTE

1. Henry Clay of Kentucky, Daniel Webster of Massachusetts, and John Calhoun of South Carolina became known as the "Great Triumvirate"; they dominated the debates over slavery and sectionalism in the decades before the Civil War. Serving together in the US Senate near the end of their careers, the three were instrumental in passing legislation that became part of the Compromise of 1850, which admitted California to the Union as a free state.

CHAPTER

1

"I will be in St. Louis Thursday morning."

—Maj. Gen. John C. Frémont

Figure 1

Born in Savannah, Georgia, on January 21, 1813, John Frémont (whose actual surname was Frémon) was a bright but unruly student. He studied science at the College of Charleston but was expelled three months before he was set to graduate. Frémont had the good fortune to meet and impress Charleston native Joel Roberts Poinsett—a famed scholar, diplomat, and naturalist—who became the young man's mentor and introduced him to the political scene in Washington City, changing the trajectory of his life.

Telegraph office, Steubenville and Indiana Railroad

Coshocton, Ohio, July 23, 1861

IN EARLY JULY 1861, John Frémont arrived in New York after spending nearly six months in London and Paris. Frémont was already famous for his explorations across North America and for his part in splitting off California from Mexico in the 1840s. However, his trip abroad was purely business—at least, it had started out that way. For a man of Frémont's achievements, it was a sad and challenging journey. With a lawyer in tow and a prospectus in hand, Frémont went to Europe to seek investors to help bail out his California mining ventures. He left the United States from the Port of New York in February 1861, just as the nation was ready to explode into war.

In May, President Lincoln appointed Frémont a major general in the United States Army and assigned him to command the Western Department—an enormous territory that included the state of Illinois and the states (and prospective states) west of there, all the way to the Rockies. The assignment became effective once Frémont stepped back on US soil. The general must've thought to himself: *Here is an assignment that would fulfill my true destiny for greatness.*

Frémont tried to perform his military duties from New York as he waited for the arrival of his family from California. Meanwhile, in Missouri, a young lawyer by the name of Chester Harding Jr. was the acting assistant adjutant who was ably managing Frémont's administrative affairs. Harding and others were urging him to proceed to St. Louis posthaste and take command in person. Then, on July 21, 1861, the Union army suffered a crushing defeat near Manassas in Virginia.

Frémont knew he would be accused of dawdling in New York. He watched as the telegraph operator tapped out his short message to Adjutant Harding, then boarded the train bound for the West.

In 1860, Jessie Frémont purchased 12 acres of prime real estate in an area of the San Francisco Peninsula known as Black Point.[1] Before Mexico lost control of California in 1848, this sharp bluff near the Golden Gate Strait was called Point San Jose. In the 1850s, the area was developed for residential use by a Massachusetts man named Leonidas Haskell. A cottage came with the land.

Jessie Benton Frémont at her Black Point home overlooking San Francisco Bay, ca. 1861. Courtesy of the California Historical Society at Stanford University, Carleton E. Watkins Collection.

Jessie had good reason to believe that her family could at last come to rest at Black Point. Since the early 1840s, she had given birth to five children. When the 1860s dawned, daughter Elizabeth (known as Lily) was nearly 18 years old. She had been born in 1842, when John was away on his first expedition to the West. The Frémonts lost a son, Benton, in 1848, and a daughter, Ann, in 1853, each in the first year of life. John Charles Jr. was born in San Francisco in 1851, and Francis Preston Frémont arrived in 1855, in Washington City.[2]

The family had lived together in California from 1857 to 1859. After John Frémont lost the presidential election in 1856, he decided to move to the Mariposa estate and attempt to manage the mines himself, a task he'd previously farmed out to others. It was a trying time for Jessie and the children, though Jessie certainly made the best of things. They lived high in the Sierra Nevada near the mines, in a frame, whitewashed home. Jessie liked to refer to it as the "White House"—with a hint of sarcasm, no doubt. But Jessie was not raised and educated to be a pioneer woman. Instead, Black Point would suit her just fine.

Jessie poured herself into making the Black Point cottage a home, and she enveloped herself in a neighborhood of friends. Black Point was a sort of outpost for New Englanders who had followed the gold fever to California. Leonidas and Sarah Haskell resided at Black Point, as did neighbors Joseph C. Palmer and his wife, Martha. These families came to California from Gloucester and Nantucket, Massachusetts, respectively. Jessie's circle of friends would widen to include budding author and poet Bret Harte, as well as famous Boston preacher and orator Thomas Starr King. An ardent abolitionist and unionist, King had moved to San Francisco in 1860 and continued his campaign against secessionism. With all of Jessie's energy behind it, the Frémont home became "San Francisco's first literary and political salon."[3] Indeed, when the novelist Herman Melville landed in San Francisco after sailing around Cape Horn, he made his way to Jessie's Black Point home.[4]

Although John Frémont had campaigned for president on a promise of "Free Soil, Free Men, and Frémont"—and although Jessie's father had, for a Westerner with Southern roots, a relatively enlightened approach to the future of slavery—one has the sense that it was Jessie Frémont, not her husband and not her father, who first crossed the threshold from racial politics to moral certitude.

John Frémont's business connections in California began with Leonidas Haskell, a successful merchant. The Frémonts' other Black Point neighbor, Joseph Palmer, was a principal in the banking house Palmer, Cook & Company; he managed the Mariposa mines under lease from the Frémonts during the early 1850s. John Frémont created connections with other men of finance and independent means, including Isaiah C. Woods, manager of the Adams Express Company; Elias L. Beard, a pioneering California agriculturist; and William T. Sherman, agent to a St. Louis banking house. Frémont also formed a close bond with George W. Wright, who, like Palmer, was a Nantucket native. He was an original partner of Palmer, Cook & Company, as well as the first person to serve in the US House of Representatives from

California. Frémont and Wright were aboard the same steamer to the East Coast in 1850, Wright to take his seat in the House of Representatives in the nation's capital and Frémont to take his in the Senate.

Then there were the lawyers. Frederick Billings, a Vermonter, arrived in California in April 1849. He is purported to be the first man to open a law office in San Francisco. By 1861 his firm, Halleck, Peachy & Billings, was by far the state's most prominent. Amid the Gold Rush, contested land claims and boundaries, and the banks and speculators who followed, there was plenty of legal work to be done. Even the firm's name signaled its prominence. Henry Wager Halleck, known derisively during his army career as "Old Brains," joined the firm in 1854. While serving in the Mexican-American War, he'd only reached the rank of captain, but during the Civil War, he would rise to the Union army's highest posts. Billings's future would prove no less impressive. He became president of the Northern Pacific Railway, and Billings, Montana, is named for him. Later, after he returned to his home in Woodstock, Vermont, Billings poured his attention into the conservation movement, perhaps his best-known legacy.

Another lawyer of note was Vermonter Trenor W. Park, who followed his wife's family to California in 1852. He was a valuable addition to Billings's firm, and later, Frémont's principal attorney. He took over the management of the Mariposa mines in 1860, primarily to protect loans made and liabilities incurred on Frémont's account as the mines waned. In the long run, Park profited immensely from his involvement with John Frémont, building a fortune that may have rivaled Billings's own.[5]

Halleck, Peachy & Billings became connected to John Frémont when Palmer, Cook & Company came on as one of Frederick Billings's early clients. While Frémont served in the United States Senate, conducted his fifth and final cross-country expedition, and ran a presidential campaign, his Mariposa holdings had been largely under the management of Joseph Palmer and his company. The mines, once a seemingly inexhaustible source of wealth, began to fail under the cost of Palmer's leadership. On top of that, Frémont was embroiled in litigation to establish his rights to the land that comprised the Mariposa mines. This troublesome issue finally ended when the United States Supreme Court confirmed Frémont's ownership in early 1856. In July of that year, though, public officials uncovered a financial fraud in which Palmer, Cook & Company was implicated, bringing about the firm's bankruptcy. An estimated 200 San Francisco commercial firms—10 percent of the total that had been in business since 1850—failed in the ensuing panic.

Late in 1860, Billings organized a trip to England and France, ostensibly to enlist new investors for the troubled Mariposa venture. For Frémont, this meant another long passage from San Francisco to New York by way of the Isthmus of Panama. About February 1, 1861, a party consisting of John Frémont and his friend George Wright, with their retinues, arrived in New York. Another contingent, which included Billings and Park, took the same route on another vessel and arrived in New York later. The combined party was to then board a transatlantic steamer bound for England, but first Frémont spoke face-to-face with president-elect Abraham Lincoln. On the night of February 19, 1861, it so happened that both Lincoln and Frémont stayed at Manhattan's Astor House.[6] As conveyed by professor Allan Nevins in his landmark 1939 biography *John Frémont: Pathmarker of the West*, the two had a cordial discussion about what role Frémont might play in Lincoln's administration. Interestingly, Frémont penned a letter from the Astor House on February 22, which must have reached Lincoln after he arrived in Washington, wherein Frémont gave Montgomery Blair a ringing endorsement for a seat in Lincoln's cabinet.[7]

Montgomery Blair. Carte de visite by E. and H. Anthony, New York, 1861–1876. Brady-Handy Collection, Library of Congress, Prints and Photographs Division.

Trenor Park had a personal stake in the enlistment of investors abroad, as did Frederick Billings. For much of their acquaintance, Billings had not represented Frémont in a personal capacity. According to Billings's biographer Robin Winks, Billings had acquired a one-eighth interest in the Mariposa mines in 1857, and by 1860, he and Park each owned one-eighth to Frémont's five-eighths. Billings took an additional one-sixteenth interest in the mines in exchange for representing Frémont and organizing the European trip.

Once the parties arrived in New York, Billings was unnerved. First, he was upset to learn that George Wright had accompanied Frémont on the trip from California, and that Wright proposed to join the others on the overseas voyage. It seems Billings was concerned that Wright—Frémont's oldest California acquaintance—would influence Frémont in a way that could temper the influence that Billings himself intended to wield. Second, and perhaps more troubling: A woman named Margaret Corbett accompanied Frémont on his trip from California, and rumors swirled about their relationship.[8] She also proposed to board the England-bound steamer, along with her young child.

If there were any question about whose financial interests were paramount on this trip, Billings is said to have remarked to Park: "If Col. Frémont allows Wright or anything else to interfere, it will be sufficient cause for you and I to look after our own interests."[9]

The Frémont/Billings party arrived in London in March 1861 and went about their planned business. For a while, Frémont and Billings split their time between London and Paris, but after Fort Sumter was fired upon in April, they focused on protecting their government back home. Frémont and Billings joined an effort already in place to acquire arms and armaments for the Union cause. Furthermore, Union agents were to outbid their Confederate counterparts to deprive the opposition of crucial arms. As far as the trip's original intent is concerned, one biographer of Frémont said simply, "[Frémont] soon found that the threat of civil war made it impossible to raise money for Mariposa on any acceptable terms."[10] Frémont returned to the United States, landing at the Port of Boston on June 27, 1861, and arriving in New York a few days later. He checked in to the Astor House, and there he waited. And waited.

The military and political tensions in St. Louis and in Missouri had not abated since the bloody incident at Camp Jackson on May 10, 1861. Nathaniel Lyon still dictated the state's Union fortunes, although he was now a brigadier general of the Missouri Volunteers. On May 17, Lyon was overwhelmingly elected to that post by the same body of men, mostly German Americans, whom he had enrolled in St. Louis before the Camp Jackson incident. His election was confirmed days later when Lincoln commissioned Lyon to this rank.

Lyon drew much of his strength and power from the Blair family. Francis Preston Blair Sr. remained in Maryland, his role in Missouri politics decidedly indirect. (Hereafter, the senior Blair will be referred to as Preston, as he had been during his lifetime.) Two of Preston's sons, Frank and Montgomery, had strong ties to St. Louis.[11]

Francis Preston Blair Sr. Carte de visite by Alexander Gardner, ca. 1862. Missouri Historical Society Collections.

In late April, the Blairs used a political bludgeon to cause the resident commanding general, William S. Harney, to be recalled to Washington, allowing Lyon to take charge in St. Louis. The timing of Lyon's capture of the Missouri Volunteer Militia was in part dictated by the knowledge that the militia had taken possession of captured US armaments, but even more so because Gen. Lyon knew that Gen. Harney would arrive in St. Louis on May 11 to resume his position of command.

Upon Harney's arrival, the fears of the Blair brothers were realized: Harney spent the rest of the month playing nice with Missouri secessionists. Harney had entered into an ill-conceived agreement with Missouri governor Claiborne Jackson to cooperate in the defense of Missouri. This did not sit well in Washington; Harney was permanently removed from command on May 30, 1861. When Lyon took over command, he rejected Harney's previous agreement but arranged for Jackson, General Sterling Price, and others to travel to St. Louis, ostensibly to discuss new arrangements for cooperation between his army and the state.[12] State officials arrived on June 11, and all repaired to a room in St. Louis's finest hotel, the Planter's House. Frank Blair was also present. The meeting ended when Lyon stood up, faced his opponents, and delivered a classic harangue against states' rights:

Rather than concede to the State of Missouri for one single instant the right to dictate to my Government in any matter however unimportant, I would see you, and you, and you, and you, and every man, woman, and child in the State, dead and buried.[13]

Frank Blair, at least, was not surprised. At a time when many people in Missouri and elsewhere had hoped to quell the coming resort to arms, Gen. Lyon was outrageously aggressive in his politics, as well as his tactics. The Blair brothers recognized this quality in him, and after Camp Jackson did their level best to provide Lyon free rein in the West.

On June 13, 1861, Lyon issued an extraordinary order that placed young Chester Harding Jr., an assistant adjutant, in charge of "carrying out the proper policy of the government" in St. Louis while the Union army awaited a commander for the Western Department. For the next six weeks, this brand-new desk soldier was the point person for the US War Department's hopes and plans for fighting a war in the western United States.

On June 14, with 2,000 of his recruits on four river steamers (including the *Iatan* and the *J. C. Swon*), Lyon set off for Jefferson City, Missouri's state capital. The force arrived there on June 15 to find that Governor Jackson, along with the rest of the government officials who supported him, had fled when they learned Lyon was on his way. With a newly constituted military force called the Missouri State Guard, Governor Jackson took position near the town of Boonville, about 50 miles upstream on the Missouri River.

The Missouri State Guard was hastily put together in May 1861, one day after the Camp Jackson incident. For the months that followed, it fought as an independent force allied with Confederate troops.[14] Although the State Guard was disorganized in its first weeks, the men who comprised it were, for the most part, seasoned soldiers. These were largely the same men and officers who had injected themselves into the Kansas strife of the 1850s.

Lyon paused only briefly in Jefferson City. His force, minus three companies left to garrison the town, reboarded the transports on June 16. The Union soldiers disembarked below Boonville at dawn the next day, soon engaging the Confederate-aligned Missouri State Guard on the road into town. Lyon's troops routed the small contingent of pro-Southern guardsmen, driving it 7 or 8 miles into the town proper. There were 81 casualties suffered in the Battle of Boonville (31 of them Union), a virtual tie with the casualty count from the war's largest battle fought thus far.

Lyon's strategy was to put the Missouri State Guard in flight to the south, where it would be met by a pincer force of two regiments of infantry—overwhelmingly German American—and two batteries of artillery, commanded by Colonel Franz Sigel. Sigel's column left St. Louis on June 12, 1861, but there were logistical challenges to overcome: The route from St. Louis to southwest Missouri was only partially serviced by a railroad. Troops and supplies left Rolla in east-central Missouri, then the railroad's terminus, by a tangle of roads that snaked through the Ozarks' high country. Still, on July 2, 1861, Sigel was where he needed to be, when he needed to be there: Neosho, a county seat a few miles south of modern-day Joplin.

Unfortunately, Lyon had been detained in Boonville while he gathered wagons and horses to support the long overland march to the state's southwest. Indeed, when Sigel's troops bedded down for their first night in Neosho, Gen. Lyon had not yet left Boonville. Lyon departed on July 3 with 2,700 infantry, 4 cannon, and a long and cumbersome baggage train. It would take him 10 days to reach Springfield, southwest Missouri's chief population center. Meanwhile, the Missouri State Guard kept moving rapidly south, its destination the extreme southwest corner of the state (where Arkansas and Oklahoma now border Missouri), where it was relatively safe to come to rest—and train and equip this new army.

At Neosho, Col. Sigel was not in regular communication with his commander, Gen. Lyon. Sigel had his own plan: His intelligence sources brought news that a small column of secessionists was south of his position. This was true. The column supported Gen. Sterling Price and his immediate staff, and it was moving toward Arkansas to confer with Confederate army officials. By the time Sigel completed preparations to attack Price's camp, he learned it had been abandoned. The main southbound column of the State Guard, operating under the command of Governor Jackson, was somewhere to the north.[15] Sigel determined to consolidate the forces under his command and march in search of Jackson, last reported to have been in Barton County, some 20 miles from his position. According to Sigel's after-action report, when he left Neosho on July 4, he thought Lyon was near to Jackson's rear. He was wrong.

On that Independence Day, Sigel marched north from Neosho to the town of Diamond Grove. After consolidating his troops there, they marched 12 miles due north to Carthage, the county seat of Jasper County. While camped on the outskirts of town, Sigel learned that the southbound force of the State Guard was 15 miles ahead of him. He roused his 1,100 men at dawn on July 5, then marched north from Carthage approximately 9 miles, where his two regiments met the Missouri State Guard's infantry, cavalry, and artillery. Jackson's force outnumbered Sigel's 4 to 1. The Union men, bolstered by excellent cannonading, fought their way back to Carthage in a textbook retreat. The Missouri State Guard fought well and valiantly. Nevertheless, the two little armies accomplished nothing except to incur 118 casualties between them. This was now the highest casualty count of any battle since the Civil War began.

Eight days after Carthage, on July 13, Gen. Lyon and about 5,000 effectives finally rolled into Springfield. Lyon initially complained to Harding via wire that stores he had ordered from St. Louis had not arrived; he sounded angry and desperate.[16] It was perhaps an effort to soften the criticism he was bound to receive for his failed march from Boonville to Springfield. While it's true that his weary troops needed to be fed, the time Lyon lost on the march meant that the Missouri State Guard had achieved its objective. Gen. Lyon had little to do in Springfield but wait while Gen. Price's command rested at Cowskin Prairie, in the state's far southwest corner. In the three weeks that followed, the State Guard would turn itself into a formidable foe.

On July 3, 1861, while Lyon was marching out of Boonville and Sigel was contemplating his next moves—and while Frémont was resting at the Astor House in New York—Adjutant General Lorenzo Thomas issued an order assigning Frémont to command the army of the Western Department. The language of the order is curious, to say the least: "The State of Illinois and the States and Territories west of the Mississippi river, and on this side of the Rocky Mountains…*will in future* constitute a separate military command, to be known as the Western Department, under the command of Major-General Frémont." (emphasis added)

Just as curious, the one man who should have known the details, Assistant Adjutant Harding, felt the need to ask Union colonel Benjamin Prentiss nearly two weeks later: "Have you official notice that General Frémont is our department commander?"[17]

As had been the case in April, when the Blair brothers engineered the removal of Gen. Harney in favor of Gen. Lyon, they had engaged in another high-stakes political maneuver, which likely affected the assignment process and its timing. On June 18, Harding received a telegram from Maj. Gen. George McClellan asserting that Missouri had been placed under his command; McClellan was also commanding the Department of the Ohio from headquarters in Cincinnati. The Blairs were aghast that military operations in Missouri could come under the control of an officer in another state, so they began a push to establish a Western Department of the army that would be headquartered in St. Louis. This effort culminated in Lorenzo Thomas's July 3 order.[18]

For the month after he appeared on the scene, McClellan technically held command of Union forces in Missouri, but his sparse correspondence with Harding reveals that he took little interest in the state. As late as July 15, 1861, as Frémont was finally making arrangements to travel to St. Louis to accept command, McClellan still believed he was commanding in Missouri. Harding stated in his July 15 cable to Prentiss, "Have you received General McClellan's dispatch of to-day? If so, what's your plan?" Prentiss responded that he had received McClellan's dispatch, but he had not been officially advised that Frémont was in charge. As for how he'd respond to McClellan's dispatch, Prentiss's plan was to do whatever "[he] could do if ordered by major-general commanding."[19] These communications seem to suggest that Thomas's order establishing the Western Department "in future" was suppressed for half of July so that McClellan would not have full knowledge of it.[20]

When the Blairs set out to reverse the conditions that had brought McClellan into the equation—after they lobbied Lincoln to establish the grand Western Department—they'd also decided to advocate for John Charles Frémont to lead it. Thanks to the Blairs, Frémont would re-enter the service of his country with a rank and responsibility that few independent observers would have thought him fit to occupy.

ENDNOTES

1. Jessie Frémont held the title for the Black Point property. See Senate Committee on Military Affairs Report no. 898 (1892). It is not clear from the record why John Frémont was not listed on the 1860 deed, but several possibilities exist, including that Jessie had inherited from her father's estate following his death in 1858 and, as a result, controlled funds in her own name. Further, John Frémont's financial viability might have been in question as the mines continued to deteriorate.

2. Three-month-old Benton Frémont died in St. Louis in October 1848, as Jessie was preparing to travel by steamboat to Westport, Missouri, to see her husband before he departed on an overland expedition. Benton is buried in St. Louis's Bellefontaine Cemetery. Also worthy of note: Francis Preston Frémont, John and Jessie's youngest child, was born in Washington City in 1855; his godparents were Preston Blair and his wife, Elizabeth Gist Blair.

3. Lois Rather, *Jessie Frémont at Black Point* (Rather Press, 1974), 24; Allan Nevins, *Frémont: Pathmarker of the West* (University of Nebraska Press, 1939), 467–468.

4. National Park Service, "Jessie Benton Frémont: Anti-Slavery Advocacy at Black Point," September 28, 2020. Melville stopped briefly in San Francisco in October 1860, during an around-the-world sailing trip that he ultimately aborted there. See also Charles A. Fracchia, "Melville in San Francisco," *The Book Club of California Quarterly News-Letter* 42 (Spring 1977): 35–39.

5. Hubert H. Bancroft, *History of California: Vol. 24, 1860–1890* (The History Company, 1890), 173–189; "Commercial and Agricultural Development in California in the Fifties," *American Trust Review of the Pacific* 13 (February 15, 1924): 34–35.

6. Abraham Lincoln was traveling by train from Springfield, Illinois, to New York City ahead of his March 4 inauguration. Two of the four military officers Lincoln invited to accompany him to Washington were John Pope and David Hunter. These men would play significant parts in the drama that unfolded in Missouri during Frémont's 100 days.

7. As to the Astor House meeting, see Nevins, 470–471. Nevins notes that the Blair family had been cool to the idea of Frémont's elevation to a high military or civilian post. For Frémont's endorsement of Montgomery Blair, see Abraham Lincoln Papers: General Correspondence, 1833–1916, Series 1. Letter, John C. Frémont to Abraham Lincoln, February 22, 1861. Library of Congress, Washington, DC.

8. Robin W. Winks, *Frederick Billings, A Life* (University of California Press, 1991), 121–123, contains a detailed description of the financial dealings that tied Frederick Billings and Trenor Park to the Mariposa operation when they departed for Europe in 1861. Mary Lee Spence provides a treasure trove about George Wright and his long friendship with John Frémont in her story "George W. Wright: Politician, Lobbyist, Entrepreneur," *Pacific Historical Review* 58 (August 1989): 345–359. Winks and Spence both address the controversy involving Margaret Corbett, as does Andrew Rolle, whose rendition contains the most detail. See Winks, 133–134; Spence, 352–353; Rolle, *John Charles Frémont: Character as Destiny* (University of Oklahoma Press, 1991), 187–188. Rolle makes a particularly convincing case that Frémont and Corbett had an affair. Two things about Corbett are important to the development of the narrative contained in Rolle's volume: first, that Jessie Frémont learned about the alleged affair, and second, that Montgomery Blair may have been enlisted, either by his father or by George Wright, to help cover it up.

9. Spence, 352. However it was that Trenor Park and Frederick Billings acquired their interests in the Mariposa mines, they certainly were entitled to protect them. After returning from Europe without successfully securing financial backing, Park continued to manage the mines until the operation was sold in 1863. Park went on to become a financier and stock speculator in New York. Many years later, Park played his hand in a high-stakes contest with Jay Gould and barely lost out. This prompted San Francisco newspaper the *Argonaut* to editorialize about the man some San Franciscans would never forget: "We remember Park, when he came to California, a boy in his teens, small in size, a wiry, active, Scotch terrier sort of man; he joined the firm of Halleck, Peachy and Billings, made a fortune from the sale of the Mariposa Estate for himself and his friends...."

10. Nevins, 471.

11. Montgomery Blair lived in St. Louis from 1839 to 1853 and served as its mayor from 1842 to 1843.

12. Sterling Price was born in Virginia in 1809. After entering politics in Missouri as a young man, he commanded Missouri militia troops in New Mexico during the Mexican-American War. He rode his fame to the Missouri governor's seat, a position he held from 1853 to 1857. Price was a natural choice to command the Missouri State Guard; then-Governor Claiborne Fox Jackson appointed him to the position in 1861, and Price held that role when the Planter's House conference took place on June 11, 1861.

13. Thomas L. Snead, *The Fight for Missouri: From the Election of Lincoln to the Death of Lyon* (J. J. Little & Co., 1886), 199–200. Thomas Snead was the adjutant general of the Missouri State Guard when he attended the Planter's House conference. Snead is important to the Civil War in Missouri for two reasons. First, in 1886, he published his account of the events that took place in his home state, a work that has been acclaimed as accurate and nonpartisan. Second, he owned the two enslaved men Frémont freed. As far as Nathaniel Lyon's states-rights speech at the conference is concerned, Snead could be excused for embellishing it to some extent, particularly because he didn't make a record of the speech until 25 years after it was given. Also see James W. Erwin, *Guerrillas in Civil War Missouri* (The History Press, 2012), 24–25 (Camp Jackson and aftermath).

14. Members of the Missouri State Guard would enroll in the Confederate army during the winter of 1861–1862.

15. After an unspecified illness surfaced just as the State Guard was preparing its battle position east of Boonville, Sterling Price took leave of his army. He was still absent two weeks later, which is why Missouri's sitting governor, Claiborne Jackson, took command of the State Guard in the field at the Battle of Carthage.

16. *Official Records of the Union and Confederate Armies, Ser. 1, Vol. 3, Ch. 10* (Government Printing Office, 1881), 494. On July 13, Lyon directed a wire from Springfield to Adj. Gen. Lorenzo Thomas in Washington that read, "My effective force will soon be reduced by discharge of three-months' volunteers to about 4,000 men, including the Illinois regiment now on the march from Rolla. Governor Jackson will soon have in this vicinity not less than 30,000. I must have at once an additional force of 10,000 men, or abandon my position. All must have supplies and clothing."

17. *Official Records*, 394.

18. Christopher Phillips, *Damned Yankee: The Life of General Nathaniel Lyon* (University of Missouri Press, 1990), 224–225.

19. *Official Records*, 495. McClellan's dispatch is not part of the record reported in *Official Records.*

20. Phillips suggests that McClellan acquiesced in a Blair plan to delegate his command responsibilities to Nathaniel Lyon. See Phillips, 224. Phillips's principal sources, which include a near-contemporaneous work by James Peckham, are not inconsistent with the notion that the Blairs left McClellan in the dark. James Peckham, *Gen. Nathaniel Lyon, and Missouri in 1861* (American News Company, 1866), 264–267. The Peckham source also provides support for the proposition that the Blairs advocated for John Frémont to lead the Western Department only after authorities in Washington refused to promote Nathaniel Lyon to a rank suitable for this assignment.

CHAPTER

2

★

"I never saw him idle one moment."

—Brig. Gen. Chester Harding Jr.

Figure 2

Chester Harding Jr. was born on October 16, 1827, in Northampton, Massachusetts. His father, Chester Harding of Boston, was one of the most celebrated portrait artists of mid-19th-century America. The younger Harding attended Harvard College and Harvard Law School, where he graduated in 1850. During the Civil War, he served generals Lyon and Frémont as assistant adjutant general, and he later commanded the 10th, 25th, and 43rd Missouri Volunteer infantries. Harding was brevetted brigadier general, US Volunteers, on May 27, 1865. He died in St. Louis in February 1875, and his remains rest under a soldier's stone at Jefferson Barracks National Cemetery.

Headquarters, 10th Missouri Volunteer Infantry

Pacific, Missouri, October 5, 1861

Col. Chester Harding Jr. sat at his desk at his Pacific headquarters, contemplating Gen. Frémont's request. The general and his entourage had arrived by rail in Pacific just days before, leading the advance of an army. Gen. Frémont had asked Harding to write a report on the affairs of the Western Department, starting from the time Frémont took charge in St. Louis. Frémont had come under attack for a variety of reasons, including the accusation that he had taken too long to assume command at St. Louis headquarters. A charge that particularly stung was that he had abandoned Gen. Lyon and his small command in the first weeks of August.

Harding reached for his ink pen, then stopped to reminisce. How his world had changed since 1850, the year he arrived in St. Louis carrying a degree from Harvard Law School. In 1852, after studying under his brother-in-law, Judge John Marshall Krum, the two entered a partnership and had offices in the McDonough Building on Olive Street.

Harding worked a desk job as assistant adjutant general for Gen. Nathaniel Lyon. Lyon was a favorite of Frank Blair and his brother Montgomery, Lincoln's postmaster general, and the brothers had the president's ear. Gen. Frémont, on the other hand, was Harding's superior officer. Here he was in Pacific, tasked with guarding the railroads that fanned out from the town. More regiments were on the way to back up Frémont as he departed on the long-awaited campaign against Sterling Price, who headed the Missouri State Guard.

Harding would choose his words carefully. He dipped his pen in the inkwell and began to write.

Gen. Lyon's army had come to rest in Springfield on July 13. Traffic on the wires from that region seemed to subside, but then Harding received some odd inquiries from the front. On July 15, Lyon's acting Adjutant General John Schofield wired in a host of complaints and suggested how other commands within and without the Western Department could spare troops to aid Lyon in southwest Missouri; he demanded 10,000 of them. Consider the absurdity of the situation: An *acting* adjutant was trying to persuade an assistant adjutant to move troops around the board.[1] In the same vein, Gen. Lyon wrote to Harding more stridently on July 17, after learning that General in Chief Winfield Scott had ordered half of one of Lyon's precious regiments re-assigned to Washington:

> If it is the intention to give up the West, let it be so; it can only be the victim of imbecility or malice. Scott will cripple us if he can. Cannot you stir up this matter...? See Frémont, if he has arrived. The want of supplies has crippled me so that I cannot move, and I do not know when I can. Everything seems to combine against me at this point. *Stir up [Frank] Blair.*[2] (emphasis added)

When it was established, the Confederate-aligned Missouri State Guard was divided geographically into nine military districts, each corresponding to one of Missouri's congressional districts, and each ruled by a brigadier general. Action was unfolding in early July in the southwest, in the 7th District of the State Guard. A civil war was about to explode in the 1st District (southeast Missouri) and in the 2nd (northeast Missouri).

By this time, Harding's attention had already turned to Missouri's far northeast, in the 2nd District of the Missouri State Guard that was under the command of Brig. Gen. Thomas Alexander Harris.[3] On July 11, 1861, Harris organized more than 1,000 pro-Southerners to surround an Illinois regiment in the town of Monroe Station, in Monroe County. They lobbed shells from a homemade cannon into the position occupied by the Union regiment. Although the contest had stalemated by the time Union help arrived, the action sent a shock wave through the area: It had severed the nearby Quincy, Illinois, rail link to the west, and men allied with Harris had also burned down a vital bridge on the Hannibal and St. Joseph Railroad, just west of Monroe Station. It would take a week to restore service on the line.

Thomas Harris left several marks on history, and one of them—the fight that brought Ulysses S. Grant into the war—flowed from the attack at Monroe Station. Grant, colonel of the 21st Illinois Volunteer Regiment, was summoned from his camp on the Illinois River, about 60 miles east of Quincy, to meet the emergency created by Harris. Grant's first service in the war zone was to guard the site of the Hannibal and St. Joseph Railroad bridge as it was being rebuilt.

Major General Ulysses S. Grant.
Photograph of a painting by
an unknown artist, 1861–1865.
Missouri Historical Society Collections.

In a letter to his wife, Julia, dated July 13, 1861, Grant reported that secessionist depredations in the area were pretty much confined to the destruction of property.[4] While railroads were his prime targets, Harris was of course still stirring up trouble in other respects. On July 14, in fact, Grant and his regiment went on a two-day "chase" of Harris to Florida, Missouri, without success.[5] Just after the regiment returned from that sojourn, Grant was ordered to the city of Mexico. As one of the most important centers of commerce on the North Missouri Railroad, Mexico was an obvious target. When he received these orders, Grant was already under orders to report to Gen. John Pope in Alton, Illinois, but the 21st Illinois Infantry was rerouted to Mexico because the situation there had escalated dramatically in the four days since Grant wrote to his wife.

John Pope, West Point class of 1842, was born into a Kentucky-Illinois clan in 1822. His father was a prominent figure in Illinois Territory politics, which brought him close to President Lincoln. On July 15, Pope issued a dispatch from Chicago to Harding in St. Louis. Pope advised that he had been in contact with Gen. Frémont in New York and was seeking approval to bring five regiments into northeast Missouri. Then, on July 16, 1861, Frémont at last spoke from the Astor House: "I have ordered Gen. Pope to take the command in North Missouri with three regiments from Alton. He moves this morning."[6] The same day, Frémont sent a similar telegram to Chester Harding. While it had to be clear to Harding that Frémont was now in command, he was still fending off McClellan's inquiries, which included concerns about the situation developing in southeast Missouri and Cairo in southern Illinois.

Once Gen. Pope formally took command—but before he arrived with his regiments—he began to deploy troops to Mexico, calling up Grant's 21st Regiment. He also sent to Mexico two companies of the 8th Missouri Volunteer Infantry, recently enrolled in St. Louis, and four companies of the 2nd Missouri Infantry, under command of Lt. Col. Frederick Schaefer. Gen. Pope was acting quickly and effectively to take control of Union interests in northeast Missouri, but events in and around Mexico were outpacing him.

On July 15, the two companies of the 8th Missouri and Schaefer's four companies left St. Charles, en route to Mexico via the North Missouri Railroad.[7] After the train passed Wentzville, 20 miles west of St. Charles, it was fired on by parties hidden in the woods along the tracks. Company officers sent out skirmishers, and the train returned to Wentzville for the night. The journey resumed the next morning; the men made slightly better progress in the daylight. For part of the route, commanders put six riflemen out front in a handcar, as well as skirmishers who "walked" the train through the gauntlet. Near the place where the men had confronted the secessionist party the day before, the train again came under fire. Immediately, five of the six men in the handcar fell wounded. The wounds sustained by Private Bill Pease proved fatal. He died that night in Montgomery City, about 40 miles northwest of the skirmish site, where the troops went into camp.[8] Pease was the first man of the 8th Missouri to be killed in action in the Civil War. He would be far from the last.[9]

On the morning of July 17—incidentally, the same day that Gen. Lyon wired Chester Harding to "stir up Blair"—the 8th Missouri buried Pease in the Montgomery City cemetery. After a somber ceremony, the men boarded the train cars and headed into Mexico, just over 25 miles away. They arrived without further incident, and two additional companies of the 8th Missouri joined them two days later.

But the carnage on the North Missouri Railroad continued. On July 18, near a place called Martinsburg in Audrain County, between Montgomery City and Mexico, a detachment of Union cavalry from the 1st Missouri Cavalry was operating independently of the infantry. One of its officers, 2nd Lt. Anton Jaeger, fell ill as he traveled to reach the 1st Missouri's command in Mexico. Also on the Mexico-bound train was a staunch Union man from nearby Danville named Benjamin H. Sharp, who had been promised a colonelcy in the Union army if he raised a regiment in Montgomery and Audrain counties.[10] The two men left the train at Wellsville, Jaeger because he was ill and Sharp because he wanted to look out for Jaeger's welfare. Sharp borrowed a buggy from a man he knew in Wellsville, and they set out for Mexico. Sharp, apparently, was not familiar with the road network north and west of there.

Enter Alvin S. Cobb, a secessionist from Cobbtown in Montgomery County. He was roaming northwest Montgomery County, where it borders Audrain County, when he and his band of followers came into contact with Sharp and Jaeger west of Martinsburg. Cobb was described by a contemporary as "a large man of magnificent physique" who carried about him a "suspicion of something sinister."[11] Cobb's imposing appearance was enhanced by an iron hook that resided where his left hand had been. Sharp took the wrong road and drove into Cobb's band of guerillas. They fired into Sharp's buggy, seriously wounding both Sharp and Jaeger. The wounded men were taken to a field north of Martinsburg and summarily executed.

The case of Lt. Jaeger is particularly jarring and heartrending. Jaeger was a St. Louis brewer who owned Jaeger's Beer Garden, a fixture of south St. Louis's German community that played a part in Lyon's march on Camp Jackson in May 1861.[12] The details of his fate were not confirmed until July 28, when his body, along with Sharp's, was found in a shallow grave. Back in St. Louis, Jaeger's wife, Eva, had waited for the news along with their three children. Their youngest son was not yet one month old.[13]

About midday on July 20, 1861, Gen. Ulysses Grant brought his 21st Illinois Infantry to town, where he was immediately confronted with an issue of the *Star Spangled Banner*, a camp newspaper reported and printed by the men of the 8th Missouri.[14] The paper, bearing the date July 19, carried news of the fighting west of Wentzville and the deadly incident in Martinsburg.

Two days after the Martinsburg killings, soldiers of the 8th Missouri took two Danville men from their homes and shot them on a prairie south of Montgomery City.[15] A third man was killed nearby. On the same day, armies in Virginia fought the First Battle of Bull Run, and Gen. Pope issued an ill-conceived order that sought to impose a levy on disloyal citizens to pay for damage done to the railroad. North Missouri was in full panic mode.

There is no record that Ulysses Grant knew at the time about the retaliatory killings in Danville. Nearly a quarter century later, when Grant penned his memoirs, this master of understatement would say: "My arrival in Mexico had been preceded by that of two or three regiments in which proper discipline had not been maintained."[16]

Throughout most of July, Gen. Frémont was guilty of dawdling in New York. Here's how we know: Early in May 1861, according to the best available evidence, Frémont was offered a senior command in the Union army. He jumped at the opportunity and made plans to return to the United States as soon as possible. From Europe, he notified Jessie in San Francisco of the news, which would have taken three weeks or more to traverse the Atlantic Ocean and North America by rail and the Pony Express. He entreated Jessie to join him in New York and to bring the children with her. But his plans didn't reach Jessie in time for her to book passage on the next scheduled steamer bound for Panama, so instead, she scheduled her departure for June 21.[17]

Jessie had made her first passage across the Isthmus of Panama in 1849, when she traveled with Lily to meet her husband after his fourth cross-country expedition. That trip was exceedingly dangerous, and it's harrowing that a six-year-old made the journey at all. But in intervening years a railroad across the isthmus had been completed that cut the trip down to three weeks and eliminated its most perilous segment. And so Jessie probably didn't give a second thought to the danger the journey entailed, as she loaded her three children—including five-year-old Frank—aboard a steamer bound for the Pacific Coast of Panama. After transferring to an Atlantic steamer named *North Star* at the Panamanian port town now known as Colón, the family continued to New York, where Jessie and the children disembarked on July 15, 1861.[18] It is no accident that Frémont ended his awkward silence the day after their arrival.

As the Frémont family reacquainted themselves in New York, Chester Harding continued to wait for Gen. Frémont to show in St. Louis. Meanwhile, Harding was confronted with a troubling situation in southeast Missouri, where aggressive enemy movements were centered on the Missouri side of the Mississippi, opposite Cairo, Illinois. In the wake of all of the confusion wrought by Frémont's continued absence from the scene of his command, on July 19, 1861, Harding telegraphed Frémont with words that laid bare the frustrations of the preceding weeks: "Expecting you here daily, I have not telegraphed before; but if you do not come at once, will you take into consideration the importance of Cairo...?"[19]

Frémont responded, "I come on immediately."

To Frémont, "immediately" did not mean "right away." It took him nearly another week to arrive on the east shore of the Mississippi River with Jessie and their three children. They ferried to St. Louis and went to the place he determined would be his headquarters: a three-story residence south of downtown known as the Brant Mansion. The lavish home had been completed in 1859 by Joshua B. Brant and his wife, Sarah Benton Brant. Sarah, known as Sally, was Jessie's first cousin. Joshua Brant had passed away in February 1861, so the mansion was unoccupied. John and Jessie arranged for the government to pay $6,000 per annum in rent.[20]

Once situated in his St. Louis headquarters, the first emergency Gen. Frémont would address was the growing menace in Cairo and southeast Missouri. He soon set off for Cairo, playing the role of a commandant of a flotilla of transports meant to resupply the Cairo garrison. It was Frémont's way to "show the flag" amid the most serious threat yet to Union control of the region: On July 28, 11,000 Confederate troops from Tennessee and Mississippi landed on the Missouri shore at New Madrid and took possession of the place. Founded in 1789, New Madrid, as its name implies, was a Spanish colonial settlement. Unlike much of this area of Missouri, some of the ground in and around New Madrid rises a few feet above the water table, creating a slight ridge that runs northward to the interior.[21] Missouri's Spanish rulers built a section of road on this ridge, and the town prospered as a trading post. In 1861, New Madrid became a key strategic point for political reasons, too: The Kentucky Legislature declared the state "neutral" in the War Between the States, a position it was able to enforce and maintain throughout the month of August. New Madrid was just a 5-mile trip by steamer from the border of Tennessee. The Confederate invasion force sidestepped Kentucky, and in so doing created a severe threat to Union interests in southeast Missouri.

On July 30, 1861, Gen. Frémont sent President Lincoln an extensive report detailing the condition of his new command. On August 1, without prior notice to Washington, he set off from St. Louis on his mission to Cairo. Perhaps predictably, Frémont did not report on his activities there, so by

August 5, Lincoln's secretary plaintively telegraphed Frémont: "The President desires to know briefly the situation of affairs in the region of Cairo."[22]

When Gen. Frémont arrived in St. Louis, he was somewhat preoccupied by Gen. Lyon's predicament in southwest Missouri. It *had* taken Lyon and his force too long to reach Springfield from Boonville. On the positive side, the largest active contingent of the Missouri State Guard had been driven to the farthest southwest corner of Missouri.[23] Depending on how things would play out, Lyon might have the strength to remain where he was.

A telegram Lyon wrote on July 13, 1861, to Adjutant General Lorenzo Thomas in Washington explained the story plainly: "My effective force will soon be reduced by discharge of three-months' volunteers to about 4,000 men.... Governor Jackson will soon have in this vicinity not less than 30,000. *I must have at once an additional force of 10,000 men, or abandon my position.* All must have supplies and clothing."[24] (emphasis added)

August 11, 1861, was the day that many of these enlistments would expire, and Lyon was at risk of losing more than half his force at once. This situation echoed that of May 10, 1861, when Lyon precipitated the confrontation at Camp Jackson on the day before he'd have to surrender his command to Gen. Harney.

Not surprisingly, Lyon seriously overestimated the force that was available to Claiborne Jackson and the Missouri State Guard. But Lyon was still at a disadvantage. With the addition of some Kansas troops who had joined Lyon on the march to Springfield, as well as Sigel's veterans from Carthage, Lyon had 5,400 effectives under his command. After consolidating at Cowskin Prairie, the Missouri State Guard was approximately the same size. However, the State Guard's Sterling Price—who, along with his staff, had evaded Sigel during the first days of July—was making progress in negotiations with Confederate forces in Arkansas. Arkansas had seceded from the Union on May 6, 1861, making it the ninth member of the Confederate States of America. Consequently, the Confederate army was organized there, operating in northwest Arkansas under the command of Brig. Gen. Benjamin McCulloch. On or about July 25, McCulloch agreed that his Confederate troops, and some Arkansas state troops who fell under his command, would advance into Missouri with Price.[25]

There's a parallel to the Confederate moves in the southeast and southwest corners of the state. On July 28, 1861, the day that Confederates took possession of New Madrid, McCulloch's army joined Price's army at Keetsville, Missouri (now Washburn), a town 5 miles inside the border with Arkansas and about 65 miles from Springfield. Gen. Frémont, in St. Louis on his third day on the job, knew about the situation in New Madrid, but he had not yet been advised of this invasion south of Springfield. In Springfield, Lyon had some intelligence that McCulloch might link up with Price, so he left the shelter of the city in an attempt to strike Price before he could unite with McCulloch's force. It wasn't until August 3, after a couple skirmishes with advance elements of Price's State Guard, that Lyon learned the junction had already been made. By this time, Frémont was in Cairo, Illinois, out of touch.

General Sterling Price.
Photograph of a painting by
an unknown artist, 1861–1865.
Missouri Historical Society Collections.

Wisely, Gen. Lyon pulled his troops back to Springfield on August 4. A prudent commander faced with such a dire situation would have prepared his tiny force to batten down and entrench in Springfield, then fight a rearguard action to cover his retreat to the railhead in Rolla. But as Lyon began to withdraw to Springfield, he did not know that the combined McCulloch-Price force was in camp along Crane Creek, barely 4 miles south of his position. While estimates vary, the strength of this army was between 10,000 and 12,000 men of all arms.[26]

This camp marked a milestone in the Trans-Mississippi war. Up until then, McCulloch had shown extreme caution in deploying enrolled Confederate troops in still-neutral Missouri. At Crane Creek, he considered withdrawing his troops to Arkansas instead of pursuing Lyon. Price confronted McCulloch at the latter's Crane Creek headquarters on the morning of August 4, 1861.

Some historians believe it was here that Price submitted himself and his Missouri State Guard to McCulloch's authority so that he could persuade McCulloch to continue the advance against Springfield. Price had probably agreed on July 30 to operate under McCulloch's command, but on August 4, he threatened to break this agreement and attack on his own. In any case, Price's gambit succeeded, and the combined forces moved together from there on August 5 or 6. They established their next camp on the banks of Wilson's Creek, about 10 miles southwest of Springfield.

Springfield stood near the highest point on the Ozark Plateau, at the junction of two important roads. One, the Springfield Road from St. Louis, followed a Native American trace once known as the Kickapoo Trail. (Some 75 years later, Route 66 would follow this same path.) The second road was carved out in the 1850s and was used by the Butterfield Overland Mail Company during its brief existence from 1858 to 1861. Springfield was an important population center, and it was crucial that it remain under Union control.

Still seeking reinforcements, Lyon waited in Springfield. On August 9, a courier from Rolla arrived with a letter from John Frémont, bearing a date of August 6. Frémont advised Lyon that no reinforcements would be coming and recommended that if Lyon didn't think he'd be able to hold Springfield, he should withdraw to Rolla. Curiously, Frémont did not give this advice the force of an order. Lyon was on his own.

Lyon penned a response to Frémont on August 9, which was similarly vague and indecisive: "I find my position extremely embarrassing, and I am at present unable to determine whether I shall be able to maintain my ground or be forced to retire." Lyon's adjutant, Maj. John Schofield, had prepared the response, but Lyon's editing created even more confusion. Because of the time it would take to deliver the message to Rolla, it doesn't seem as though it was intended to elicit a response from Frémont.

During the afternoon of August 9, Gen. Lyon determined that he would retire to Rolla, but before he did, he would attack Price and McCulloch at Wilson's Creek.[27] Covering his retreat by attacking at Wilson's Creek might have been an acceptable tactic, but Lyon's plan was poorly conceived and poorly executed. In 1990's *Damned Yankee*, Lyon's principal biographer, professor Christopher Phillips, put forth an insightful analysis of Lyon's decision: Lyon's most serious error was in devising a two-pronged attack, which divided his force in the face of a superior enemy. The idea came from Franz Sigel, a highly schooled veteran of European conflicts and the Battle of Carthage. In Phillips's estimation, Sigel foisted the plan upon Lyon.

Many (if not most) of the troops whose terms were expiring were Sigel's Germans. Gen. Lyon was concerned that unless Sigel acquiesced in the plan of attack, his troops would leave the field. So it was that Lyon marched on the night of August 9. Sigel did likewise, but taking a roundabout route to reach the south end of the field where the McCulloch-Price army was camped. Sigel had with him the batteries he'd used effectively at Carthage. Lyon's attack came at 5am on August 10, 1861, completely surprising the slumbering Southerners. The roused troops were rattled, to be sure, when Sigel's fire came on from their rear.

Death of General Lyon, August 10, 1861 (cropped). The moment of the mortal wounding of Brig. Gen. Nathaniel Lyon at the Battle of Wilson's Creek, August 10, 1861. Drawing by Henri Lovie, 1861. The Miriam and Ira D. Wallach Division of Art, Prints and Photographs: Print Collection, The New York Public Library.

Sigel abandoned the field prematurely, and he and his force retreated in the direction of Springfield. McCulloch and Price then focused on Lyon, with about 4,000 infantry and 14 cannon defending a hill to the north.[28] On that hill, known ever since as Bloody Hill, Nathaniel Lyon was shot fatally through the chest, at the head of his troops and at the climax of the battle. He was the first Union general killed in action in the American Civil War.

On July 25, 1861, the day Gen. Frémont arrived in Missouri, something transpired in the far southeast corner of the state—a harbinger of Frémont's many headaches to come. In the State Guard's 1st Military District, at a campground south of present-day Dexter in Stoddard County, soldiers assembled to elect a new commander. The first brigadier of the 1st District was Nathaniel Watkins of Jackson, Missouri. An aging soldier and planter who was a half-brother to Kentucky senator Henry Clay, Watkins had accepted the post when the State Guard was formed. By July 1861, however, he had become disillusioned. The aims of Missouri secessionists now went well beyond Watkins's own motivations when he first took command, so he resigned.

Virginia-born Meriwether Jefferson Thompson, the former mayor of St. Joseph, Missouri, had by then started a crusade to procure a meaningful officer's commission. He went to Memphis to confer about joining the Confederate ranks, but in late July learned of Watkins's resignation and the now-open position in the State Guard. He bought a new horse, a white charger he named Sardanapalus after a Byron poem. In his memoir, *The Civil War Reminiscences of General M. Jeff Thompson*, he related that he arrived at the State Guard camp in Stoddard County donned in "a wool hat with a white plume in it, red sash, and a very large iron scabbard, sabre, pistol, and a bowie knife in my belt."[29] Thompson, most often referred to as "Jeff" or "M. Jeff"—and later, "Missouri's Swamp Fox"—won the election to brigadier general. The activities of this peculiar man, with his penchant for theatrics and self-promotion, would literally move armies over the course of the next 100 days.

ENDNOTES

1. John McAllister Schofield, West Point class of 1853, was the son of a Baptist minister. After teaching at West Point, he was appointed as an instructor of mathematics at Washington University in St. Louis in 1860. Schofield re-entered active army service in 1861 as Gen. Lyon's chief of staff. He would end his army career as the commanding general of the US Army, a position he held from 1888 to 1895. Schofield was the fourth in a line of officers that also included Ulysses Grant, William Sherman, and Philip Sheridan, who served in that position during the last third of the 19th century.

2. *Official Records of the Union and Confederate Armies, Ser. 1, Vol. 3, Ch. 10* (Government Printing Office, 1881), 397.

3. Thomas Alexander Harris attended the United States Military Academy for two years, beginning in 1843, the year Ulysses Grant graduated. As a young teen in the 1830s, Harris purportedly fought in the Mormon War. He was commissioned a second lieutenant during the Mexican-American War, just as that conflict was ending. Harris was elected brigadier general of the 2nd Division of the Missouri State Guard, a post he resigned in November 1861 to take a seat in the Confederate Congress.

4. Ulysses S. Grant, *Selected Letters, 1839–1865* (Literary Classics of the United States, 1990), 968–969. In this letter, Ulysses writes to Julia from West Quincy, Missouri, "Secessionists are thick through this part of Missouri but so far they show themselves very scary about attacking. Their depredations are more confined to burning R. R. bridges, tearing up the track and where they can, surround [*sic*] small parties of Union troops."

5. Florida, Missouri, located on the Salt River in Monroe County, was once a prosperous town, notable as the birthplace of Samuel Langhorne Clemens—better known as Mark Twain—in 1835. In mid-July 1861, at the head of his 21st Illinois regiment, Col. Grant led a 25-mile, round-trip march to Florida, where he expected Harris to be. When he arrived at the crest of a hill that overlooked the town and the valley that separated him from it (as he vividly remembered 25 years later): "[T]he marks of a recent encampment were plainly visible, but [Harris's] troops were gone. My heart resumed its place. It occurred to me at once that Harris had been as much afraid of me as I had been of him. This was a view of the question I had never taken before; but it was one I never forgot afterwards." Ulysses S. Grant, *Personal Memoirs of U. S. Grant* (Charles L. Webster & Company, 1885), 164.

6. *Official Records*, 187. Alton, Illinois, 20 miles north of St. Louis, dominates the high ground north and east of the confluence of the Missouri and Mississippi rivers. Its commercial and strategic importance was guaranteed in the 1850s when the Chicago and Alton Railroad became the first to connect the Mississippi River to the Great Lakes.

7. The North Missouri Railroad linked St. Charles to Macon, Missouri, in 1859. Located on the Missouri River about 20 miles northwest of St. Louis, St. Charles was founded as a French settlement in 1769. It served a jumping-off point for wagons headed from St. Louis to points west. The North Missouri Railroad connected St. Louis and St. Charles to St. Joseph, Missouri, when the Hannibal and St. Joseph Railroad was completed in 1859. By the time of the Civil War, "St. Joe" was the westernmost point that rail reached from the east.

8. Chester Childs, ed., *Star Spangled Banner* 1, no. 1 (July 19, 1861).

9. Most soldiers of the 8th Missouri who were stationed in Mexico while Grant was there belonged to companies raised in central Illinois. These companies filled out a regiment largely composed of Irishmen from St. Louis. Throughout its existence, the regiment lost over 200 men, who were either killed in combat or died from disease. See National Park Service, "Battle Unit Details, Union Missouri Volunteers, 8th Regiment, Missouri Infantry."

10. Benjamin Sharp was a Missouri legislator in 1861. A Virginia native, Sharp was a member of the first class admitted to the Virginia Military Institute in Lexington when the school opened its doors in 1839. Purportedly, only 13 graduates of VMI served in the Union army during the Civil War, and Sharp was the only one killed in action. Legend notwithstanding, Sharp did not graduate from VMI, and he died before he was commissioned an officer of the Union army. Edward A. Miller, "VMI Men Who Wore Yankee Blue, 1861–1865," *VMI Alumni Review* (Spring 1996): 8.

11. Joseph A. Mudd, *With Porter in North Missouri* (The National Publishing Company, 1909), 204.

12. Jaeger's Beer Garden was a popular spot in St. Louis's Soulard neighborhood. One of the German American units, the 1st Regiment US Reserve Corps, trained at Jaeger's, and on May 10, 1861, it marched from that point to Lindell's Grove. See Robert J. Rombauer, *The Union Cause in St. Louis in 1861* (Nixon-Jones Printing Co., 1909), 227.

13. Henry Almstedt Papers, Missouri Historical Society Collections. Among these papers is a letter written by William Martin of Martinsburg, dated July 29, 1861, which describes finding the bodies of the two men. For personal details, see Eva Jaeger, widow's pension application no. 352070, service of Anton Jaeger (Washington, DC: National Archives).

14. An original copy of the first issue of *Star Spangled Banner* is held at the Mexico–Audrain County Library.

15. *History of St. Charles, Montgomery and Warren Counties, Missouri* (National Historical Company, 1885), 618–620.

16. Ulysses S. Grant, *Personal Memoirs of U. S. Grant* (Charles L. Webster & Company, 1885), 165.

17. Allan Nevins, *John Frémont: Pathmarker of the West* (University of Nebraska Press, 1939), 472.

18. Jessie and Lily's 1848 westbound trip across the Isthmus of Panama is colorfully described in Steve Inskeep's *Imperfect Union: How Jessie and John Frémont Mapped the West, Invented Celebrity, and Helped Cause the Civil War* (Penguin Press, 2020), 200–204. To put Jessie's risk in proper context: In 1852, Ulysses Grant led a company of the 4th US Infantry on this route and lost one-third of his command in the process. See Grant, *Personal Memoirs*, 132–133. For Jessie's arrival date in 1861, see the passenger manifest for the steamship *North Star*, which docked at the Port of New York on July 15, 1861 (Washington, DC: National Archives).

19. *Official Records*, 400.

20. Measured in 2025 dollars, the annual rent on the Brant home was approximately $190,000. Although certainly not pertinent to the propriety of Frémont's dealings, note that in 1839, Lt. Col. Joshua Brant of the Quartermaster Corps resigned his army commission, having been found guilty of purchasing fraud. In *Pathmarker*, Nevins defended Frémont's transaction in 1861 as reasonable and in the best interest of the service, 493.

21. Missouri's Bootheel is an alluvial area of about 1,000 square miles, situated between the Mississippi and St. Francois rivers, below the line that Congress had established as the state's southern boundary. An influential landowner by the name of John Hardeman Walker successfully persuaded the territorial legislature to add this area to Missouri's petition for statehood.

22. *Report of Joint Committee, Part 3*, consisting of a telegram from John J. Nicholay submitted as evidence through the testimony of Gen. Frémont, 103. Frémont returned to St. Louis the following day, August 6, 1861, as he was issuing orders from that place on that date.

23. Cowskin Prairie is located a half mile east of the border of Missouri and Oklahoma, formerly Indian Territory, and about 2 miles north of Arkansas.

24. Christopher Phillips, *Damned Yankee: The Life of General Nathaniel Lyon* (University of Missouri Press, 1990), 248–250.

25. Edwin C. Bearss, *The Battle of Wilson's Creek* (Wilson's Creek National Battlefield Foundation, 1992), 19–20.

26. Crane Creek's valley has hardly changed in a century and a half. The site of the encampment of the Southern forces before Wilson's Creek can be viewed from the Wire Road Conservation Area. This valley also saw a skirmish in February 1862 at the beginning of the Pea Ridge campaign, and it was the starting point of the greatest forced march in Civil War history: the march of Gen. Francis Herron's Army of the Frontier on Prairie Grove, Arkansas. See Gregory Wolk, *A Tour Guide to Missouri's Civil War: Friend and Foe Alike* (Monograph Publishing, 2010), 230–231.

27. Phillips, 248–249.

28. Bearss, 161–162.

29. Unpublished memoir of M. Jeff Thompson, in possession of the State Historical Society of Missouri and quoted in Doris Land Mueller's *M. Jeff Thompson: Missouri's Swamp Fox of the Confederacy* (University of Missouri Press, 2007), 30.

CHAPTER 3

"General Frémont was the unruly child of the Republican Party."

—Lt. Col. Camille Ferri-Pisani

Figure 3

Lt. Col. Marcel Victor Paul Camille Ferri-Pisani of the French Army was aide-de-camp to Prince Napoleon. This Napoleon, nicknamed "Plon-Plon," was the nephew of Napoleon Bonaparte and a cousin to the sitting emperor of France, Napoleon III. Ferri-Pasini himself would rise to the rank of major general of the French Army after serving in the Franco-Prussian War from 1870 to 1871. The letters he wrote and sent to Paris during his 1861 tour of the United States—including one he penned from St. Louis—were translated and published by *American Heritage* magazine in 1957.

The Planter's House Hotel

St. Louis, September 5, 1861

ON THE EVENING OF September 4, a party of dignitaries arrived on the east bank of the Mississippi River. So far on his American tour, Prince Napoleon of France—a nephew of Napoleon Bonaparte—had visited Abraham Lincoln in Washington and crossed the battle lines in Virginia to meet some Confederate generals. The prince looked forward to meeting John Frémont, a man with French lineage who was among the most famous men in the United States.

The city left a poor first impression on the dignitaries from Paris. Frémont had planned a rousing welcome on the St. Louis levee. At 8pm a regiment of infantry and several batteries of artillery assembled there, along with the general's cavalry escort known as "Frémont's Body-Guard." But when the visitors' train arrived at the depot on the east side of the river, an enterprising man with a fine carriage persuaded the prince—who was unaware of Frémont's official arrangements—to enter his coach. As a result, the prince's party never saw the assemblage on the levee. What's more, Gen. Frémont had booked rooms at Barnum's Hotel on 2nd Street, but the man with the carriage conducted the party to the Planter's House Hotel on Broadway. The visitors were enjoying dinner there when one of Frémont's aides found them. At 9pm, Lt. Col. Ferri-Pisani had the unenviable task of riding to Gen. Frémont's headquarters to present the prince's regards.

The next day, the party's first full day in St. Louis, got off to a better start. It began with Gen. Frémont's grand arrival at the Planter's House, led by his splendidly attired Body-Guard. Lt. Col. Ferri-Pisani was struck by the brilliant staff of senior officers whom Frémont had assembled—men from places such as Bavaria, Switzerland, and the Rhineland—each looking his part. But would this fine-looking army fight?

In mid-August 1861, the full scope of the disaster at Wilson's Creek was coming to light. Nearly a quarter of Lyon's men had been killed, wounded, or captured. The survivors abandoned Springfield in such haste that the body of their dead leader had to be buried in the rose garden of a loyal congressman.[1] No railroad was available to evacuate troops and supplies; no telegraph line had been established that could be used during the retreat to the Rolla railhead. A rider arrived in Rolla at noon on August 12, and news of Lyon's defeat and death soon lit up wires across the nation.

Battle of Wilson's Creek. Chromolithograph by Kurz and Allison, 1893. Missouri Historical Society Collections.

Almost as soon as the news reached Washington, the Blairs—the sons and the father—began to slowly lay siege to the reputation of John C. Frémont. They called into question Frémont's military judgment because he did not reinforce Gen. Lyon at Wilson's Creek. Before the month was over, the charges continued to escalate until Frank Blair was ready to call for Frémont's removal. It is true that the Blairs had used Nathaniel Lyon very adroitly and successfully to further their short-term goals—seemingly, to remove the influence of Gen. Harney and to blunt a secessionist bid for Missouri neutrality. That the Blairs could have held such a sentimental view of Gen. Lyon's sacrifice, though, denies the essence of what made a Blair a Blair: family.

Elizabeth "Lizzie" Blair Lee was Preston Blair's second child and his only daughter who survived infancy.[2] A prolific letter writer, she had this to say in the wake of Wilson's Creek: "All my forebodings of last night are fulfilled this morning [August 15, 1861]—Cary Gratz is killed—His beautiful infancy was a great pleasure to my childhood & his fine manly character has made him a very dear kinsman to me...."[3]

Lizzie Lee was lamenting the loss of Cary Gist Gratz, the captain of Company F, 1st Missouri Infantry. A Union fighter, he was a first cousin to Lizzie, Montgomery, and Frank Blair. Upon learning about the death of Capt. Gratz, members of the Blair family must have felt enormous angst, especially Frank: He had no doubt recruited Cary to join his 1st Missouri regiment, and he was absent from the field of battle at Wilson's Creek because he was attending a session of Congress.[4]

Back in St. Louis, Gen. Frémont's first reaction to the news from Wilson's Creek was to declare martial law throughout the city and county. On August 14, 1861, Frémont appointed Maj. Justus McKinstry to be his provost marshal and directed that whatever McKinstry decided would be done. The declaration, which was consistent with a directive from the secretary of war, was used to suppress two newspapers, but its significance ends there.[5]

On August 16, Frémont recalled Maj. Franz Kappner of the Engineer Corps to St. Louis from Cape Girardeau, Missouri. Since the time of the Civil War, the town has been the largest river port between St. Louis and Memphis. Frémont had ordered Kappner to Cape Girardeau on July 28, within days of reaching St. Louis, to superintend the construction of a ring of forts to protect that city. "Cape," as it was known then and now, was thought even at this early juncture to be under threat by the Confederate forces that had entered Missouri through New Madrid. The works in Cape Girardeau were important enough that Frémont halted to confer with Maj. Kappner as Frémont made his way to Cairo during the first week of August. In the wake of Wilson's Creek, Frémont ordered Kappner back to St. Louis to lead what Frémont viewed was an urgent task to fully fortify the city. Kappner, for his part, left the Cape Girardeau fortifications in good hands.[6]

We last saw Missouri's Swamp Fox, Jeff Thompson, in camp in Stoddard County, where on July 25 he was elected brigadier general of the 1st District of the Missouri State Guard. Thompson accepted the position in a rousing speech that included this exclamation: "I am a rip-squealer, and *my name is fight!*"[7] Thompson had absolutely no experience as a soldier. It seems what he did have was an extraordinary talent for motivating men and for confusing adversaries—along with a very healthy sense of self. Over the course of the first two weeks of August, before he had the opportunity to engage Union troops in pitched battle, Thompson's fight was with the high command of the Confederate army in the western theater. Atop the chain of command was Confederate Maj. Gen. Leonidas Polk, an 1827 graduate of West Point, and more recently, the Episcopal bishop of Louisiana.[8] He operated from headquarters in Memphis.

Fortifications at St. Louis, MO. Fort No. 1 (cropped). View of Union entrenchment at Marine Avenue and Chippewa Street, ca. September 1861. Drawing by Henri Lovie, 1861. The Becker Collection, Boston College Libraries.

Putting aside his West Point education, Gen. Polk had no more experience as a soldier than Thompson did. Still, Polk was not the weakest point in this Confederate structure of command. It was Gen. Gideon Pillow of Tennessee, who commanded forces in his home state and ferried regular CSA troops to New Madrid. Pillow clothed this tiny force in the oversize name the Army of Liberation—meaning the liberation of Missouri, of course. While Gen. Pillow did have some professional experience, particularly front-line service in the Mexican-American War, it seems that even those who fought alongside him were left with an unfavorable impression. In the judgment of history, Pillow regularly vies with Braxton Bragg for the title of worst Confederate general. A short list of his personal characteristics would include these adjectives: ceremonious, irritable, intractable.[9]

In early August, Gen. Frémont had Polk and Pillow to contend with, as Gen. Lyon was moving toward his doomed clash with Confederates south of Springfield. The pattern was established: Price in southwest Missouri persuaded CSA general Benjamin McCulloch to join him at a time when Missouri's allegiance to the Union remained a question mark. Jeff Thompson was doing the same by enticing Pillow into the southeast. And in southern Missouri, Confederate general William J. Hardee was occupying the town of Greenville in Wayne County, where he posed a threat to a critical railhead that Frémont would need to supply most of the territory between New Madrid and Springfield.

William Hardee was a famous American soldier before the Civil War.[10] In Missouri in 1861, he'd assembled an army composed of enrolled Confederate troops and state-sanctioned military units, perhaps 4,000 effectives in all. Hardee was supplying himself from Pocahontas, Arkansas, about 80 miles south of Greenville. When he came to rest in Greenville in early August, he was in position either to move on that railhead—40 miles to the north, just above Ironton—or on Cape Girardeau, about 60 miles to the east by good roads. Soon after Hardee arrived in Greenville, Gen. Pillow started a turf war with him, signaled by this note to Gen. Polk on August 5: "You promised me the co-operation of Hardee's force."[11] Pillow used this argument to lobby for permission to move north from New Madrid so he could link up with Hardee en route to Pillow's preferred point of attack, Cape Girardeau.

The railhead that Hardee's Confederates coveted was just above Ironton in Iron County, Missouri, a place called Pilot Knob. A town had grown up in the shadow of a mountain by that name, where there was an industrial-scale exploitation of rich iron ore deposits. An iron furnace was built in Pilot Knob in 1848. The railroad-building boom in 1850s Missouri—which produced the Hannibal and St. Joseph and the North Missouri railroads—also included the St. Louis and Iron Mountain line. Pushed by St. Louis commercial interests to tap natural resources in St. Francois County and its environs, the road reached its pre–Civil War terminus at Pilot Knob in 1858. Ironton, 2 miles south of Pilot Knob, was designated the county seat when Iron County was formed in 1857. The terrain that the Iron Mountain line serviced was not at all like the prairie lands the northern Missouri railroads traversed; rather, the Iron Mountain line snaked through hill country for most of its 100-mile run from St. Louis. All combined, these factors made the railroad and the cities of Pilot Knob and Ironton critical strategic assets for the Union army.

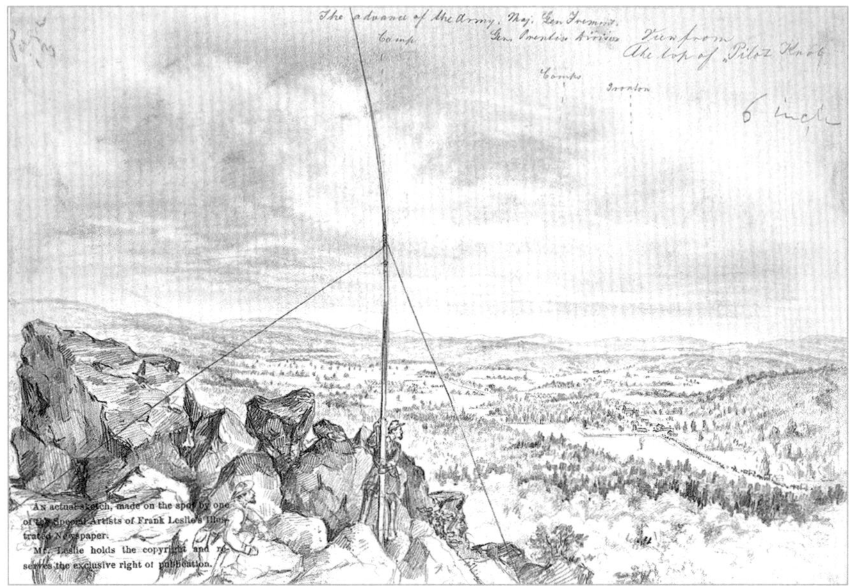

Entrance of Prentiss at Ironton. View from the top of Pilot Knob Mountain when Brig. Gen. Benjamin Prentiss relieves Brig. Gen. Ulysses Grant, August 17, 1861. Drawing by Henri Lovie, 1861. The Miriam and Ira D. Wallach Division of Art, Prints and Photographs: Print Collection, The New York Public Library.

On August 7, 1861, Ulysses Grant was dispatched to Ironton from his camp in Mexico, Missouri, which he had occupied for more than two weeks. His orders on August 7 were addressed to him in auspicious terms: "Brigadier-General GRANT, Charged with the Command of the Ironton Force." Grant put himself and his regiment on the train cars of the North Missouri Railroad, and he was in St. Louis within 24 hours. That evening, Grant and his men bunked at Jefferson Barracks, along the Iron Mountain Railroad south of the city. He and his regiment arrived at their new post at Ironton in the evening of August 9, where Grant relieved Col. Benjamin Gratz Brown.[12]

Whatever the original intention was in deploying the Ironton force, in retrospect it seems clear that its impetus was Hardee's presence at Greenville. Grant did mount an expedition to probe south from Ironton in search of Hardee's advance, but by August 16, authorities in St. Louis no longer saw Hardee as a threat. On August 17, Grant was surprised when another newly minted brigadier stepped off the train from St. Louis with orders to take command at Ironton. Grant's successor in Ironton was Gen. Benjamin Prentiss of Quincy, Illinois, a Mexican-American War veteran whose specialties were law and politics. Grant was on a train to St. Louis by the end of that day, intent on disputing Prentiss's claim of seniority.[13]

With the benefit of hindsight, as of August 9—just before Lyon's engagement at Wilson's Creek—Frémont considered Hardee's force south of Ironton to be the most urgent, looming threat to his command. But if Nathaniel Lyon was determined to bring on a battle in the southwest, a battle he did not need to fight, Frémont was powerless to reverse his course.

When it came to pure bullheadedness, Gen. Hardee gave not an inch to Pillow. Throughout the three weeks Hardee spent in Missouri, he did not move to consolidate his force with Pillow's. In fact, he did not move from Greenville, period, except for one brief retrograde movement to Arkansas. During this same time, Jeff Thompson, who'd been the ranking general of the Missouri State Guard in the sector since July 26, ferried his men from place to place at will; he seemed to always have an excuse that orders from either Pillow or Hardee prevented him from following the orders of the other. Thompson could pull Pillow anywhere he wanted him to go, so long as Pillow could take credit—and Pillow held similar sway over Gen. Polk. Finally, Gen. Thompson was the only commander of the lot to exhibit a singleness of purpose. His objective: Get the Army of Liberation up and out of the swamps, onto the high ground around Cape Girardeau. Then, attack and defeat the Yankees who were fortifying the town.[14]

Thompson nearly succeeded. Only one all-weather road ran north from New Madrid: the old Spanish road along Sikeston Ridge. Thompson generally operated from a rather formidable range of hills 10 miles to the west, but when circumstances were right, he moved his camp along the slightly elevated land mass of Sikeston Ridge. The ridge road ran north from New Madrid for some 32 miles, to a point surrounded on three sides by a lake; at this juncture, the road crossed a bridge that spanned a narrow arm of that lake. Just north of the bridge was Benton Hill, the high ground Thompson coveted. The road split north of the bridge. To the east it followed Benton Hill through the town of Benton until it reached Commerce, a port town on the Mississippi. Head on, the road continued north for another 25 miles to Jackson. For persons traveling north, Benton Hill was the first high ground above Memphis that bordered the west side of the river. At points north of Commerce, Benton Hill was within cannon range of Cape Girardeau.

Gen. Thompson coaxed Gen. Pillow northward along Sikeston Ridge, until on August 17, the 1st Mississippi Cavalry Regiment, CSA, reached the high ground and went into camp (ironically, on the country estate of Nathaniel Watkins, Thompson's predecessor). The 4th Regiment, Tennessee Infantry, under the command of Col. Rufus Neely, also reached this point on or before August 17, as did two companies of Thompson's own cavalry. Thompson came forward from Sikeston on August 18, establishing his camp and headquarters at the town of Benton in Scott County. On that day, Thompson hauled an old 6-pounder gun 7 miles east to Commerce, took the town, then fired on boats plying the Mississippi. Though mostly symbolic, Thompson's act was enough to halt traffic on the river for a day. In the eyes of distant beholders, Thompson had outflanked the 5,000 Union troops in Cairo and Bird's Point. This induced the desired panic in Cape Girardeau, and it rippled north to St. Louis.

A few days later, from his St. Louis headquarters, Gen. Frémont issued an order to Gen. Prentiss of Illinois, who was still in command at Ironton. Frémont's order of August 25 began with these words: "A report has just reached me that 4,000 rebels are fortifying Benton, Mo., and 1,500 more are encamped behind the hills 2 miles below Commerce, opposite Big Island. To disperse these forces a combined attack by your troops and those stationed at Cape Girardeau has been determined upon."[15]

Then unbeknownst to Frémont, the work of Pillow's Army of Liberation had come to an end. Relations between Gen. Polk and the Confederate high command had taken an ugly turn. On August 20, Hardee sent a dispatch to Polk from Greenville flat-out refusing to advance in support of Pillow's plans. That same day, Pillow told Polk he had misgivings about Polk's direct order to withdraw Neely's 4th Tennessee Infantry from its position near Benton. The next day, Pillow went over Polk's head, to Confederate secretary of war LeRoy Pope Walker, and made his case for keeping Neely's regiment. After Gen. Polk threatened to prefer charges against Pillow, Pillow finally acceded to Polk's authority and ended the controversy.[16] By the time Gen. Frémont ordered Gen. Prentiss to attack the rebels at Benton, some Confederate troops still lingered near Sikeston. Of course, Gen. Thompson was still in the neighborhood with his State Guard troops, and he still presented a potent threat to good order.

Confusion reigned on the Union side as well. Three days after Frémont sent his order to Prentiss, he issued another one to Ulysses Grant that began with virtually the same words. How things unfolded—and what happened as a result—suggests that the national administration, together with Frémont's command in St. Louis, was nearly as inept as Polk's operation in Tennessee.

When Lincoln called for Illinois men to meet the state's quota for enlistments in April 1861, the response was so overwhelming that Illinois companies helped fill regiments in other states. Up until August 5, 1861, Illinois had two soldiers who had attained the rank of brigadier general: John Pope and Stephen A. Hurlbut. On August 5, the US Senate confirmed 37 new brigadiers of volunteers, whom Lincoln had nominated to the rank. Among them were three Illinoisans: Ulysses Grant; Benjamin Prentiss; and another politician, John McClernand. Obscure army traditions dictated that officer commissions could be backdated, so the ranks of Grant, Prentiss, and McClernand—and many of the other 37 men—were all made effective on the same day, May 17, 1861. While this system may have been productive in the peacetime army, at no other time in American history would so many generals be left to determine seniority by reference to a single date.

Frémont's words in his order to Prentiss on August 25 conveyed the urgency of the situation in the cities of Benton and Commerce. On that day, however, it appears that Frémont was comfortable that Prentiss, taking charge of small commands in Ironton and Cape Girardeau, would be up to the task. On the other hand, there was Gen. Grant, who was now in Jefferson City after Prentiss relieved him. Frémont had sent Grant there after he returned to St. Louis from Ironton. It has never been clear why Frémont did this; one reasonable conclusion is that Grant was parked in Jefferson City, pending determination of Grant's claim that he outranked Prentiss.

Gen. Grant was a faithful and honest correspondent to his wife, Julia. We know from a letter he wrote from Jefferson City on August 26 that he was crestfallen by the circumstances of his departure from Ironton: "When I was ordered away from Ironton nearly all of the commanders of regiments expressed regret I am told."[17]

Late in the morning of August 28, 1861, Grant was surprised when an Indiana colonel by the name of Jefferson C. Davis walked into his Jefferson City headquarters. Davis presented an order from Frémont that directed Grant to proceed immediately to St. Louis for "special orders." Grant was on an eastbound train within hours. Early the next day, Grant began a letter to his wife: "I have a moment to drop you a line...but this time I cannot inform you where I am going. I know there is a Steamer laying at the Wharf, loaded with troops, ready to start whenever I go aboard."[18]

Whatever created this stunning turnaround happened over several hours at the Brant Mansion in St. Louis during the afternoon of August 28. Grant detrained at the Pacific Railroad terminal at 7th and Cerre streets and walked the three blocks to Frémont's headquarters. According to the only description still extant, Grant passed through the well-guarded entrance to the building's basement, where he was relegated to a bench to wait and see why he was there.[19]

Meanwhile, Frémont had assembled senior staff on the floor above. While staff engaged in high-level strategic talks with their commander, Grant was brought into the room. After he left the meeting and the mansion, Grant carried with him an order that read: "You are instructed to proceed forthwith to Cape Girardeau and assume command of the forces at that place." As in the order Frémont sent to Prentiss on August 25, Frémont warned Grant of the enemy forces thought to still occupy Benton and the hills around Commerce. Importantly, though, the order also laid out plans for an aggressive campaign on several fronts, including a movement upon neutral Kentucky.

At the same time, Frémont dictated a communiqué to Benjamin Prentiss in Ironton that left no doubt whatsoever that Grant had seniority, and that Prentiss would henceforth subordinate his actions to Grant's command:

> When you were ordered to go to Ironton and take the place of General Grant, who was transferred to Jefferson City, it was under the impression that his appointment was of a later date than your own. By the official list published it appears, however, that he is your senior in rank. He will, therefore, upon effecting a conjunction with your troops, take command of the whole expedition.[20]

History has placed Ulysses Grant's life under a microscope. Some aspects of his life have become a matter of legend, one that's been colored by a notion that this "everyman" could not have succeeded on his own merit. The decision made in St. Louis that vaulted Grant into renown is attributed by some to connections he'd forged during his brief residence in Galena, Illinois—specifically, favors from Galena congressman Elihu Washburne.

Grant's woeful experiences in the weeks and days before his assignment to Cape Girardeau belies the notion that Grant had a guardian angel, whether Washburne or anyone else.

Justus McKinstry posited an alternate version of Grant's promotion. McKinstry knew Grant from the Regular Army in California. According to Bruce Catton's *Grant Moves South*, when McKinstry was on his way to the staff meeting in the Brant Mansion on August 28, he greeted Grant as he was waiting in the basement. When the discussion upstairs turned to appointing an officer to command a drive south, McKinstry said, "I know just the man, Sam Grant, who is waiting downstairs."[21] It's a fascinating story, but most likely, the simple and correct answer is that Ulysses Grant was the senior brigadier whom Frémont had available, and Grant was not otherwise usefully engaged.

Many historians would agree that putting Grant in charge was the best decision Frémont made during his 100 days in Missouri. Within the next 48 hours, however, Frémont would make a decision that was probably his worst.

ENDNOTES

1. Lawrence O. Christensen, William Foley, and Gary Kremer, eds., *Dictionary of Missouri Biography* (University of Missouri Press, 1999), 615.

2. Virginia Jeans Laas collected and annotated Elizabeth Lee's letters in *Wartime Washington: The Civil War Letters of Elizabeth Blair Lee* (University of Illinois Press, 1991). References to individual letters shall be to their author, place, and date, and to the page number where the letter appears in Laas's work.

3. Elizabeth Blair Lee to Samuel Lee, Philadelphia, August 14, 1861; Laas, 71.

4. Although he lacked combat experience, in 1861 Blair worked hard to obtain a significant army command. Ultimately, he proved he could be a soldier of supreme competence. During the Civil War, Blair would rise to the rank of major general of volunteers, commanding an entire army corps during Sherman's Atlanta campaign and March to the Sea.

5. "Martial Law Proclaimed in St. Louis," *New York Times*, August 15, 1861; "Broadside Proclamation of Martial Law in the City and County of St. Louis," Missouri Historical Society Collections. See Thomas F. Carroll, "Freedom of Speech and of the Press during the Civil War," *Virginia Law Review* 9, no. 7 (May 1923): 516–551.

6. The completion of the forts surrounding Cape Girardeau was left in the hands of two men. One was Henry Flad, an engineer who would later become chief assistant engineer for the construction of the Eads Bridge in St. Louis. The second man was John Wesley Powell, then a young lieutenant in the 20th Illinois Infantry. Powell would go on to lead the first exploration by European Americans of the Grand Canyon and serve as director of the US Geological Survey.

7. Gen. Thompson's phrase "I am a rip-squealer" is of unknown origin, but it's probably a variant of the expression "ring-tailed squealer," which seems to refer to something superlative.

8. Leonidas Polk graduated in 1827 from West Point, where he befriended classmate Jefferson Davis. In 1830, he entered the ministry of the Episcopal Church and ultimately rose to the post of Episcopal bishop of Louisiana. Jefferson Davis persuaded Polk to join the army, which he did in 1861, entering the service as a major-general of the Provisional Army of the Confederate States. After rising to the rank of lieutenant-general, the "Fighting Bishop" was killed in Georgia in 1864. As bishop, Polk founded the University of the South, which still operates in Sewanee, Tennessee. Leo J. Goodsell, "Leonidas Polk," in *Tennessee Encyclopedia* (University of Tennessee Press, 1998), published October 8, 2017; last updated March 1, 2018, https://tennesseeencyclopedia.net/entries/leonidas-polk.

9. Ulysses Grant held Gideon Pillow in absolute contempt. Writing years later about the prospect of facing Pillow at Fort Donelson, Tennessee, Grant said, "I had known General Pillow in Mexico, and judged that with any force, no matter how small, I could march up to within gunshot of any intrenchments he was given to hold. I said this to the officers of my staff at the time." Ulysses S. Grant, *Personal Memoirs of U. S. Grant* (Charles L. Webster & Company, 1885), 196.

10. William J. Hardee graduated from the United States Military Academy in 1838. He fought in the Mexican-American War and received two brevet promotions for gallantry. Later in his military career, Hardee returned to West Point, where he served as the commandant of cadets from 1856 to 1860. While on assignment to West Point, Hardee wrote *Rifle and Light Infantry Tactics*, probably the most widely used infantry-tactics book of the Civil War era. "William J. Hardee," in *American Battlefield Trust*, https://www.battlefields.org/learn/biographies/william-j-hardee.

11. *Official Records of the Union and Confederate Armies, Ser. 1, Vol. 3, Ch. 10*, 630.

12. In *Personal Memoirs*, Ulysses Grant wrote, "Brown himself was gladder to see me on that occasion than he ever has been since," 169. This tongue-in-cheek remark referenced the fact that Brown was the vice-presidential candidate on the opposing ticket when Grant ran for a second term as US president in 1872. Kentucky-born Benjamin Gratz Brown was a first cousin to Frank Blair Jr., who was coincidentally the opposing candidate for vice president in 1868, when Grant ran the first time.

13. In *Personal Memoirs*, Grant acknowledged that Prentiss's orders did not technically relieve him, but that by law, "even the President did not have authority to assign a junior to command a senior of the same grade," 170.

14. For readers who would like to explore the Confederate incursion into Missouri through New Madrid in more detail, *Official Records* has an extraordinary date-ordered section that lays out the communications among Polk, Pillow, and Thompson, 631–670. The communications recorded in *Official Records* for the week of August 5, 1861, leave no doubt that Thompson adroitly and successfully played Polk, Pillow, and Hardee against one another in his bid to capture Cape Girardeau, 631–644.

15. *Official Records*, 453–454.

16. Gen. Gideon Pillow lived up to negative expectations in his dealings with his superiors and subordinates over the matter of Neely's regiment. In the first place, the Confederate high command determined it would abandon its foray into Missouri; on August 15, 1861, Maj. Gen. Polk advised Pillow: "[I]t is your duty to cross the river into Tennessee with your whole command at once." Two days later, on August 17, Polk allowed Pillow some leeway in his timing, but very soon thereafter Pillow violated a direct order to send Neely's command to its assignment in Tennessee. *Official Records*, 662–663. Pillow was being encouraged by Gen. Thompson to join in an attack on Cape Girardeau. *Official Records*, 661–662; 664. It appears that, all the while, Neely's command was off with Jeff Thompson on Thompson's mission to Commerce. *Official Records*, 685.

17. John Y. Simon, ed., *The Papers of Ulysses S. Grant, Volume 2: April–September 1861* (Southern Illinois University Press, 1967–1985), 140–141.

18. Simon, 148–149.

19. Grant's experience at St. Louis headquarters was representative of Frémont's normal practice. Throughout the 64 days that Frémont commanded from the Brant Mansion and before he took the field in late September 1861, countless visitors complained of waiting in the basement.

20. *Official Records*, 142–143.

21. Bruce Catton, *Grant Moves South* (Little, Brown & Company, 1960), 37–38.

CHAPTER 4

*"I am like a deeply built ship;
I drive best under a stormy wind."*

—Jessie Benton Frémont

Figure 4

Jessie Benton Frémont was born in Virginia in 1824 and raised in Washington City, as her father, Thomas Hart Benton, served out his 30-year tenure in the US Senate. Along with her husband, she authored reports that chronicled Frémont's great expeditions to the West. These works immortalized Frémont and his sidekick, Kit Carson, and laid the groundwork for a modest body of literature she produced during her lifetime. Among them is *The Story of the Guard: A Chronicle of the War*, a spirited defense of her husband's activities in 1861 Missouri.

The White House

Washington City, September 10, 1861

THE GENERAL'S WIFE WAITED in the Red Room for her audience with Abraham Lincoln. Measured by intelligence, by force of will—indeed, by birthright—no woman in 19th-century America was more prepared to confront a sitting president than Jessie Frémont was on this day.

Ten days had come and gone since John Frémont issued an order declaring martial law in Missouri. In the twilight of the 11th day, Jessie Frémont checked into Washington City's Willard Hotel at the corner of 14th Street and Pennsylvania Avenue. She'd left army headquarters in St. Louis and crossed half a continent in two days, toting a letter defending her husband's August 30 order and his honor. She would demand that President Lincoln hear and understand that the most controversial phrase in John Frémont's order—the one that offered freedom to enslaved persons—was the most indispensable:

> The property, real and personal, of all persons, in the State of Missouri, who shall take up arms against the United States, or who shall be directly proven to have taken an active part with their enemies in the field, is declared to be confiscated to the public use, and their Slaves, if any they have, are hereby declared Free men.

From her room at the Willard, Jessie forwarded a note to the White House that asked to present her husband's letter to Lincoln. Lincoln's response arrived before midnight: "Now, at once."

Her anger, hyped by exhaustion from her journey, was a product of the realization that the Blairs had abandoned her husband and were working to undermine him. The door of the State Dining Room swung open, and Abraham Lincoln entered the Red Room. Jessie Benton Frémont stood, erect and defiant, to face the president. Lincoln would say of the meeting that ensued: "[She]...attacked me so violently with so many things that I had to exercise all the awkward tact I had to avoid quarrelling with her."

On August 30, 1861, Ulysses Grant boarded the side-wheeler *City of Louisiana* for Cape Girardeau. His progress had been delayed for a day. While stationed in Jefferson City, Grant had decided whom he would appoint to his staff. One of the men—lawyer William Hillyer, whom Grant knew from his time working in real estate—lived in St. Louis and joined Grant on the trip south. John Rawlings and Clark Lagow, both of Galena, Illinois, would round out Grant's personal staff. The *City of Louisiana* was one of the swiftest vessels on the river, but even so, the passage to Grant's assigned destination took most of the day.[1]

Early in the morning of August 30, about the time Grant and Hillyer boarded the steamer, Jessie Frémont was walking into the first-floor war room at the Brant Mansion. Drawing on Frémont's memoir, Nevins described what happened: "Shortly after daybreak, Mrs. Frémont found Gen. Frémont at his desk. He had sent for Mr. Edward Davis, of Philadelphia, who arrived as she came…. The General said, 'I want you two but no others.'"[2]

Then, Gen. Frémont read aloud the text of a proclamation he'd written. While it declared martial law across the entire state of Missouri, it first concentrated on the military situation in northern Missouri. Frémont suggested in his writings that he drafted the document by himself, but it's likely that John Pope also had a hand in it. Pope had been in St. Louis during that time, and he was becoming frantic that the area he'd been charged with protecting had gone to the devil. Pope's order of July 21, 1861—stating he would levy the local populace to repair damage to the railroads—seems to have grown in importance in his mind as the days and weeks went by. He had become obsessed with the idea that his plan could tame the insurgency in northeast Missouri. From his headquarters in Mexico, Pope proposed that he would occupy each and every one of the county seats northeast of Mexico, even reporting on August 4 that "by a simultaneous movement I shall to-night or to-morrow morning occupy in force the county seats of the nineteen counties." This did not happen—perhaps because the Battle of Athens erupted the next day, or perhaps because it was just an impossible thing to do.[3]

On August 10, Gen. Pope ordered a regiment of Iowa cavalry to "march slowly" through five northeast Missouri counties, "occupying in turn the county seats of each long enough to restore peace." Finally, on August 25, 1861, Pope wrote a rambling letter to Frémont that touted the success of his plan, a letter that was probably both written and delivered within the walls of the Brant Mansion. The letter made a stunning, if unintentional, admission: Occupying Union forces had only enforced Pope's draconian regime in one county.[4]

Frémont released his proclamation to the public on August 30. It read in part:

> The lines of the army of occupation in this State are for the present declared to extend from Leavenworth, by way of the posts of Jefferson City, Rolla, and Ironton, to Cape Girardeau, on the Mississippi River.
>
> All persons who shall be taken with arms in their hands within these lines shall be tried by court-martial, and if found guilty will be shot.[5]

Historians, generally, do not dwell on this part of Frémont's declaration, but a few words for the sake of context are appropriate. It is noteworthy that Frémont had already assumed Ulysses Grant's conquest of Cape Girardeau, even though Grant was still on his way there, and the body of troops he would need were still marching from Ironton. Coupled with Frémont's earlier direction to Grant that he should prepare to assault Columbus, Kentucky, Frémont's assumption suggests that Union authorities were anticipating the end of Kentucky's neutrality. Noteworthy as well, Frémont announced an Army of Occupation, which applied only to the territory that Frémont already had (or soon would have) under control. Frémont's line in the sand was there to protect his army north and east of the line he drew from Leavenworth to Cape Girardeau—largely, the part of the territory where Pope was operating. Of course, the notion that citizens of north Missouri who were found in possession of firearms would be executed was preposterous.

But it was this phrase from Frémont's August 30 proclamation that ignited a firestorm: "and their Slaves, if any they have, are hereby declared Free men." With that phrase excluded, Frémont's order was not much different from Congress's First Confiscation Act, which President Lincoln had signed into law earlier that month. In fairness to Gen. Frémont, his proclamation differed in essence only because he spelled out what was hidden between the lines of that act.

The First Confiscation Act stated that whenever any slave was employed, by the order or consent of the master or an agent of the master, in the work upon "any fort, navy yard, dock, armory, ship, entrenchment, or in any military or naval service," the master would "forfeit his claim" to the labor of the slave. In its last sentence, the act said that whenever such a master attempted to enforce his right to such labor, "it shall be a full and sufficient answer to such claim that the person whose service or labor is claimed had been employed in hostile service against the Government of the United States...."[6] One may fairly ask: If the master may not enforce the servitude of the enslaved person, is not the enslaved person free?

Colonel Frank Blair Jr.
Photograph by E. Anthony,
New York, 1864–1865.
Missouri Historical Society Collections.

Frank Blair was in St. Louis when Frémont issued his proclamation, having returned to the city after the special session of Congress concluded on August 6. Within a week, an omen of future strife between the Frémonts and the Blairs surfaced. Congressman Blair, it seems, was obsessed with the welfare of Colonel Blair, the soldier. The lawyer in Frank Blair thought he could evade the Ineligibility Clause of the United States Constitution,[7] which states that military officers are "officials" of the United States and therefore prohibited from serving in either house of Congress. Frank Blair's plan—proposed in an August 1861 letter to Jessie Frémont that Preston Blair authored—was that Gen. Frémont would use his influence with Missouri's provisional governor to obtain for Frank a position in the Missouri militia: "I want you to have Frank made a Militia Major General."[8] Preston Blair made this his first condition if the Blairs and the Frémonts were to form a "co-partnership in the West," one that would in turn promote Gen. Frémont's interests. The elder Blair also noted in this letter that President Lincoln had offered Frank a general's commission, but Frank declined it because that would cause him to vacate his seat in Congress, and "Frank felt he might be useful in Congress."[9]

On September 1, Frank Blair penned a letter to his brother Montgomery, in which he let loose on the man Jessie Benton had married.[10] Gen. Frémont, he said, "should be relieved of his command and a man of ability put in his place—The sooner it is done the better." He then recited a litany of charges against Frémont, including that he'd abandoned Nathaniel Lyon, plus an extremely dubious charge that two additional regiments would have turned the tide at the Battle of Wilson's Creek.

If it is presumed that Frank intended this message for Montgomery's eyes only and not for the public record, it may help gauge Frank's state of mind at a crucial point in time. One particular part stands out: Speaking much like a modern politician, Frank warns Montgomery that "The views I have given of this matter are fast becoming public opinion [in St. Louis]." As Frémont's chief antagonist, Frank Blair would be the main source of Frémont's loss of public support. Additionally, Frank's remarks omitted the part of Frémont's proclamation that offered freedom to enslaved people. Evidently speaking of the proclamation's military measures, Frank noted that it "is the best thing of the kind that has been issued."[11]

Abraham Lincoln had a different reaction. He penned a letter on September 11 that, on its surface, seems to represent a good-faith effort to elicit Frémont's cooperation. It was important and secret enough, however, that Lincoln did not trust it to the military telegraph. Instead, he dispatched a messenger to deliver it to St. Louis. Lincoln gave short shrift to the matter of executing gun-toting Southerners and simply ordered Frémont to ask him before shooting anyone. Lincoln's attention focused on the so-called "emancipation order," and his letter to Frémont reveals both what and why:

> Liberating slaves of traiterous [*sic*] owners, will alarm our Southern Union friends, and turn them against us perhaps ruining our rather fair prospect for Kentucky. Allow me therefore to ask, that you will as of your own motion, modify that paragraph so as to conform to [the First Confiscation Act].[12]

Whatever—or whoever—it was that prompted Frémont to include the phrase that offered freedom to the enslaved, his timing was absolutely atrocious. The Commonwealth of Kentucky—the birthplace of Abraham Lincoln, Jefferson Davis, and Frank and Montgomery Blair—was one of the last border states to decide the question of secession. Lincoln was encouraged by the results of Kentucky's legislative elections in early August, which left unionists with a three-quarters margin of control in the House and a similar margin in the Senate.[13] Gen. Polk had to decide in this new light if his army would be the first to break Kentucky's policy of neutrality. Ironically, perhaps, the August election results made his decision easier. For all practical purposes, the question of Kentucky's future in the Confederacy had been decided. Still, the North drew some benefit in public perception because its soldiers were not the first combatants to enter Kentucky in force. Fortunately, as well, John Frémont and Ulysses Grant were ready to move into the state in the blink of an eye.

Jeff Thompson, the Missouri State Guard general who created the panic that brought Ulysses Grant to the fore, also had an opinion about Frémont's proclamation. While Tennessee and Mississippi troops were leaving the scene by way of New Madrid, Thompson established a fortified camp at the north end of Sikeston Ridge, commanding the bridge that crossed the lake on the way to high ground—a good choice for defensive purposes. Thompson named the site Camp Hunter.

On September 2, 1861, Thompson issued a proclamation of his own, a scathing critique of Frémont's martial law edict. (See the appendix, page 198, for the full text.) For the most part, Thompson focused on the new rules of engagement that had been designed, it seems, to placate Gen. Pope as he clamped down in northern Missouri. Said Thompson:

> Therefore, know ye, that I, M. Jeff. Thompson, Brigadier General of the first military district of Missouri...do most solemnly promise that for every member of the Missouri State Guard, or soldier of our allies, the armies of the Confederate States, who shall be put to death in pursuance of the said order of General Frémont, that I will "hang, draw and quarter" a minion of said Abraham Lincoln.
>
> [...]
>
> I intend to exceed General Frémont in his excesses....[14]

At the same time Thompson issued his bombastic challenge, he unknowingly caused a hitch in the plans of the man sent to drive him away:

Ulysses Grant. Just north of Camp Hunter, the road forked to the right, passing through Benton before ending at Commerce on the river. The left fork proceeded due north from the junction for 25 miles to Jackson, the county seat of Cape Girardeau County. This was how the stage was set for Grant and Prentiss (the latter marching east from Ironton) to attack the Missouri State Guard and the Confederates who were known to be camped near Benton. The road from Jackson, the left fork, was the route that would put Grant's forces below Benton, in the enemy's line of retreat. For this reason, Prentiss was ordered to halt his six regiments at Jackson and wait there until Grant joined him to take command.[15]

Prentiss left Ironton on August 27. On the evening of September 1, Grant learned that Prentiss's troops had reached Jackson. The next morning, Grant saddled up outside his hotel on Main Street and proceeded two blocks north toward the road to Jackson, when he noticed a commotion on Themis Street, one block west. Grant saw a column of Union horsemen. He redirected his horse and galloped around the block to meet the column head-on. Sure enough, it was Benjamin Prentiss and his staff. As ordered, Prentiss had left his regiments at Jackson, but contrary to orders, he had left them there headless. One would suppose Gen. Prentiss had misunderstood his orders, but in fact Prentiss had intentionally come to Cape Girardeau to assert his purported seniority over Grant.

When Prentiss announced his intentions, a heated argument ensued. Grant wouldn't budge from his position. Rather than submit to Grant's authority, Prentiss demanded that Grant arrest him. Grant refused, so Prentiss placed himself under arrest. He remained in Cape at least until September 3, when orders arrived from Frémont that Prentiss was to report to St. Louis headquarters.[16] Grant preferred charges of insubordination against Prentiss and complained bitterly that the offensive against the enemy at Benton—one that Frémont's orders had dictated—had to be called off because of Prentiss's antics.[17]

Grant's offensive was indeed canceled, but other events soon intervened to render the plan Frémont had composed five days earlier in St. Louis a matter of ancient history. On September 3, 1861, Gen. Gideon Pillow invaded Kentucky with 6,000 Confederate troops, most of whom had populated Pillow's Army of Liberation in Missouri.

Despite the fervent hope of most Kentucky legislators, the state's self-proclaimed neutrality was destined to collapse under its own weight. There were many reasons that this was so, but at least in western Kentucky, one was a matter of geology. Politics had dictated that Confederate defenses along the Cumberland and Tennessee rivers had to be sited in Tennessee so as not to infringe on Kentucky's sovereignty, so Fort Henry, for example, was built in a flood-prone river bottom. In August 1861, Confederates were contemplating a similar mistake on the Mississippi River, as they began to fortify Island No. 10 near the border of Tennessee and Missouri. Geology pointed instead to a bluff known as the Iron Banks, which loomed nearly 200 feet above the Kentucky side of the Mississippi River, about 25 miles inside Kentucky's border with Tennessee. Explorers Jacques Marquette and Louis Joliet named this prominence Les Rivages de Fer, as they assumed its reddish color meant iron was present in the bluffs.

Columbus, Kentucky, sat in the shadow of the Iron Banks, but the town was of great strategic value for another reason: It was the railhead of the Mobile and Ohio Railroad. When the line to Columbus was completed in April 1861, it marked the first time a through route stretched from Chicago to the Gulf of Mexico. Still, goods and passengers arriving at Cairo via the Illinois Central Railroad had to be ferried to Columbus to complete the journey south. The technology to build a bridge through the massive wetlands around the confluence of the Ohio and Mississippi rivers did not yet exist. The commercial opportunities that this new rail link enabled during times of peace became liabilities once the Civil War broke out: Here was a choke point for the movement of men and materiél. In anticipation of the railroad reaching Columbus from the south, Missouri business interests got behind the construction of a line that would terminate at Belmont, Missouri, directly across the river from Columbus.

On September 3, Gen. Pillow entered Kentucky and made a beeline for Columbus. Gen. Polk would join him there in the following days with additional troops from Memphis. But first, Pillow detached perhaps half of his force to march on Paducah, a strategic city on the Ohio River that controlled the mouths of the Cumberland and Tennessee rivers.[18]

Frémont wanted Grant's permanent headquarters to be located in Cairo, Illinois, with temporary headquarters in Cape Girardeau, while Grant carried out the campaign against Thompson in Benton. Gen. Grant moved to Cairo on September 4, 1861. It was there that Grant learned of Pillow's movement aimed at Paducah from Charles de Arnaud, a man whom Frémont had hired to spy on Pillow's operations.[19] From then until the end of the Civil War, Grant showed how quickly he could move an army when circumstances demanded it. By the next evening in Cairo, the brand-spanking-new general had two regiments and four pieces of artillery loaded on three steamboats. Two gunboats stood at the ready. The flotilla cast off at 10:30pm and arrived in Paducah 10 hours later, on September 6.

Steamboats at Cairo, Illinois. Union gunboats *Lexington* and *Tyler* anchored south of Cairo. Drawing by Henri Lovie, August 8, 1861. The Becker Collection, Boston College Libraries.

Just seven days after he'd boarded the *City of Louisiana* in St. Louis, it was now Grant's turn to make a proclamation. He came ashore at the wharf in Paducah and declared, "I am here to defend you against this enemy and to assert and maintain the authority and sovereignty of your Government and mine."[20] From that day on, Paducah remained firmly in Union hands.

★ ★ ★

Gen. Frémont had a direct role in all of these developments. Faced with insurrection to the north, enemy incursions in the southeast, and the Confederate invasion of Kentucky, his hands were already full. But on August 25, 1861—31 days into Frémont's reign in Missouri—it was time for Sterling Price to again flex the muscles of the Missouri State Guard. They ventured out of Springfield.

Since his victory at Wilson's Creek two weeks before, Price had the southwest under his unmolested control. He might have moved earlier, but he'd tried to goad Benjamin McCulloch and his Confederates into joining him in a Missouri offensive, as he had done successfully before Wilson's Creek. McCulloch would have none of it; by the end of August, with Hardee and Pillow withdrawing to Arkansas and Tennessee, there was no chance that McCulloch would leave his base in northwest Arkansas.

Moving north along the Missouri-Kansas border, the State Guard first advanced to Missouri's Vernon County, opposite Fort Scott in Kansas. Its immediate objective was to punish the Kansas troops, under command of the notorious James Lane, who were using Fort Scott as a base to carry out raids on Missouri. On September 2, 1861, Price and Lane fought a sharp skirmish along Dry Wood Creek in Vernon County, known as the Battle of the Mules.[21] The skirmish was indecisive, but as Price left the scene still heading north, his ultimate objective was becoming clear: Day after day he was moving closer to Lexington, a thriving port city on the Missouri River some 50 miles downriver from Kansas City. By maneuvering through the wide gap between the Kansas forces to the west and Jefferson City to the east (where Jefferson Davis was in command), Price would split the Union defenses in two. And, logistically, there was nothing that Frémont was going to do about it.

The week Frémont issued his martial law proclamation was consumed with activity. On September 4, Frémont took a visit from William T. Sherman, an old California acquaintance with a new command at Louisville, Kentucky. Over September 5 and 6, Frémont entertained Prince Napoleon of France, and Benjamin Grierson of Illinois dropped in to headquarters to make the case that his friend Benjamin Prentiss should have seniority over Grant.[22] On September 6, a band of renegades partially destroyed the Salt River Bridge, once again stopping rail traffic on the Hannibal and St. Joseph Railroad, and a similar incident was reported near Rolla on the Southwest Branch of the Pacific Railroad.[23] At some point before the week's end, Lincoln's messenger arrived with the president's plea asking Frémont to moderate his August 30 order.

John Frémont might well have taken Lincoln's plea to conform his order to the First Confiscation Act to heart. After all, Lincoln had said it was written in "a spirit of caution and not of censure." What happened instead nearly boggles the mind. In response, Frémont wrote a letter dated September 8 that amounted to the same sort of petulant nonsense that followed his court-martial for insubordination some 14 years before. Frémont defended his reasons for issuing the August 30 proclamation, as well as his need to have enough discretion to make mistakes. Frémont believed that "If I were to retract [the proclamation] of my own accord it would imply that I myself thought it wrong and that I had acted without the reflection which the gravity of the point demanded."[24] Frémont insisted that Lincoln override his proclamation and do so publicly, which he did on September 11, 1861.

Because President Lincoln sent his September 2 missive—the one asking Frémont to modify his "emancipation order"—by special messenger, Frémont's response would be a tit for tat. Jessie Frémont hand-carried Frémont's defiant letter to Lincoln in Washington. It was not a pleasant experience for either one of them. As Jessie recollected many years later, she was summoned to the White House before she could bathe or change from her traveling clothes. After the president entered the room, she reported that he was discourteous to her, not even offering her a seat. For his part, Lincoln had this to say: "General Frémont should not have dragged the Negro into [the proclamation]—that he never would if he had consulted with Frank Blair. I sent Frank there to advise him."[25]

Jessie Frémont said that Lincoln had promised a response to the letter the following day. Instead, Preston Blair paid her a visit, and he was livid. In his view, Frémont had grievously erred by not letting Preston's eldest son, Montgomery Blair, manage affairs in Missouri. The senior Blair also evidently let it slip that his son Frank had written a letter to Montgomery charging Frémont with incompetence. Moreover, Jessie learned that Montgomery Blair had boarded a westbound train for St. Louis three days earlier, intent on counseling Gen. Frémont back to his senses.

Preston Blair summed up his meeting with Jessie Frémont this way: "She has proved to be to us what [Thomas] Benton proved to be at the close of his life when his inveterate ambition mastered all his faculties."[26] The bonds between the intertwined families, ones that stretched back to the Jackson administration, were now severed forever.

Jessie's trip to Washington City was no mean feat, even for a woman who had traversed the Isthmus of Panama on numerous occasions. Jessie was relatively unfamiliar with the workings of modern transportation in the eastern United States. She had been living in California since 1857. In the meantime, railroads had proliferated across the landscape, especially in the Midwest, as the great eastern lines fought to reach the Mississippi Valley. Jessie's father's dream of a railroad to the Pacific, with St. Louis at its head, had secured a foothold even before she left for California. The Pacific Railroad—its name reflecting the unbridled confidence of its promoters—had nearly reached Tipton, Missouri, 160 rail miles west of St. Louis, by the end of 1857.

However, the connections that St. Louis would need from the east were lagging. It was not until April 1857 that the first through route by rail from the Eastern Seaboard finally reached St. Louis. This was thanks to a combination of carriers that had built west from the Ohio River opposite Parkersburg, Virginia, the westernmost reach of the great Baltimore and Ohio Railroad. Not long after, the Pennsylvania Railroad line extended to St. Louis, eventually connecting Pittsburgh to Indianapolis to St. Louis. The Mississippi River had not been bridged before the Civil War, so these lines terminated at East St. Louis. When the Civil War began, the Baltimore and Ohio Railroad shut down for about 10 months because it crossed Virginia soil and was a target for Confederate raiders.

Jessie had traveled east on September 8 in the company of a maid. After meeting with old Preston Blair, Jessie gave the maid a cyphered telegram to give to John in St. Louis, warning him that Montgomery Blair was on the way to meet him, and he was not to be trusted. Jessie also told her husband about Frank Blair's September 1 letter to Montgomery that advocated for Frémont's removal from his post. She had become obsessed with the missive, and it would fuel one of the next escalations in the Benton-Blair war.

ENDNOTES

1. The *City of Louisiana* arrived at Cape Girardeau the evening of August 30. John Y. Simon, ed., *The Papers of Ulysses S. Grant, Volume 2: April–September 1861* (Southern Illinois University Press, 1967–1985), 159.

2. Allan Nevins, *John Frémont: Pathmarker of the West* (University of Nebraska Press, 1939), 500.

3. *Official Records of the Union and Confederate Armies, Ser. 1, Vol. 3, Ch. 10,* 426–427.

4. *Official Records,* 435.

5. *Official Records,* 466–467. See appendix.

6. United States Congress. *The Statutes at Large and Treaties of the United States of America, from December 5, 1859, to March 3, 1863. With References to the Matter of Each Act and to the Subsequent Acts on the Same Subject, Vol. 12* (Little, Brown, 1863), 319. See appendix.

7. United States Constitution, article 1, section 6, clause 2.

8. Abraham Lincoln Papers. Letter, Francis P. Blair Sr. to Jessie Benton Frémont, August 13, 1861. It appears that the senior Mr. Blair addressed nearly the same letter to Gen. Frémont, although that letter is not preserved in the Library of Congress. See Allen Nevins, *The War for the Union, Vol. 1: The Improvised War, 1861–1862* (Konecky & Konecky, 1971), 324–325.

9. Ibid.

10. Abraham Lincoln Papers: General Correspondence, 1833–1916, Series 1. Letter, Francis P. Blair Jr. to Montgomery Blair, September 1, 1861. Library of Congress, Washington, DC.

11. Abraham Lincoln Papers. Letter, Francis P. Blair Jr. to Montgomery Blair, September 1, 1861.

12. Abraham Lincoln Papers. Letter, Abraham Lincoln to John Frémont, September 11, 1861.

13. Lowell H. Harrison, *The Civil War in Kentucky* (The University Press of Kentucky, 2009), 11.

14. *Official Records,* 693. See appendix.

15. Grant, *Personal Memoirs,* 165.

16. *Official Records,* 147–148.

17. Grant, *Personal Memoirs,* 173; Simon, 140–141.

18. Joseph W. McCoskrie, *The War for Missouri, 1861–1862* (The History Press, 2020), 94–95. Berry Craig, *Kentucky Confederates: Secession, Civil War, and the Jackson Purchase* (The University Press of Kentucky, 2014), 132.

19. Grant, *Personal Memoirs,* 174; Simon, 193.

20. Simon, 194–195.

21. This small battle was fought along Dry Wood Creek, 12 miles east of the Kansas border. Combatants of the victorious Missouri State Guard nicknamed the clash "Battle of the Mules" because the Union commander retreated in such haste that he left his mules on the field. "Battle of Dry Wood Creek," *Civil War on the Western Border* (Kansas City Public Library, 2013–), https://civilwaronthewesternborder. org/timeline/battle-dry-wood-creek.

22. Bruce J. Dinges and Shirley A. Leckie, eds., *A Just and Righteous Cause: Benjamin H. Grierson's Civil War Memoir* (Southern Illinois University Press, 2016), 52–53.

23. *Official Records,* 474.

24. *Official Records,* 478.

25. Nevins, 517.

26. Elizabeth Blair Lee to Samuel Lee, Bethlehem, September 17, 1861; Laas, 78–81.

CHAPTER 5

*"I am grieved & cut to the heart by
Frémont's treatment of Frank."*

—Elizabeth Blair Lee

Figure 5

Elizabeth Blair Lee, known to friends as "Lizzie," was the second-oldest child and only daughter of Preston Blair and Eliza Violet Gist. She was born in 1818 in Frankfort, Kentucky. In 1843, Elizabeth married a young naval officer named Samuel Phillips Lee, a distant cousin of Robert E. Lee. Like many Navy wives, she was often apart from her husband, but she purportedly promised that she'd write him every day he was away from home. Promise or no promise, Elizabeth left behind a massive historical record in her letters, which were published in part in 1991.

The Mary Blair Cottage

Bethlehem, Pennsylvania, September 19, 1861

THE WEATHER BEGAN TO chill this week in the hills above Bethlehem, something Elizabeth "Lizzie" Blair Lee was unaccustomed to. She had spent nearly her entire life in and around Washington City, where September was just about as hot as August. She had left there in July, soon after the Union's loss at Bull Run, as her father, Preston Blair, had suggested. There was a palpable fear among many Washingtonians that the rebels would soon overrun the capital, and besides, Lizzie rarely rejected her father's advice, which he gave freely and often. Lizzie's four-year-old son, Blair, was with her during this uprooted summer.

Lizzie and Blair visited Philadelphia for a time, staying longer than she expected, and then headed to a place her sister-in-law was renting near Bethlehem, Pennsylvania. This was Lizzie's intended destination when she left Washington a few weeks before. Mary Jessup Blair was the widow of Lizzie's brother James. Mary had rented a summer cottage that year to escape the heat of Washington with her three children. Lizzie and Blair arrived in Bethlehem in late August 1861; after three weeks, they left to return to Philadelphia.

As Lizzie packed her things, she was still fuming about the events of the day before. The nerve of that woman. Jessie Benton had been like family. Back in Washington, Jessie had grown from a precocious five-year-old into a young woman before Lizzie's very eyes. From the early 1830s into the 1840s, hardly a month went by that the Bentons and the Blairs were not together.

The family never saw what Jessie did in that husband of hers. She married too young. Over the years, as Jessie seemed to drift away from the family, Lizzie thought John Frémont was to blame. Before Jessie left Bethlehem, though, it was clear to her that Jessie was no victim in that marriage.

Soon after Gen. Frémont issued his martial law edict of August 30, he and his staff began to vet cases of enslaved persons who might qualify for manumission, a process that required independent fact-finding. As his proclamation dictated, Frémont would only emancipate those whose owners were "directly proven" to have aided enemies of the United States in the field. Ultimately only two men were granted freedom under the terms of the edict: Hiram Reed and Frank Lewis, two of the crewmen aboard the *J. C. Swon* when the Union steamer *Iatan* captured it on May 25, 1861, following the May 10 attack at Camp Jackson.[1]

Within two weeks of Frémont's August 30 edict, orders of manumission were delivered to Reed and Lewis. They were dated September 12 and read in part: "I declare Hiram Reed [and Frank Lewis] heretofore held to service or labor by Thomas L. Snead to be free and forever discharged from the bonds of servitude."

Thomas Snead was a Virginian who moved to St. Louis in 1850. Snead was most certainly aiding the enemy in the field: During Wilson's Creek and after, Snead was Sterling Price's adjutant in the Missouri State Guard. As for the enslaved men, not much is known of Frank Lewis, except that he was a dozen years younger than Hiram Reed. Reed was born into slavery on May 4, 1830, probably in or near Louisville. His mother had been enslaved by the extended family of Henry Miller Shreve, the central figure in the rise of steam-powered navigation on America's inland waterways, and the man for whom Shreveport, Louisiana, is named.

With his glory days in the past, Shreve moved with his family to St. Louis in the early 1840s. He built an estate north of the city limits and took up farming. By this time, Shreve and his wife, Mary, were caring for their orphaned granddaughter, Harriet Vairin Reel. She was the only child of the Shreves' oldest daughter, also named Harriet, who died during childbirth in 1833. Young Harriet's father, John, died five years later. As Hiram Reed remembered it, this younger Harriet Reel was his "missus," even though Hiram was three years her senior.[2]

In 1853, when she was 20 years old, Harriet Reel married Thomas Snead. The 1860 US Census listed Hiram Reed as Snead's sole property.[3] One year later, when Reed received the signed order of manumission from Frémont, he became the first person ever freed by the military authority of the United States.

September 12, 1861, was not just a random date on John Frémont's calendar. Recall that Montgomery Blair was traveling to St. Louis on a westbound train that nearly crossed paths with Jessie Frémont's eastbound one. Frémont had received the maid's cyphered telegram the day before, alerting him to Blair's upcoming visit.

Accompanying Montgomery Blair on this journey was Montgomery C. Meigs, the US Army's quartermaster general. It is well to remember that Montgomery Blair had deep St. Louis roots. He moved there as a young man to practice law under the tutelage of his father's ally Thomas Hart Benton, Jessie Frémont's father. From 1842 to 1843, Montgomery Blair was St. Louis's mayor and then became a city judge. In 1853 he returned to Washington, where he continued to practice law. He and his family occupied Blair House on Pennsylvania Avenue, which Preston Blair bought in 1837. Today, it retains the family's name and functions as the president's guest house for visiting dignitaries.

Blair House in Washington, DC. Unknown photographer, 1918–1920.
Library of Congress, Prints and Photographs Division.

Montgomery Meigs was an old soldier and a prodigious engineer. Before the Civil War, he was the superintendent of construction during the US Capitol Building's massive expansion that produced a new House and Senate chambers, and ultimately, the Capitol dome. Meigs filled the role with great distinction from 1853 to 1859.

Meigs was a rising star in President Lincoln's eyes when the Civil War began. A former captain in the Regular Army, Meigs was promoted to colonel of the 11th Regiment, US Army, effective May 14, 1861. The next day, he was promoted to brigadier general and installed as the army's quartermaster general. By all accounts, Meigs was an excellent choice for the job, which begged for the precision of a master engineer, and he served a long and successful tenure.[4] Throughout his army career, Meigs maintained a reputation for utmost honesty and rectitude, so it's clear why Meigs was elevated to quartermaster general. Less clear is why he was pegged to join Montgomery Blair on his trip to St. Louis (unless one considers that the two were brothers-in-law).

Meigs kept handwritten journals for decades, many of them written in so-called Pitman shorthand. According to the translated version of Meigs's notes from September 10, 1861, Meigs was told the night before that he was to go to St. Louis with Montgomery Blair. On the train the next morning, Blair advised him that the reason for the journey was "to look into the affairs of the Q. M. Dept. at St. Louis, great complaints of extravagance having been made." Meigs knew Justus McKinstry, the current quartermaster, because he was in the class ahead of McKinstry's at West Point. Once Blair and Meigs reached St. Louis, though, they had just one meeting with Frémont and McKinstry, on the morning of September 13.[5]

A remarkable thing happened the next day. Preston Blair sent Lincoln a telegram proposing that he relieve John Frémont of his post and appoint Montgomery Meigs as commander of the Western Department. Preston Blair's telegram screamed that "things are deplorable and action must be decisive and prompt to save the state."[6] It seems beyond reasonable doubt that the reason Montgomery Blair brought Montgomery Meigs to St. Louis was to supersede Frémont if the Blairs could persuade Lincoln to fire Frémont on the spot.

Blair and Meigs departed St. Louis at 8am on Monday, September 16. Their train arrived in Washington City on Wednesday at 11am. At 4pm, Blair and Meigs were in front of the president and his cabinet. Gen. Meigs recorded in his notes that Montgomery Blair had been indignant during the meeting.

Frémont had arrested Frank Blair on September 15 for communicating outside the chain of command via the September 1 letter Montgomery Blair delivered to President Lincoln that urged Frémont's removal.[7]

But another issue was weighing on Meigs's mind. Even days before the Washington meeting, newspapers in the eastern states were reporting that Meigs was going to take Frémont's place and lead the army of the Western Department. Meigs complained bitterly to the cabinet about Montgomery Blair publicizing the purpose of the trip, saying, "[Montgomery Blair] had made it impossible for me to take the place with any usefulness to the Country or myself."[8] According to his notes, Meigs also told the cabinet what he suspected was the real reason they'd come to St. Louis: "[Frank Blair's] letters, with others, were the cause of the visit...." These "others" were St. Louis politicians who had written letters filled with complaints about Frémont, letters composed at least a week before Blair and Meigs left Washington for St. Louis.[9]

When the two arrived in St. Louis on September 12, something else mysterious was underway. A career army officer named David Hunter, who'd recently been appointed a major general of volunteers, was there. At the suggestion of Montgomery Blair, Frémont had summoned Hunter from Chicago via telegram on September 5, and Hunter arrived in St. Louis two days later. Montgomery Blair carried a handwritten note from Abraham Lincoln addressed to Gen. Hunter that said:

> Gen. Frémont needs assistance which it is difficult to give him: He is losing the confidence of men near him, whose support any man in his position must have to be successful. His cardinal mistake is that he isolates himself, & allows nobody to see him; and by which he does not know what is going on in the very matter he is dealing with. He needs to have, by his side, a man of large experience. Will you not, for me, take that place? Your rank is one grade too high to be ordered to it; but will you not serve the country, and oblige me, by taking it voluntarily?[10]

David Hunter would have a significant role in the events to come in Missouri. A month after arriving in St. Louis, he was in the field commanding a division of nearly 10,000 men.

After Jessie Frémont met with Preston Blair in Washington City on September 11, she did not immediately return to St. Louis. She had friends and acquaintances she wanted to see in Washington after a very long absence. Jessie also had a mission that would take her to Bethlehem, Pennsylvania, where she would meet her favorite among the Blairs, her old friend and confidante, Elizabeth "Lizzie" Blair Lee.

Lizzie and her four-year-old son, Blair, joined Mary Jessup Blair and her three children in the summer house near Bethlehem during the third week of August. Mary's late husband, James, was the middle brother in the Blair clan; he died suddenly in 1853 while Mary was pregnant with their third child. A naval officer, James Blair had spent some time in California in 1850 during a leave of absence, and John and Jessie Frémont became well acquainted with James and Mary over that time. Indeed, when Mary Blair grew lonely for her husband, it was Jessie Frémont who brought Mary and her two children with her through the isthmus route to California, a shared experience that may have brought Mary Blair nearly as close to Jessie Frémont as Jessie was to Elizabeth Blair Lee.

Although it is not known what prompted Jessie to visit Lizzie and Mary, it's hard to imagine that Jessie had planned this excursion prior to her disastrous meeting with Preston Blair. Whatever the case, Jessie had likely sought out this tight circle of Blair women she'd known most of her life as a counterweight to her feelings of disappointment in two generations of Blair men.

But Jessie would find neither solace nor sympathy in Bethlehem. Elizabeth Lee reported the following when she wrote her husband, Samuel, about the events of September 18:

> Jessie is here putting all the blame on the Cabinet for the delinquincy [*sic*] in the Western department.... In a word they hate & fear Frank & are also hostile to everybody in the administration who is supposed to stand between them & imperial power.... I talked 3 hours & sounded her to the bottom[,] her natural secretiveness [and] Benton cunning giving way under the passion I provoked.[11]

Translation: Over the course of three hours, Lizzie and Jessie had a terrible argument. Lizzie won.

Elizabeth Lee's bout with Jessie Frémont may have been more contentious than the letter to her husband revealed. John Frémont's order for the arrest and confinement of Frank Blair for sidestepping the chain of command in St. Louis was issued late on September 15. Perhaps the order was timed so that it would become public only after Blair and Meigs left on their Washington-bound train. Elizabeth Lee's letters indicate that she had some advance notice of the order before Jessie arrived in Bethlehem, but the full details did not reach her until after Jessie had departed.

The charges against Frank Blair for going around the chain of command stemmed from the scathing September 1 letter he'd written to his brother Montgomery about John Frémont, the tenor of which Preston Blair revealed to Jessie on September 11. Notably, Frank Blair's letter did not come entirely out of the blue. After he'd returned to St. Louis at the close of the first session of the 37th Congress, he made the rounds of acquaintances and constituents, and he seems to have gotten an earful about Frémont's administration. His letter is littered with complaints—some petty, some serious—but none of which should have been said about the man who commanded the military force Blair was enlisted in. But that was part of the rub: Frank Blair's military service from May 1861 and beyond was not backed by a commission in the US Army; rather, Blair was an officer of a unit specially enrolled by Nathaniel Lyon in St. Louis.

Before Jessie left Washington, she took issue with the letter and demanded that the president release it. Lincoln declined to do so, saying, "I do not feel authorized to furnish you with copies of letters in my possession, without the consent of the writers."[12] Next, John Frémont made good on the threat of arrest and took Frank Blair into custody in St. Louis. On September 19, Montgomery Blair agreed to release the letter, commenting to Gen. Frémont in the process that the letter "is not unfriendly." As a quid pro quo, Gen. Frémont released Frank Blair.

Frank Blair was not chastened by this first arrest and confinement, and he felt no remorse for his actions. Instead, he spent the next week drafting in longhand a formal charge against Frémont, his superior officer. Speaking like a prosecutor, Blair had written out a total of 22 specifications, divided unevenly into five "charges." It is difficult to assign importance to these charges based upon the order they're presented in, and the language has a feverish character to it. Still, "Charge 1, Specification 1" is surprising:

> In failing and neglecting from the third day of July, eighteen hundred and
> sixty one, until the twenty sixth day of July, eighteen hundred and sixty one,
> to repair to the City of St. Louis, in the State of Missouri, the Head Quarters
> of the Western Department, and there enter upon the duties belonging to

him, as the Military Chief of said Department, to the serious injury of the public service therein, and the loyal people thereof.[13]

There was no previous indication that Frank Blair had been vexed by Frémont's late arrival to St. Louis; this specification suggests that his disillusionment with Frémont started very early on. There were other allegations amid his charges that one might expect, among them Frémont's habit of secluding himself in his headquarters and his supposed failure to support and reinforce Nathaniel Lyon at Wilson's Creek. By the time he wrote the charges, Blair could also complain about Frémont's alleged inadequate response to Sterling Price's threat to Lexington. Lastly, Frank Blair took issue with his commanding officer for "surround[ing] himself with men of disreputable character, his former dependants [sic] and hangers on from the State of California," singling out Leonidas Haskell for special mention.

Particularly noteworthy about Frank Blair's "indictment" of Gen. Frémont is the fact that he only briefly referred to Frémont's emancipation order of August 30 and that he didn't mention Frémont's act of emancipating the two enslaved men at all. This comports with the language Frank employed when he first responded to the order in his infamous September 1 letter to his brother Montgomery. While Frank did criticize the order, it was on the grounds that Frémont did not amend it to comply with the president's demand. A second specification accused Gen. Frémont of circulating printed copies of his original proclamation in direct disobedience to Lincoln's order withdrawing it.[14]

When Frank Blair filed the charge with the US War Department on September 26, Frémont had him arrested once again and confined him to the brig at Jefferson Barracks.[15] Although this should have been enough, Frémont filed countercharges accusing Blair of insubordination. Gen. Frémont finally ordered Blair's release on October 1.

Beyond the drama of Montgomery Blair's trip to St. Louis, even more was happening on the opposite side of the state. Starting from the site of the Battle of Dry Wood Creek on September 2, 1861, Sterling Price's Missouri State Guard was advancing slowly but inexorably north toward Lexington. Price's march took him in and through the counties of Vernon, Bates, Henry, Johnson, and Lafayette—approximately a distance of 135 miles. Gen. Price had with him about 15,000 men of all arms. On September 12, when Blair and Meigs arrived in St. Louis, Price was near Warrensburg, driving Union defenders 30 miles north toward Lexington. The State Guard skirmished south of town over several days and went into camp there until all of Price's troops came up. The Missouri State Guard left their camps on September 18, moved on the town, and surrounded it.

Meanwhile, the Kentucky Legislature declared its fealty to the Union. One could say that Frémont's gambit worked and that Lincoln's fears of a Confederate Kentucky were exaggerated. But in truth, when the Confederate army became the first to break that state's neutrality, it also broke the back of secessionism in Kentucky.

ENDNOTES

1. In May 1861 the steamboat *J. C. Swon* was employed by Missouri secessionists to transport arms and armaments intended for the militia encampment in St. Louis. Union forces captured it on the Missouri shore opposite Harlow's Landing, Illinois, on May 22, 1861. John Thomas Scharf, *History of Saint Louis City and County, From the Earliest Periods to the Present Day: Including Biographical Sketches of Representative Men* 1 (L. H. Everts and Co., 1883), 398. The incident was reported in the May 25, 1861, edition of the *New York Times*, wherein it was stated that a watchman, a mate, and several hands were on board at the time of capture.

2. "Hiram Reed, Nantucket's Former Slave, Celebrates His 50th Year of Freedom," *Boston Daily Globe*, July 24, 1910. In his interview with the *Boston Daily Globe* reporter, Reed misidentified his place of birth as St. Louis; he was born near Louisville. Henry Shreve is credited with building and operating the first true Mississippi steamboat in 1824. Florence L. Dorsey, *Master of the Mississippi* (Houghton Mifflin Co., 1941), 137–138. Shreve is buried in St. Louis's Bellefontaine Cemetery, a stone's throw from the estate he established north of St. Louis.

3. United States Census, St. Louis township, 1860.

4. Gen. Meigs succeeded future Confederate general Joseph E. Johnston. Johnston resigned his army commission when his home state, Virginia, seceded in 1861. Meigs is also remembered as the man who established Arlington National Cemetery, which he sited on the ancestral home of Robert E. Lee's family.

5. John G. Nicolay Papers: Research File, ca. 1860–1942. Nicolay, one of President Lincoln's personal secretaries, transcribed several diaries of Lincoln's contemporaries, including one kept by Montgomery Meigs. Meigs's diary entries documenting his 1861 trip to St. Louis with Montgomery Blair can be accessed electronically beginning at https://www.loc.gov/resource/mss34736.01308/?sp=94&st=image&r=-0.001,1.006,0.629,0.356,0. See Images 94–97. Library of Congress, Washington, DC. This resource exists only in Nicolay's handwriting.

6. Abraham Lincoln Papers: General Correspondence, 1833–1916, Series 1. Telegram, Montgomery Blair to Abraham Lincoln, September 14, 1861. Library of Congress, Washington, DC. See appendix.

7. John G. Nicolay Papers. Transcription of diaries of Lincoln's associates, including diary of Montgomery C. Meigs, Mar.–Sept. 1861. Image 96.

8. John G. Nicolay Papers. Image 97.

9. William E. Parrish, *Frank Blair: Lincoln's Conservative* (University of Missouri Press, 1998), 120. Professor Parrish notes that Frank Blair first showed the letter he proposed to send to his brother Montgomery to three prominent St. Louisans. At least one of those men sent a letter to Montgomery that parroted Frank's complaints about Frémont. Abraham Lincoln Papers: General Correspondence, 1833–1916, Series 1. Letter, Samuel T. Glover to Montgomery Blair, September 2, 1861. Library of Congress, Washington, DC.

10. Roy P. Basler, ed., *The Collected Works of Abraham Lincoln* (Rutgers University Press, 1953), 513.

11. Elizabeth Blair Lee to Samuel Lee, Bethlehem, September 17, 1861; Laas, 78–79.

12. Allan Nevins, *Frémont: Pathmarker of the West* (University of Nebraska Press, 1939), 510.

13. Abraham Lincoln Papers. Charges and specifications by Frank Blair against Maj. Gen. John C. Frémont, October 2, 1861.

14. The recorded facts strongly indicate that, after President Lincoln withdrew Frémont's proclamation, Frémont had it printed and distributed in areas of southwest Missouri. If true—as it appears to be—this would constitute insubordination and warrant severe sanction or dismissal.

15. Abraham Lincoln Papers. Letter, Francis P. Blair Jr. to Montgomery Blair, October 1, 1861.

CHAPTER 6

*"Where the vultures are,
there is a carcass close by."*

—Gen. William T. Sherman

Figure 6

William Tecumseh Sherman was born in Lancaster, Ohio, on February 8, 1820. After his father died when he was nine years old, he was reared in the household of prominent Ohio politician Thomas Ewing. Sherman served in the Regular Army until he resigned his commission in 1853. When he re-entered the army in 1861, Sherman's first significant assignment was as brigadier general commanding the Department of the Cumberland from headquarters in Louisville, Kentucky. Sherman's ties to St. Louis date back to 1853 and endured throughout his life and even in death: He died in New York City on February 14, 1891, and is buried in St. Louis's Calvary Cemetery.

Jeffersonville Railroad Depot

Jeffersonville, Indiana, October 16, 1861

THE TRAIN FROM INDIANAPOLIS was late. Gen. Sherman paced the platform back and forth, cigar clamped in his teeth, smoke intermittently shrouding his head. Here, at the depot, he was waiting for Secretary of War Simon Cameron. Cameron was on a fact-finding tour of the West in the company of the army's Adjutant General Lorenzo Thomas.

Sherman had more than an inkling of what had sent Cameron and Thomas to Missouri. The last time Sherman was in St. Louis, the Frémont administration was coming under a growing, angry cloud. There was Frémont's damned proclamation at the end of August, but troublesome rumors were flying in every direction: That Frémont conducted affairs of his department like a potentate, that soldiers and senators and citizens waited for days to meet with him, and on and on. Sherman himself had sought an audience with Frémont during his trip to St. Louis and got one easily. Then again, the men knew each other from California before and during the Gold Rush; perhaps Sherman had received special treatment.

On his previous trip to St. Louis, on September 4, 1861, Sherman approached Frémont's headquarters. He was astonished when he was greeted at the door by Isaiah Woods from California. Sherman had last seen Woods in 1855 in San Francisco, where he'd worked for the Adams Express Company and lost clients hundreds of thousands of dollars in that year's banking crisis. Sherman would learn that Palmer, Haskell, and Beard were also in town, all involved in army acquisitions and federal contracting "opportunities."

Sherman heard a distant whistle—the train from Indianapolis. Jolted back to present, he reflected on the troubles facing his command. The first commander of the Department of the Cumberland was Kentuckian Robert Anderson, who had famously defended Fort Sumter. Gen. Anderson had resigned on October 5, citing physical and mental exhaustion. Now in charge, Sherman was also exhibiting signs of distress.

Those who followed Frémont to St. Louis in 1861 came from widely different means and from many different places. Not all of them owed their allegiance to the "Pathfinder" because of their California connections, but that was certainly the case for Palmer, Woods, Haskell, and Beard. By and large, these men had earned their reputations for sketchy business practices during the Gold Rush days. None were in California to pan for gold. All were there to "mine the miners." Their unsavory reputations festered through the 1850s and would become more fodder for Frémont's enemies and detractors who criticized his leadership.

Joseph C. Palmer was and remained the most significant of John Frémont's California friends, even though Palmer and his firm had played a role in the declining fortunes of Frémont's Mariposa mines. But Frémont seemed to hold no ill will toward Palmer or his banking firm. While the Mariposa estate was causing grief for John and Jessie Frémont, Palmer's firm was embroiled in controversy after controversy. California's super-heated economy was dealt a significant blow in early 1854, when San Francisco's real estate bubble burst. By April of that year, property values had dropped more than 50 percent. Blame was heaped upon Palmer, Cook & Company for missing a payment of interest on state bonds, which the firm was contractually bound to deliver to New York.[1] Following a financial crash that brought down Adams Express, charges against Frémont's friends Woods and Haskell were tossed about—including that they had entrusted more than $160,000 to Palmer's firm—but years of litigation would fail to pin this allegation on Palmer, Cook & Company or its principals. Finally, in July 1856, the firm went bankrupt after another public scandal, once again involving California state bonds. In its wake, Palmer's company left liabilities estimated at $3.5 million (about $132 million in 2025).[2]

After this bankruptcy, it is possible that Palmer got involved in Frémont's presidential campaign, which began in earnest when the new Republican Party nominated Frémont as its candidate in June 1856. George Wright, Palmer's fellow Nantucketer and California partner, was now out of Congress and spent much of 1855 promoting Frémont's candidacy in eastern states. But Palmer's reputation was so toxic that he became a liability to the campaign, so he likely laid low as Election Day 1856 approached.

Although gold had been found in California in January 1848, it took another eight months for a *New York Herald* story to break the news out east. The inhabitants of Nantucket Island—where Palmer, Cook, and Wright heard about the discovery—were in a better position to respond quickly than any other community in New England.

Joseph Palmer's father, Lot Palmer, had immigrated to Nantucket around 1800 from a Quaker settlement in Rhode Island called New Compton. Lot met his wife, Ruth, in Nantucket. When Joseph was born to the couple in 1819, the island was still near its peak as the whaling capital of the world, making it one of America's wealthiest communities per capita. But a massive slaughter of sperm whales—the only source of sperm oil, used to light homes—resulted in a shortage of these creatures in Atlantic waters. In response, Nantucket's seamen innovated, learning to extract and process oil at sea. No longer required to return to port to carry out this process, the sailors extended their field of harvest to the far reaches of the Pacific Ocean, often leaving for years at a time. But eventually the rest of the world learned the trade as well, contributing to Nantucket's gradual decline throughout the 1800s. The town of New Bedford, Massachusetts, was also growing and supplanting Nantucket's role in North America—plus, Nantucket had suffered a devastating fire in 1846 that consumed a large part of the island's wharf area.

So when news of gold in California hit Nantucket, the island's economic conditions meant that it had whaleships in abundance, many of them idle. Idle, too, were masters and crews who were experts in the craft of whaling and accustomed to long Pacific voyages. The first whaleship to depart Nantucket for the gold fields was the *Aurora*, which sailed in January 1849 with a crew of 12 and 24 passengers. The *Aurora* arrived at San Francisco Bay on July 1, 1849, and was followed by at least 10 more vessels from the island, most of them converted from whalers into passenger and freight carriers. By 1850 approximately 650 Nantucketers had arrived in California, among them Joseph Palmer and his soon-to-be partners in the banking business.[3] In May 1850, the 3 were among 11 founders of the Mariposa Mining Company. In late September of that year, California achieved statehood.

Isaiah Churchill Woods, the man who met Sherman at the door of Frémont's Chouteau headquarters on September 4, had by then firmly established himself in the San Francisco press as the "notorious" I. C. Woods. His background was much like Joseph Palmer's: Woods was born in 1825 in Saco, Maine, a port city 90 miles north of Boston. Woods's family moved to

New Bedford, Massachusetts, where his father (the senior Isaiah) captained vessels engaged in New Bedford's whaling trade. Captain Woods died at sea in 1839, when his oldest child and namesake was 14. According to biographer Albert Shumate, in 1847 young Woods managed to acquire a trading vessel, the schooner *Sagadahoc*, and set sail for the South Pacific.[4] Within a year, the *Sagadahoc* docked at Honolulu. This was a tremendous stroke of luck for Woods, as word of the California gold discovery reached Honolulu long before it reached New England. With his schooner full of trade goods, Woods immediately headed for the Golden Gate Strait. Woods's good fortune, which placed him in San Francisco in November 1848, left him in a position well ahead of the masses in the rush to California.

I. C. Woods had the trade goods where they were needed most, and he made a small fortune selling them in San Francisco. Like many who would follow, Woods also disposed of his ship and began investing in Bay Area real estate. Serendipity again intervened in Woods's favor when, about a year after he landed in San Francisco, Daniel Hale Haskell of Boston arrived to establish an office for the Adams Express Company. According to early San Francisco lore, Haskell opened his business on a lot controlled by I. C. Woods, which Woods had improved only to the extent of building a "small shanty."[5] The block that contained this property would, over the next several years, evolve into a major financial epicenter of California, largely a result of the phenomenal success enjoyed by Adams Express.

In 1854, Woods parlayed his position into a partnership with Daniel Haskell and Adams Express founder Alvin Adams. It was a reorganization of the company's California operations into a stand-alone entity, a sort of franchise. By the time 1855 dawned, Adams Express was regarded as California's leading business organization. As Shumate noted, "It handled more money, dealt with more people, and furnished more services to industry and commerce than any other."[6]

Then came the crash. Intertwined bank-to-bank relationships produced a run on the banks in San Francisco, which in turn created a panic that culminated on Friday, February 23, 1855: California's original Black Friday. One of the California banking institutions based in St. Louis—Page, Bacon & Company—suffered severe losses in a railroad venture in the eastern US. It temporarily shut down its St. Louis office in the hope of preventing a run by its depositors. When this news reached the West, a shock wave engulfed the company's San Francisco office and rippled through almost all of California's financial houses, until Adams Express itself was devastated. Adams Express in California closed its doors on Black Friday, never to reopen them.

William Sherman had witnessed all of these goings-on. He was posted to California when he resigned his army commission in 1853. His first civilian job was to represent the West Coast interests of the bank of Lucas, Turner & Company in St. Louis. Decades later, Sherman recalled the major role he played in the 1855 crisis. To save his own bank, Sherman refused to vouch for Page, Bacon & Company's solvency, in its last-ditch effort to avoid the collapse of the market. Sherman's bank survived the crisis intact, one of few banking houses in the city to do so. Sherman would boast in his memoirs that Lucas, Turner & Company "for the extent of our business, [was] stronger than the Bank of England, or any bank in New York City."[7]

In August 1855, I. C. Woods boarded the steamer *Audubon*, bound for Australia. His departure set off a firestorm in the San Francisco press. While Woods had been embroiled in litigation flowing from the financial crash, it's doubtful that he left with a hoard of cash, as the rumor mill suggested. Within a couple years, Woods was back in the express delivery business.

Yet another expressman with New England roots, James E. Birch hired Woods to superintend Birch's new San Antonio–San Diego Mail Line. Building upon an earlier venture that only carried mail across a part of this route, Birch intended to introduce overland passenger coach services. Woods, setting out from San Antonio in July 1857, conducted a cross-country trek of the proposed route. Woods was to meet Birch when he arrived in San Diego, but the 30-year-old Birch died when the SS *Central America* sank off the coast of South Carolina.[8] The full responsibility for operating the new line now fell to Woods. Mail riders—and later, passengers—had to transfer to muleback to cover 100 miles of desert on the route, and the venture soon acquired the nickname the "Jackass Mail." During his stewardship, which probably concluded in 1859, Woods faced a host of challenges, and the San Antonio–San Diego Mail Line ended its existence in total failure. Still, Woods's Jackass Mail was the first to cross the Sierra Nevada. Enterprises of a similar nature, including John Butterfield's Overland Mail Company (1858–1861) and the Pony Express (1860–1861), leapfrogged each other in the race to be the fastest carrier of mail and messages to California. But a revolution in communications took away the most lucrative business of these competitors on October 24, 1861, when a cross-country telegraph line was completed.

I. C. Woods joined Gen. Frémont's staff in St. Louis, and by September 1861, he was a colonel and Frémont's director of transportation. Although this seems to comport with Frémont's general pattern of rewarding his friends, just below the surface there's another prevalent pattern of conduct: the self-interested dealings of two generations of the Blair family. Either Preston Blair or his son Montgomery had persuaded Frémont to bring Woods on board in St. Louis. As it turns out, Montgomery and his deceased brother, James, had close professional and personal ties to Woods's brothers-in-law. As of 1861, Montgomery still held property in partnership with one of them, Eugene Casserly, who would go on to be a US senator from California.[9]

Residence + Head Quarters of Gen'l Fremont, in St. Louis. Drawing of the view of Brant Mansion from the northeast corner of Chouteau Avenue and 8th Street by Alexander Simplot in *Harper's Weekly*, August 31, 1861. Missouri Historical Society Collections.

Rounding out the list of the California men who drew Sherman's interest were Leonidas Haskell and Elias Beard, who held smaller roles in Frémont's Missouri administration. Haskell was a seventh-generation American, descended from the immigrant William Haskell of England, who settled in the Massachusetts Bay Colony around 1635. By the 1640s, a major branch of the Haskell family had been firmly established in Gloucester, where Leonidas was born in 1823. Leonidas and his wife, Sarah, had not known the Frémonts until Jessie purchased the home at Black Point in 1860, but from then on the four were fast and good friends. Haskell had acquired the 13-acre Black Point site using the proceeds from the sale of a ship he brought from Gloucester in 1849, as well as earnings from a general merchandise business he started. He developed and sold houses and parcels on his Black Point tract and continued his mercantile business until he and Sarah had become quite wealthy. It is fair to surmise that Frémont beckoned Haskell to St. Louis in August 1861 to serve him as a trusted friend. While in St. Louis, Haskell was a captain on Frémont's staff, acting as the city's police director.

Lastly, Elias Lyman Beard: He was born near Lyons, New York, in 1816, the son of a contractor who worked on the Erie Canal. Young Elias went West with his father in the 1830s, working first in Michigan and then building canals in Indiana. Around 1840, he was hired to construct and improve Mississippi River docks in Memphis, Tennessee, but the project left Beard financially embarrassed. He set out for San Francisco, crossing Mexico by land and then taking passage on a Pacific steamer. He arrived in May 1849.

Beard joined brothers John and William Horner in a partnership to acquire 30,000 acres of prime agricultural land in Alameda County, across the bay near present-day Oakland. This was a part of the historic Mission San Jose, a large Spanish grant to the Catholic Church that the Mexican government had secularized after Mexican independence. The Beard-Horner venture achieved spectacular success that lasted for most of the 1850s: Its farm produce fed workers in the mines as well as the burgeoning population of San Francisco.

By 1858, Beard's success as a grower had run its course. Again in financial straits, Beard visited John Frémont and procured a position at the Mariposa mines. All things considered, it seems likely that Beard joined Frémont in St. Louis because he needed a job. On September 4, 1861—the day Sherman visited St. Louis—Gen. Frémont put Beard to work constructing military fortifications on the city's periphery.

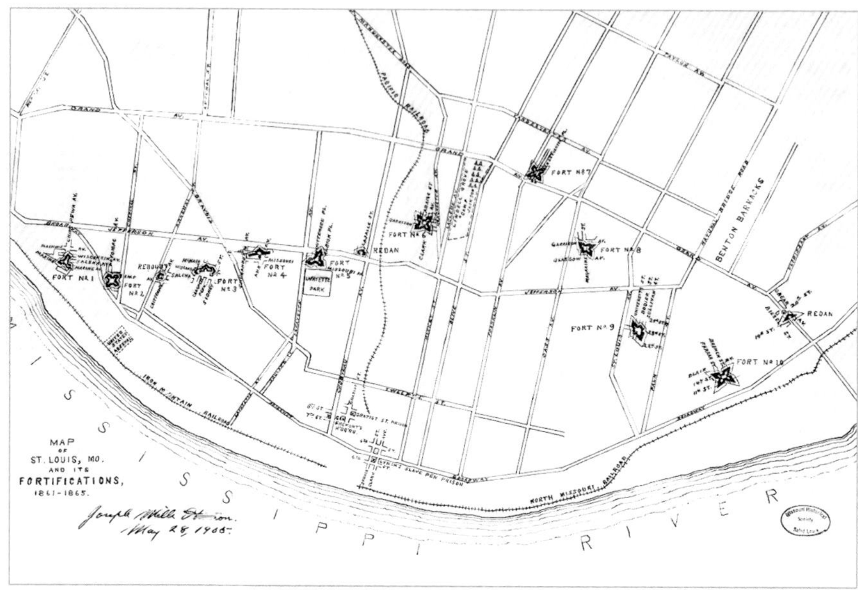

Map of St. Louis, MO. and Its Fortifications, 1861–1865.
Missouri Historical Society Collections.

Another man with Nantucket roots made his way onto Frémont's staff: Capt. Edward M. Davis, the aide whom Frémont summoned along with Jessie as he contemplated his August 30 emancipation proclamation: "I want you two but no others."[10] Davis was a Quaker and an ardent abolitionist, the son-in-law of women's rights icon Lucretia Coffin Mott. Mott, too, was a Quaker with strong antislavery sentiments. She was born on Nantucket on January 3, 1793, into a family that traced itself directly to the first Europeans who wed on the island. At 18, she married James Mott of Philadelphia, a union that produced six children. Their daughter Maria married Edward Davis in 1836.[11]

It would be easy to overstate the importance Nantucket had on the evolution of John and Jessie's emancipationist views, but there is still this to consider: In 1855, Jessie and the children spent a considerable amount of time on the island as her husband's run for president was beginning to take shape. John Frémont was in Washington for the birth of Francis Preston Frémont on May 17, 1855. It had been a difficult pregnancy and birth for Jessie. She rented a cottage on Nantucket to recuperate, and she and the children spent most of the summer and autumn there. According to journalist and historian

Sally Denton, it's here that Jessie helped solidify the elements of the new Republican Party by enlisting her father's friend Preston Blair to switch his allegiance away from the Democratic Party.[12]

Among Gen. Frémont's purported faults was the excessive pomp and circumstance he brought to his St. Louis command. The epitome of this was Frémont's Body-Guard, a peculiar cavalry unit that earned much scorn within and without the army. Through their extensive travels in Europe, John and Jessie Frémont had developed an inordinate fascination with the Continent's mores. The general's high military rank and extravagant surroundings should have been all the Frémonts could want from his stint in the army—after all, in many respects, St. Louis was the American city with the most European flavor.

The 1860 Census ranked St. Louis eighth in population among American cities, and other sources reported that it had a higher proportion of foreign-born persons than any other major city in the nation.[13] Waves of immigrants from Ireland, fleeing famine, and from Germany, escaping a political crackdown after the failed revolutions of 1848, made up a large part of the citizenry. St. Louis also had expatriates from all parts of the Austro-Hungarian Empire, which had seen widespread revolutions in the late 1840s. The story of the Body-Guard brings into focus some colorful Hungarian nationals who joined Frémont in 1861.

One of Gen. Frémont's very best officers was Gen. Alexander (Sándor) Asboth. Asboth would eventually lead one of Frémont's divisions on the battlefield, but in August and September 1861, he was Frémont's chief of staff. Frémont asked Asboth if he could recommend an officer to serve as his chief of cavalry, and Asboth's response came without hesitation: his countryman Charles (Károly) Zagonyi.[14]

Zagonyi had been a cavalry officer during the Hungarian War of Independence of 1848–1849 and served as a commander of an elite cavalry force under the famed Polish general József Bem.[15] When the War of Independence failed, Zagonyi joined Bem in exile in Ottoman Turkey and later emigrated to New York. Zagonyi was trained in the Huszár tradition of light cavalry (*hussar*, in modern parlance), a feature of Eastern European warfare that originated in Hungary in the 1400s. There was a tradition across Europe that a high-ranking general would raise a mounted "Body-Guard" to see to his personal protection. When Zagonyi suggested to Gen. Frémont that he, too, should have a Body-Guard, Frémont naturally seized upon the idea.

Major Charles Zagonyi. Photograph by Mathew Brady Studio, ca. 1860s. National Portrait Gallery, Smithsonian Institution; Frederick Hill Meserve Collection.

Zagonyi would raise three companies of cavalry, 100 troopers in each, from sources far afield. The first company was converted from one recently raised in Cincinnati, the 5th Independent Company of Ohio Volunteer Cavalry. A second company was recruited in Kentucky, across the river from Cincinnati. The third company was populated with overflow from Ohio and Kentucky, plus men recruited in St. Louis. Late in August the Body-Guard began a month of training at a camp in south St. Louis before receiving their weapons and distinctive uniforms and headgear. They escorted the general and his wife donned in these ostentatious outfits, which only added to the public's perception of Frémont's extravagance. Soon, the Body-Guard was derided as Frémont's "sidewalk cavalry" and "the kid glove brigade."[16]

★ ★ ★

On September 4, 1861, before Gen. Sherman dropped by Frémont's St. Louis headquarters, he went to the Planter's House to meet an old acquaintance from Ohio. A fellow West Pointer long retired from the army, Robert Renick was working as a merchant in St. Louis. Renick warned Sherman about the sentries and guards he would face when he approached Frémont's headquarters. As Renick observed, Frémont "had a more showy court than any real king."[17] Sherman was scheduled to leave for Louisville on September 5, but his commanding officer persuaded him to leave earlier, so he just missed the ruckus at the riverfront that accompanied Prince Napoleon's arrival.[18]

Reverend James Crane of Illinois visited St. Louis in August 1861, and in a magazine article he wrote 35 years later, he described the scene as "a whole host of little moguls and august Italian and Hungarian lieutenants, and orderlies and captains and corporals, and carriers and riders and musketeers, and swordsmen, waiters, and ushers, doorkeepers, hostlers, and bootblacks, which Frémont had as a body-guard."

ENDNOTES

1. William T. Sherman, *Memoirs of General William T. Sherman* (D. Appleton & Co., 1891), 129–132; Albert Shumate, *The Notorious I. C. Woods* (Arthur H. Clark Co., 1986), 47–53.

2. Bill Mero, "The Looting of California: Bankers, Corruption and Theft," Contra Costa County Historical Society, https://www.cocohistory.org/essays/the-looting-of-california-bankers-corruption-and-theft.

3. Helen L. Winslow, "Nantucket Forty-Niners," *Historic Nantucket* 4, no. 3 (January 1956): 6–28.

4. Shumate, 26–27.

5. A. L. Stimson, *History of the Express Companies* (Baker & Godwin Printers, 1881), 111.

6. Shumate, 37.

7. Sherman, 132.

8. The SS *Central America* was lost at sea during a hurricane on September 12, 1857, off the coast of South Carolina. Of the nearly 600 passengers and crew, only 149 people survived. An estimated $40 million in gold consigned to New York from California was also lost in the sea disaster, the worst one in American history up until that time. R. J. Duhse, "Last Cruise of the SS *Central America*," *Naval History* 4, no. 1 (January 1990).

9. *Report of the Joint Committee on the Conduct of the War, Part 3: Department of the West* (US Government Printing Office, 1863), 212–213; Shumate, 102.

10. Allan Nevins, *Frémont: Pathmarker of the West* (University of Nebraska Press, 1939), 500. Nevins includes an extensive quote from an unpublished manuscript, intended for a continuation of a memoir published during Frémont's lifetime. The manuscript is in the possession of the Bancroft Library at the University of California, Berkeley.

11. "Lucretia Mott," National Women's Hall of Fame, https://www.womenofthehall.org/inductee/lucretia-mott.

12. Sally Denton, *Passion and Principle: John and Jessie Frémont, the Couple Whose Power, Politics, and Love Shaped Nineteenth-Century America* (Bloomsbury Publishing, 2007), 232.

13. Campbell Gibson, *American Demographic History Chartbook: 1790 to 2010,* http://demographicchartbook.com.

14. Edmund Vasvary, *Lincoln's Hungarian Heroes: The Participation of Hungarians in the Civil War, 1861–1865* (The Hungarian Reformed Federation of America, 1939), 86–88.

15. Known as the hero of three nations, Józef Bem fought for Poland against Napoleon and with Hungarian insurgents in 1848–1849. When the Hungarian revolt failed, he fled to Turkey, where he was named a marshal of the Turkish army.

16. Michael E. Banasik, ed., *Confederate Tales of the War in the Trans-Mississippi, Part 1: 1861* (Press of the Camp Pope Bookshop, 2010), 138, note 14; Joseph W. Morton, ed., *Sparks from the Camp Fire or Tales of the Old Veterans* (Philadelphia: Keystone Publishing Co., 1892), 115.

17. Sherman, *Memoirs,* 212.

18. James L. Crane, "Grant as a Colonel, Conversations Between Grant and His Chaplain," *McClure's Magazine* 7 (June 1896): 40–45.

CHAPTER 7

*"Out of provisions, out of ammunition...
they yet fought on."*

—Franc Bangs Wilkie

Figure 7

Franc Bangs Wilkie was born in Saratoga County in upstate New York in 1832. In 1856 he and a college classmate moved to Iowa, where they started a newspaper. During the Civil War years, he wrote articles under his own byline, as well as commentary using the pseudonym "Galway." Postwar, Wilkie had a long and distinguished career with the *Chicago Times*. He was the first president of the Chicago Press Club and purportedly broke the story of the Great Chicago Fire in 1871. Wilkie died at home in 1892 and is buried in the Chicago suburb of Elgin.

The City Hotel

Jefferson City, October 1, 1861

WHEN FRANC WILKIE ARRIVED in Missouri's capital city the day before, he checked into the City Hotel, where he found a disconsolate Junius Henri Browne. Browne was already a legend among war correspondents, thanks to his reporting for the *Cincinnati Gazette*. Now that the action was taking place in the western theater—in Missouri, to be precise—the New York and Boston papers were rushing to get the story. Browne had been hired by the *New-York Tribune*, and Wilkie hoped to tread a similar path. He'd set off from Iowa about 100 days earlier, joining the men and boys who volunteered to fight with the 1st Iowa Infantry. ("Embedded" might be the term we would use today.) They departed by river steamer in June, bound for the war zone in Missouri. Wilkie was to dispatch reports to the *Dubuque Herald*, his hometown paper, for publication.

The 1st Iowa marched from Hannibal to Boonville before joining Nathaniel Lyon there for the march to Springfield and Wilson's Creek. The men of the 1st Iowa fought bravely at Wilson's Creek, and Wilkie reported their actions and progress to his Iowa audience. His account of the Battle of Wilson's Creek—one of the first to reach the North—was a sensation. In the wake of his newfound fame, Wilkie was hired by Henry Jarvis Raymond, the co-founder and editor of the *New York Times*.

After Wilson's Creek, Wilkie returned to Dubuque but soon left for St. Louis to await further developments and assignments. He arrived in the city on September 3, 1861, during the week that Gen. Frémont entertained the likes of William Sherman and Prince Napoleon of France. It was also the day Confederates invaded Kentucky.

John Frémont's 100 days in Missouri coincided with developments in the eastern United States and with landmark events in Gen. George B. McClellan's career. For example, McClellan received his first significant command on July 25, 1861, the same day Frémont arrived in St. Louis to take command west of the Mississippi. On November 1, 1861, Lincoln elevated McClellan to the position of general in chief of the Union armies, and on the very next day, Frémont lost his command altogether. It is inevitable that Frémont's plight in Missouri would be compared to the plight of Gen. McClellan and his Army of the Potomac—a comparison that casts a favorable light on Gen. Frémont.

McClellan came fully on to the national scene following the Union disaster at Bull Run, as the Lincoln administration desperately organized a defense of the capital city. Men who'd survived the battle were still trickling into Washington and its suburbs. They were demoralized. McClellan had achieved some small-scale victories in Virginia, and he was known as an adept organizer, but his positive characteristics were far outweighed by a sense of caution that could paralyze him. In the parlance of the day, he suffered from "the slows." Even so, he took the demoralized army in and around Washington and established the nucleus of the famed Army of the Potomac.

General George McClellan in uniform, seated next to a camp box and drum. Steel engraving from an original painting by Alonzo Chappel, taken from an 1862 book published by Johnson, Fry and Co. Missouri Historical Society Collections.

McClellan arrived in Washington on July 27, 1861, taking over command from Irvin McDowell, the general who oversaw the Bull Run campaign. McClellan established a line of forts along a range of small hills overlooking Long Branch, a tributary of Four Mile Run in northern Virginia.[1] On the opposite (south) side of the valley of Long Branch, the old Leesburg Pike ran northwest, from Alexandria on the Potomac toward Leesburg to the north. McDowell had overseen the fortification of some major points in northern Virginia, but as of August 1, Washington City was dangerously exposed. McClellan's new Union line north of Long Branch filled a gap near Bailey's Crossroads, a Virginia suburb of Washington. It was not long before Confederate forces advanced to within shooting distance of McClellan's line. They occupied several positions south of Long Branch, including Munson's Hill—the area's most prominent height. They remained there for two months.

Munson's Hill: Secession Fort. The Confederate fort at Bailey's Crossroads, Virginia, with Leesburg Pike in the foreground. Drawing by Arthur Lumley, September 1861. The Becker Collection, Boston College Libraries.

Gen. McClellan might have deserved a grace period in his new role defending the capital, but to his detriment, the most pernicious of his personal traits came to the surface almost immediately. After hearing preposterously inflated Confederate troop strength estimates from spy Allan Pinkerton,

McClellan sat, immobile on his Long Branch line and elsewhere in the Virginia suburbs. Pinkerton reported that 150,000 Confederates were within marching distance of the capital; the fact was, McClellan, with 122,000 effectives, had at least a 2 to 1 advantage throughout August and September—and maybe as much as 4 to 1. Yet he did not move until September 28. Compounding the frustration of Lincoln's administration, the Confederates had hoisted the "Stars and Bars" above their fort on Munson's Hill, and it was visible from Washington. This alone should have compelled McClellan to attack.

With great fanfare, on September 28, 1861, the Army of the Potomac moved upon Munson's Hill.[2] What came next would animate the Washington press corps for a week or more: McClellan's attackers found that the Confederates had abandoned the works some time earlier, and guns that seemed to be trained on Washington City were nothing more than logs stripped of their bark and painted black. Although this artifice predated the Civil War, it may be that the press used this occasion to coin the derisive term "Quaker gun" as a way to mock McClellan's performance at Munson's Hill.[3]

Sterling Price's State Guard had laid siege to the town of Lexington, Missouri, on September 18—the same day Blair and Meigs returned to Washington from St. Louis. Lexington would turn into a disaster for Frémont, although some would contend that the true disaster was on the battleground of public relations. Gen. Frémont was trying to make good of this bad situation. On the day McClellan embarrassed himself at Munson's Hill, Frémont was in Jefferson City, 100 miles from his St. Louis base, assembling an army to chase Gen. Price. Outside of Washington, McClellan's hurdles were but a fraction of those faced by Fremont, but there were similarities: McClellan had crept out of the Washington defenses only to find his foe had already left his front. Frémont had decided to run down Price wherever it would take him, but Price had already outpaced Frémont when Price left Lexington. Yet McClellan's star was ascending, while Frémont had begun a professional death spiral. How did this happen?

During the lead-up to Lexington, around September 17, 1861, Franc Wilkie of the *New York Times* attached himself to the command of Gen. Samuel D. Sturgis in Utica, Missouri. Sturgis was involved in a vain attempt to reinforce the Union soldiers who were hunkered down in Lexington, when he brought a small infantry force from northeast Missouri. Time was short.

It was already late in the day when Frémont sent a proper force to garrison the critical town of Lexington. Critical, because any foothold Price might grab on the bank of the Missouri River would give him the power to stop traffic on that strategic waterway. Lexington's position on the south bank of the Missouri River made the city a tempting target. Moreover, Lexington's citizens were largely Southern in character, so Gen. Price had reason to believe his army would be welcomed there.

In St. Louis, Gen. Frémont was occupied with multiple issues, many of his own making. He still had to contend with the gap that Gen. Price was skillfully exploiting west of Jefferson City. As of mid-September, Jefferson City remained the westernmost outpost that St. Louis could rely upon in efforts to thwart Price. Col. Jefferson Davis, who had relieved Ulysses Grant on August 28, was still commanding in Jefferson City and doing a good job with the resources he had. He'd secured Boonville on September 13, 1861, where a small engagement left unionists in charge of the city and its fortifications.[4]

One of Col. Davis's resources had arrived in Jefferson City in mid-July: the Chicago Irish Brigade, properly known as the 23rd Illinois Volunteer Infantry Regiment. Around September 9, Frémont ordered these men to move west from Jefferson City and take position in Lexington. The so-called brigade was soon joined by the 13th Missouri Infantry, near full strength at 840 men, plus 500 men of the 1st Illinois Cavalry, and a similar number of Home Guards from Kansas City. James Adelbert Mulligan, colonel of the 23rd Illinois Infantry, now had perhaps 3,000 effectives under his command. Mulligan chose the site of a Masonic college for his citadel, high on a bluff. Working furiously, on September 11 his men began to construct earthworks, preparing for a siege in which they might be outnumbered 5 to 1.

The advance units of Price's army, and the commanding general himself, arrived late in the day on September 11. They went into camp about 5 miles southeast of Lexington. The next morning, Price moved west along the Salt Pond Road in the direction of the city. Three miles in, he was stymied when confronted by a small detachment of Mulligan's infantry who guarded a bridge on the road. The Union men burned the bridge. Price withdrew a short distance, then tried an approach to the city several miles west, which was also unsuccessful. Finally, well into the day, Price drove north on the Lexington Road, where his men collided with a significant detachment from the 13th Missouri Infantry. The fight—a skirmish, really—was centered in the city's historic cemetery south of town. Colorfully and aptly, to this day it is known as the Battle Over the Dead. Gen. Price's forces drove the defenders back into Mulligan's entrenchments, and as twilight approached, he was able to post two cannon in position to bombard the Union entrenchments at will.

Price's aggressiveness on September 12—a rare showing from him—was wasteful and unnecessary. The bombardment itself, while no doubt frightening for some of the men in the Union trenches, depleted the artillery supplies Price had on hand. Much of the guard's ordnance stores were with Price's supply train near Osceola, Missouri. In 10 days, the wagons had only gotten about 50 miles from where they started, and they still had 90 miles to go.[5] Gen. Price withdrew from his forward position and moved south to the county fairgrounds, where he would wait for the next five days. The Missouri State Guard's presence outside Lexington turned up the heat on Gen. Frémont in St. Louis as the nation fixated day after day on the plight of Mulligan's Irish Brigade.

Sterling Price moved on Mulligan's position on September 18. The day was punctuated when the Irish Brigade charged up and out of the trenches, attempting to dislodge enemy sharpshooters who had taken a nearby house. Mulligan's outbreak failed. Then, with all of Mulligan's men back in position, Price tightened his grip. The Missouri State Guard worked its way around the left and around the right until Mulligan's infantry was sealed in the trenches. These maneuvers blocked the defenders' access to drinking water, and nearly as important, they blocked any means of reinforcement from the north. Sturgis's force, coming on from Utica, got close to Lexington, but they turned away when they were warned that a State Guard party had crossed the river to pursue them.

Price's final play at Lexington came on September 20, 1861. The evening before, one of Price's officers noticed a large quantity of hemp bales on the Lexington wharf, accumulating until they could be transported downriver. The officer suggested that the bales be used as moveable fortifications. Price agreed, and on the morning of the September 20, the bales were hauled up the bluff, soaked in water, then rolled up toward the Union earthworks. There was some firing at and from the bales, but in the end no final assault was necessary. Out of food and water, the Union defenders surrendered that afternoon. The fighting resulted in another memorable moniker: the Battle of the Hemp Bales.

Amid difficult logistics and controversies surrounding his leadership, Frémont did just about everything that could have been done to save the defenders of Lexington. Despite these efforts, Price took 3,000 Union prisoners there, most of them members of the Irish Brigade. The non-commissioned soldiers were soon paroled, while the officers were placed under guard and detained in Lexington. For his part, Col. Mulligan was offered a parole but refused it, standing on the principle that the Missouri State Guard was a foe not recognized by his government.[6] Instead of throwing Mulligan in irons, Gen. Price showed extreme deference to the colonel, even allowing Mulligan's young wife to join him in Lexington. "Old Pap" may have taken a liking to 19-year-old Marian Nugent Mulligan, but whatever the case, he lent the couple his carriage and team, and they rode around the city like mini-celebrities.

The Battle of Lexington. Unknown artist, 1861–1865.
Missouri Historical Society Collections.

Gen. Frémont reacted to the surrender of Lexington on September 23 by writing to an officer in Washington, intending for his words to reach Abraham Lincoln. The letter has some similarities to Frémont's correspondence from the Astor House in July 1861, when he was expected to take command in Missouri. It was a mixture of exaggeration and bravado, delivered too late: "Re-enforcements, four thousand strong, under Sturgis, by capture of ferry-boats, had no means of crossing the river in time. Lane's force from the southwest, and Davis's from Southeast, upwards of eleven thousand in all, could not get there in time. *I am taking the field myself.*"[7] (emphasis added)

It was September 30, 1861, when Price evacuated Lexington. Price was a cautious man, to be sure, but it must be noted that the Missouri State Guard was dangling dangerously far from its base. Frémont had taken the field himself during the week that passed since his September 23 dispatch to Lincoln. On September 30, Frémont was just getting comfortable in Jefferson City. He'd managed to reinforce Sedalia, Missouri, on the Pacific Railroad 60 miles west of the capital. Sedalia was uncomfortably close to Price's route of retreat through Warrensburg. Clearly, it was time to go. Gen. Price left a small force at Lexington to guard the prisoners, then departed with Col. and Marian Mulligan.

James Mulligan was exchanged in late October 1861 and returned to Chicago in November to a tumultuous welcome.[8] This speaks volumes regarding the state of Union fortunes during the first six months of the war. In July, the Union suffered a major loss in Virginia. The next month brought the loss at Wilson's Creek, and the month after that, the Union surrendered a small army at Lexington. From July through September, nothing had occurred in any theater of the war to bolster the hopes of citizens of the North, and the North would take its heroes where they could be found. So it was that Col. James Mulligan and a few thousand Union soldiers held out in Lexington for two days. Then they surrendered. Chicago celebrated.

Franc Wilkie, the new reporter for the *New York Times*, had followed Samuel Sturgis's column as it marched to the relief of Lexington from the railroad at Utica. When Sturgis turned away from the beleaguered city, his force was in Richmond, Missouri, 6 miles north of Lexington. It was September 19. As Wilkie described, "Believing that among all nations the position of a correspondent is held sacred, and confiding in the magnanimity of Gen. PRICE, I determined to throw myself in his hands, state my business, and request permission to witness the battle."[9]

This statement was contained in the story that Wilkie filed with the *Times*, along with a curious line that suggests Sturgis's command had left Wilkie behind in Richmond: "Here a few bottles of wine were cracked at the expense of a citizen...and then the command moved on...." Others have said that Wilkie was more than a little buzzed when he presented himself to Sterling Price in Lexington: "Wilkie managed to get drunk enough to imagine himself invincible," Brayton Harris wrote in *Blue & Gray in Black & White: Newspapers in the Civil War*.[10] However it was that Wilkie got up the courage to do this, his story from Lexington filled half of the front page of the October 2, 1861, edition of the *New York Times*. His editor lauded Wilkie's feat as "unparalleled in the history of journalism."[11]

Writing on October 1, 1861, from Jefferson City, Wilkie got to the heart of the matter of John Charles Frémont, describing him as succinctly, perhaps, as anyone ever has:

> I believe that Gen. Frémont is a hard worker; he labors incessantly to promote the cause in which he is engaged; he leaves nothing undone that can be done by personal effort, or advanced by personal sacrifice; yet in spite of all of this, things seem to advance with supernatural slowness.[12]

ENDNOTES

1. National Park Service, *Civil War Defenses of Washington: The Civil War Years*; last updated October 29, 2004, npshistory.com/publications/cwdw/hrs/chap4-1.htm.

2. "Munson's Hill Evacuated by Rebels," *New York Times*, September 29, 1861.

3. "Munson's Hill," *New York Times.*

4. On September 13, Col. William B. Brown led a band of Missouri State Guard troops in an attack on the Union position in Boonville. Boonville legend has it that an enslaved man belonging to Brown reported the plans for the attack, took up a musket in the Union trenches, and killed William Brown in the charge. Gregory Wolk, *A Tour Guide to Missouri's Civil War: Friend and Foe Alike* (Monograph Publishing, 2020), 131.

5. The State Guard's forward movement began near the site of the Battle of the Mules, along the Missouri-Kansas border.

6. Albert Castel, *General Sterling Price and the Civil War in the West* (Louisiana State University Press, 1968), 55–56.

7. *Official Records of the Union and Confederate Armies, Ser. 1, Vol. 3, Ch. 10* (Government Printing Office, 1881), 184.

8. "The Siege of Lexington, the Surrender of Col. Mulligan," *Chicago Tribune*, September 25, 1861, in Theodore J. Karamanski and Eileen M. McMahon, eds., *Civil War Chicago: Eyewitness to History* (Ohio University Press, 2014), 73.

9. Michael Banasik, ed., *Missouri in 1861* (Camp Pope Bookshop, 2001), 184.

10. Wilkie made the remark about wine in a September 10 letter to his editor from Lexington. Banasik, 184. Wilkie's drunken state is also noted in Albert Castel's *General Sterling Price and the Civil War in the West* (LSU Press, 1993), 52. For the Brayton Harris quote, *see Blue & Gray in Black & White: Newspapers in the Civil War* (Potomac Books, 1999), 128.

11. "Wilkie, Franc," *Encyclopedia Dubuque*, https://www.encyclopediadubuque.org/index.php/WILKIE,_Franc.

12. Banasik, 194.

CHAPTER 8

★

*"I knew I was doomed when
I consented to go to St. Louis."*

—Simon Cameron

Figure 8

Born in 1799 in Pennsylvania, Simon Cameron was an astute politician whose career—often marked by financial scandals—waxed and waned over the years. His power was ascendant in 1860, and Lincoln promised him a seat on his cabinet to satisfy Pennsylvania interests. Lincoln appointed him secretary of war, even though many of his advisers balked at this decision in light of Cameron's reputation. Cameron's primary contribution to American political culture, perhaps, is the quote for which he is best remembered: "An honest politician is one who, when he is bought, will stay bought."

The American Embassy

St. Petersburg, Russia, July 1, 1862

Now minister to czarist Russia, Simon Cameron had been US secretary of war when the Civil War began. In 1862, he occupied a key post in the country's diplomatic corps. From his office, amid the opulence of Peter the Great's west-facing city, Cameron could look back from a distance at the turmoil that had gripped America during the previous nine months. He chuckled to himself. Cameron was not in exile in St. Petersburg; rather, he had engineered a deal to gain the position he now enjoyed. Purportedly, Cameron selected the Russian post as a trade-off for his "cooperation" with Lincoln's desires. Ironically, or perhaps not, among Cameron's many prewar monikers was the "Czar of Pennsylvania."

The events in Missouri throughout September and October 1861 foreshadowed a split in the nascent Republican Party. The party's Free Soil members began to separate from those who were serious about ending slavery in the South. Cameron, who had already served Pennsylvania for two non-sequential terms in the US Senate, played a critical role in 1860, when he delivered his state's convention delegates to Abraham Lincoln. Always tending toward the abolitionist view, Cameron became increasingly fixed in this position as he watched the Lincoln administration drift in the direction of the Blairs. Cameron had a poor hand to play in 1861, but he played it brilliantly.

Cameron went to Missouri in mid-October to examine the charges lodged against Frémont. It was an unsavory task, particularly for a man who favored emancipation. After he returned to Washington, Cameron issued his comeuppance: his year-end report on the US War Department's operations. In the report, he recommended the administration create "an army of slaves." Lincoln was apoplectic when he read the passage and demanded its removal from the report. But Cameron had already mailed out copies of it, including one that went to the *New York Times*.

At long last, on September 27, 1861, John Frémont began his campaign against the Missouri State Guard. The official kickoff that day occurred when Frémont and his staff and the musicians of his Body-Guard boarded the train at the Pacific Railroad terminal in St. Louis.[1] The rail trip from St. Louis to Jefferson City should have taken about 4 hours. It took 10. Halfway through, at the German settlement of Hermann, Frémont and his staff detrained to attend a dinner hosted by the town's city fathers. As one eyewitness described, "[A]midst the shouts of an enthusiastic little crowd, the General passed into a room decorated with flowers, through the centre of which was stretched a table groaning under the weight of delicious fruits and smoking viands."[2]

Another man on the ride to Jefferson City commented favorably on the band, which he said played at every station along the route.[3] The train arrived at the Jefferson City depot late in the evening of September 27. The commanding general and his staff repaired to a hotel to await the dawn.

Franc Wilkie, the journalist who rode a drinking spree into a brush with history at Lexington, was not a unique character by any means. He'd reported on the Battle of Wilson's Creek, and after a visit back home he made his way to St. Louis. Just after he arrived at his hotel on September 3, he ran into two other journalists whom he knew casually.[4] Wilkie was a "cub" to these veteran reporters from New York, Thomas W. Knox and Albert Deane Richardson, who thought they had a rube on their hands. So Knox and Richardson told Wilkie he ought to pay Gen. Frémont a visit: "Frémont will not like it when he learns that you have been in town for several days without calling on him." So Wilkie went over to headquarters and waited for five hours before leaving in disgust.[5] He had been pranked.

Another reporter of renown, Junius Henri Browne of Horace Greeley's *New-York Tribune*, was in Jefferson City, waiting out Price's siege of Lexington for two weeks before Frémont and his entourage arrived. Browne described his first days in the nearly deserted city: "I sauntered [the streets] listlessly and gloomily, wondering when my brother Bohemians...would make their appearance at the dreary capital."[6] The national press soon flooded in, and the city became the nexus for the North's appetite for news about the war. Richardson and Knox, representing the *New-York Tribune* and the *New York Herald*, respectively, came on, as did Richard Colburn of the *New York World* and George Beaman of the *Missouri Democrat*, among others. The two major national illustrated newspapers of the day, *Frank Leslie's Illustrated Newspaper* and *Harper's Weekly*, were soon represented in Jefferson City, as well as sketch artist Henri Lovie of *Frank Leslie's*, a Prussian immigrant who had become an artist of note in Cincinnati, and his counterpart, Alexander Simplot of *Harper's*. These reporters and artists were the men whom Browne called his "brother Bohemians," and they reveled in it.

The men gathered in Jefferson City were among the first Americans to work in a new profession: war correspondent.[7] The name that Browne applied to them had a fascinating backstory, one that has been traced to the 1851 novel *Scènes de la vie de bohème* by Parisian author Henri Murger, which itself inspired Giacomo Puccini's opera *La bohème*. Murger's work was all the rage among Manhattan's literati in the 1850s, which perhaps explains how it transitioned from a tale of tragic lovers to a crew of single men let loose in Missouri. In a 2006 article, Columbia University professor Andie Tucher concludes that the phrase "bohemian brigade" was coined in Jefferson City by these correspondents to describe this new career.[8]

In the days before Frémont's grand entrance on September 27, 1861, the journalists and artists had formed a bond. All or most of them had moved into a dilapidated hotel on High Street, a rooming place and tavern. For as long as two weeks, boredom was the only enemy Browne's bohemians faced in Jefferson City, but they fought it nearly to its death with shenanigans and high jinks. In Richardson's view, the journalists "held high carnival."[9] They raced borrowed horses. They harassed poor Tom Knox when he preferred to sleep during the day. According to Richardson, "There was little work to be done; so they discussed politics, art, society and metaphysics, and would soon kindle into singing, reciting, 'sky-larking,' wrestling, flinging saddles, valises and pillows."[10]

Gen. Frémont established his Jefferson City headquarters on a high shelf of land 1 mile southwest of the capitol building. He and his staff moved to this place on September 29, once tents had been erected and a telegraph link established.[11] Meanwhile, troops continued to stream into position. The buildup centered on Sedalia, 60 miles west of the city. It occupied a critical place for a reason that did not exist in any previous war: the railroad. Established in October 1860 while the Pacific Railroad continued its march west, Sedalia welcomed its first passenger train on January 17, 1861. Railroad-building came to an abrupt halt in the run-up to the Civil War, making Sedalia the end of the line—and it remained so until after hostilities ceased in 1865.

Sedalia's position was the reason Brig. Gen. Franz Sigel was dispatched there on September 23. Six weeks before his assignment to Sedalia, Sigel had botched his appearance at Wilson's Creek, but nevertheless he retained a reputation for aggressiveness. His 3rd Division began to consolidate at Sedalia and its vicinity shortly before his arrival. A cavalry scout from the 3rd Division was the first to confirm that Sterling Price's army had started its withdrawal from Lexington; indeed, nearly the entire State Guard had, by October 1, passed through Warrensburg on its way south.[12] During this same time frame, Frémont assigned commanders to four other divisions: Gen. David Hunter to the 1st; Gen. John Pope to the 2nd; Gen. Alexander Asboth to the 4th; and Justus McKinstry, whom Frémont promoted to acting major general of volunteers, to the 5th.

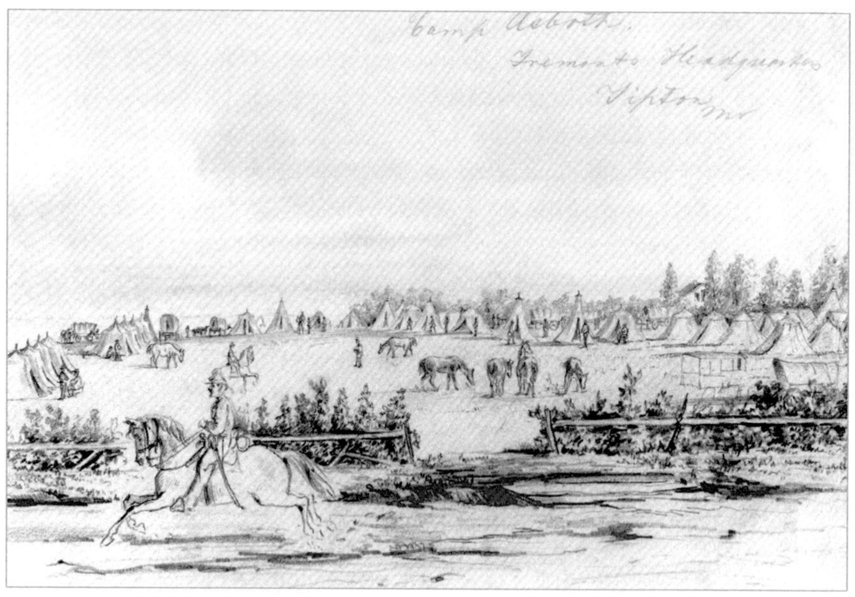

Camp Asboth, Fremont's Headquarters, Tipton Mo. Drawing by Henri Lovie, October 1861. The Becker Collection, Boston College Libraries.

As Frémont was getting himself situated in Jefferson City, a massive troop movement was underway. From the time Col. Mulligan surrendered at Lexington on September 20 until Gen. Frémont left Jefferson City for points west on October 8, more than 30,000 men reached their assigned destinations along the Pacific Railroad. The divisions of Asboth and Hunter were at Tipton, Missouri, 35 train-miles west of Jefferson City. McKinstry's division was at the hamlet of Syracuse, Missouri, just 6 miles west of Tipton. Sigel was at Sedalia. Meanwhile, the troops that would form Pope's 2nd Division were pouring in from the north and east, and they posted at various locations near Georgetown, Missouri, north of the Pacific Railroad. Within a week after October 8, more than 38,000 men were in place along this line. Most had arrived by rail from St. Louis via Jefferson City.

Gen. Frémont's Jefferson City headquarters was soon outfitted as a suitable command center. Frémont named the place Camp Lillie, in honor of his oldest child and only daughter, Elizabeth.[13] Gen. Frémont saw to it that a telegraph key was at his beck and call at Camp Lillie; it was an extraordinary feat undertaken and completed by a man named George H. Smith, Frémont's telegrapher. To accommodate Frémont's wishes, Smith buried a mile-long cable down the middle of Broadway in a matter of days. This is just one of several mostly forgotten innovations that Frémont brought to the fore during his brief assignment to Missouri.[14] While Frémont's detractors would be loath to recognize it, the movement of 38,000 men under exigencies of war was truly unprecedented. On the other hand—and herein lies a clue to the enigma of John Frémont—even in times of great success, he could not resist sowing doubt about his seriousness and competency. There was no good reason for Frémont to bring the telegraph to his headquarters rather than putting his headquarters near where the telegraph was already located.

The same might be said of his idea to direct the business of the Western Department from a tent city in the hills above Jefferson City. In this case, Frémont did have a good reason, but it was all for the sake of appearances. Frémont had blurted on September 23 that he was "taking the field myself." The response from the Lincoln administration was swift and emphatic: "Your despatch [*sic*] of this day is received. The President is glad you are hastening to the scene of action. His words are, he expects you to repair the disaster at Lexington without loss of time."[15]

Most of the Union soldiers who passed through Missouri's capital that fall only camped for a day or two at Jefferson City. Still, throughout the first week of October, there was a constant presence of infantry troops that measured in the thousands. All through his stay, Frémont kept his Body-Guard close to him; the troopers camped in the well-watered valley of Wears Creek, just north of and down the slope from his headquarters.

Camp Lily, Frémont's Headquarters, Jefferson City, Mo. Drawing by Henri Lovie, October 5, 1861. The Becker Collection, Boston College Libraries.

Camp Lillie was, quite literally, a stage set. Frémont's presence there confirmed that he had "taken the field," but the scene had an unseemly air of extravagance about it. Ten or twelve officers' tents were arranged in a semicircle, with Frémont's tent at its center.[16] When viewed from the south, Camp Lillie's backdrop was a vista that encompassed the capital city and the Missouri River bluffs in the far distance. On October 1, Jessie Benton Frémont arrived with Lily and little Frank on a special train from St. Louis, an act intended to move the national press—and by some accounts, it did. John C. Frémont Jr. had arrived with his father a few days before. The family would stay in Jefferson City until John Sr. took his leave on October 7, 1861, when he'd march at the head of the last of his departing troops.

On October 5, Henri Lovie sat facing the headquarters' tents and drew the scene at Camp Lillie.[17] Here is Jessie, huddled with Lily and Justus McKinstry, while John Jr. and Frank cavort nearby. Another group of officers, identified by Lovie only as "Hungarians," engage in conversation. After the drawing was received in Boston and fully engraved, it appeared in *Frank Leslie's Illustrated Newspaper.*

Frémont's departure to the west, as reported by Franc Wilkie, was full of the same sort of ballyhoo that had accompanied Jessie's arrival in Jefferson City a week earlier. Wilkie's report, which appeared prominently in the October 12 *New York Times*, reeks of sarcasm, although the *Times* editors and the paper's reading public likely took it all in as if it were gospel. Just before noon on October 7, at the base of the hill, troopers of the Body-Guard readied their mounts, and soon Frémont and his staff rode to the heart of the city. Jessie took the general's carriage from Camp Lillie into town, where she parted with him, no doubt playing her leading-lady role with dramatic flair. At that point, "[T]he General and Staff rode on at a brisk trot, followed at a slower pace by the body guard and the baggage train."[18]

Frémont's cavalcade left the fairy-tale war of Jefferson City and entered the not-so-hospitable real world. After a 7-mile march, the men filed into a valley where Frémont established his first camp, which he called Camp Lovejoy.[19] The next day, Frémont moved another 14 miles, to the town of California, before arriving at Tipton, Missouri, on October 9, 1861. In all, the trek stretched just over 30 miles and took two and a half days. But the entire route was serviced by the Pacific Railroad, which had already carried thousands of troops with their equipage and rations. This outrageous waste of effort could be written off as more of Frémont's theatrics, but it's just as likely that Frémont simply needed the practice.

Frémont is rightly lauded as a leader of men. He gained legendary success as the "Pathfinder of the West." But up until October 1861, the largest force Frémont had ever led in battle was in December 1846 during the Mexican-American War, when he brought the California Battalion into Santa Barbara. There, Frémont had fewer than 500 men, and his attack resulted in a bloodless capitulation. He now contemplated leading 38,000 soldiers on an overland march that had no precedent in American history.[20] What's more, rumors circulated freely in the eastern press that Lincoln was about to replace him at the helm.[21]

On October 8, Secretary of War Simon Cameron was preparing to travel to St. Louis. Lincoln had drafted him and Adjutant General Lorenzo Thomas to make the trip, ostensibly to further investigate the charges regarding Frémont's fitness for command. It was the same mission, in effect, that caused Postmaster General Montgomery Blair and Gen. Meigs to travel to St. Louis the month before. But in this second instance, Lincoln had given Cameron discretionary authority to fire Frémont. Cameron even carried an order signed by General in Chief Winfield Scott that would relieve Frémont, if Cameron saw fit to do so.[22]

Cameron and Thomas arrived in St. Louis at 2:30am on Friday, October 11. The next afternoon, the men boarded a train and reached Jefferson City by evening. The travelers rose early on October 13, reboarded the westbound train, and arrived in Tipton by 9am.[23] Tipton in 1861 was a thriving community that had benefitted from the western progress of the Pacific Railroad, much as Sedalia later benefitted when it was the end of the line. Founded after the railroad reached there in 1858, Tipton's place in history was cemented that year by the arrival of John Butterfield's Overland Mail Company's route to San Francisco. Gen. Frémont established his Tipton headquarters in a building that was constructed in 1858 as Rose Hill, a school for girls, but was now vacant. Tipton's star was fading. Still, the road network established by Butterfield's venture still existed in 1861, and it would serve Frémont in the days ahead.

The visitors from Washington enjoyed breakfast with Gen. Frémont and his senior staff. Secretary Cameron, along with Gen. Frémont and a cavalry escort, then mounted up and galloped off for the next station 6 miles to the west. This was Syracuse, where Justus McKinstry's 5,000-man-strong division was camped. Cameron let his decorum slip on the ride to Syracuse when he accepted an officer's challenge to race, and he surprised some with his skill as a horseman. Whatever glee this episode engendered was spoiled when two riders from Frémont's escort seriously wounded themselves by accidentally discharging their weapons. When the party reached Syracuse, Cameron reviewed McKinstry's troops. One of the bright spots of Cameron's trip, from Gen. Frémont's perspective, was that Cameron found them well equipped and supplied.

Lorenzo Thomas did not accompany Cameron and Frémont to Syracuse; it seems his agenda required him to interview Frémont's subordinates in Tipton. With Frémont out of the way, Thomas went directly to Gen. Hunter.

Gen. David Hunter had been summoned to St. Louis in early September 1861 and was present when Blair and Meigs arrived from Washington and when the two met with Gen. Frémont on September 13. Montgomery Blair privately delivered the president's note that encouraged Hunter to mentor Frémont: "He needs to have, by his side, a man of large experience. Will you not, for me, take that place?" But a good deal more was going on behind the scenes. Gen. Hunter was home in Chicago, recovering from a wound he received at the First Battle of Bull Run, but managed to get himself to St. Louis within two days after being summoned. According to participants' sworn testimony some months later, Hunter was sitting in Frémont's basement when Montgomery Blair suggested that he should join the meeting that had already begun. When all is said and done, Hunter's contribution to the September 13 conversation is not in dispute. He trashed the campaign plans that Frémont had put together, preferring to express the company line that Frémont should concentrate on the threat to Lexington before Sterling Price got there.[24]

When Thomas met Hunter in Tipton, it was as though Hunter had prepared a script: He had a list of petty complaints that mostly concerned Frémont's discretion as he faced a mountain of logistical problems to get his forces on the road. Hunter complained that he had to march to Tipton on a dirt road, *and it rained.* When he left Jefferson City, Hunter was "directed to take 41 wagons with him, when he had only 40 mules." Hunter received his order to march in the direction of Springfield two days after the order was dated. The complaints went on and on. Hunter's whining devolved into a charge that some firearms were defective, and (as if Hunter could have known) these were rifles that Gen. Frémont had acquired in Europe. He also said he'd just received a "private letter" from John Pope, which he shared with Thomas. According to Pope, the division commander who had more than 9,000 troops in camp north of Sedalia, moving them as ordered was an "utter impossibility" due to a want of supplies and transportation.

When the time came, Cameron showed Frémont the order relieving him of his command. Frémont, in Cameron's words, "was very much mortified, pained and, I thought, humiliated."[25] Gen. Frémont begged for the chance to bring Gen. Price to battle. Cameron pulled the order back, acceding to Frémont's request, mumbling something to the effect that he would hold the order until he had returned to Washington. This was truly an astonishing development. In contrast to Montgomery Blair's half-baked effort in September, Lincoln's October plan to replace Frémont seemed to have all of its *T*s crossed, and Cameron had inexplicably thrown a wrench into it.

Their business done, on the afternoon of Sunday, October 13, Cameron and Thomas began their return trip to St. Louis. They traveled most of the night, then checked into the Planter's House upon their arrival. The next morning the two of them presented some brief patriotic remarks to troops and citizens assembled outside the hotel before crossing the Mississippi to board an eastbound train. On their way back to Washington, Cameron and Thomas visited Indianapolis to meet with Governor Oliver Morton, and then they proceeded to Louisville, where Gen. Sherman had recently taken command.

ENDNOTES

1. *Diary of the Paymaster of Frémont's Body Guard*, November 29, 1861, including transcription by J. Kaufman and D. Northcott, Missouri Historical Society Collections.

2. William Dorsheimer, "Frémont's Hundred Days in Missouri, Part 1," *Atlantic Monthly* 9, no. 53 (January 1862): 116–117.

3. *Diary of the Paymaster*, 2.

4. Franc B. Wilkie, *Pen and Powder* (Ticknor and Company, 1888), 49–51.

5. Wilkie, 49. Wilkie's delightful story of his visit to Frémont's headquarters may have grown more interesting over time; of course, he was aware of the experiences others had endured in trying to visit the general.

6. Junius Henri Browne, *Four Years in Secessia: Adventures Within and Beyond the Union Lines* (O. D. Case and Company, 1865), 23–24.

7. The men in Jefferson City had a British predecessor, a man named Billy Russell of the *London Times*, who reported the Crimean War from the front.

8. Andie Tucher, "Reporting for Duty: The Bohemian Brigade, the Civil War, and the Social Construction of the Reporter," *Book History* 9 (2006): 131–157.

9. Albert D. Richardson, *The Secret Service, the Field, the Dungeon, and the Escape* (American Publishing Company, 1865), 189–192.

10. Richardson, 190.

11. William R. Plum, *The Military Telegraph during the Civil War in the United States* (McClurg & Company, 1882), 115–116.

12. Warrensburg, Missouri, is 90 miles due west of Jefferson City. When Price reached that point, his retreat could no longer be blocked. It was now a chase.

13. Elizabeth's name was variously spelled Lily, or Lilly, or Lillie. For consistency's sake, this manuscript refers to her as Lily and the camp as Camp Lillie.

14 Frémont was instrumental in establishing and promoting the Western Sanitary Commission and worked tirelessly to assist James Eads in his venture to build iron-clad gunboats. By good authority, Frémont himself innovated converting train cars into rolling ambulances—a first. See Galusha Anderson, *The Story of a Border City during the Civil War* (Little, Brown & Co. 1908), 297.

15. *Official Records of the Union and Confederate Armies, Ser. 1, Vol. 3, Ch. 10*, 185.

16. A Sibley tent, patented in 1856, was conical in shape, while a Frémont tent was squared off and could hold nearly twice the number of soldiers.

17. Henri Lovie, "Camp Lily, Frémont's headquarters, Jefferson City, Missouri," October 4, 1861, accessed February 1, 2025, https://beckercollection.bc.edu.

18. "Departure of Frémont's Army," *New York Times*, October 12, 1861.

19. Camp Lovejoy was named for Col. Owen Lovejoy, an Illinois congressman and younger brother of Elijah Lovejoy, an abolitionist newspaper publisher who was murdered in Alton in 1837 for his views on slavery.

20. The only Civil War troop movement by rail that preceded Frémont's was Joseph E. Johnson's movement of 10,000 Confederates by rail from the Shenandoah Valley to Manassas, Virginia.

21. Pamela Herr and Mary Lee Spence, eds., *The Letters of Jessie Benton Frémont* (University of Illinois Press, 1993), 280, note 7.

22. On October 7, 1861, General in Chief Winfield Scott signed General Order No. 18, which would have relieved Frémont of his post. Notes in the Abraham Lincoln Papers point to an oddity: Order No. 18 was reissued without change on October 24, 1861. See http://www.loc.gov/resource/mal.1244800.

23. Rudi Keller, *Life during Wartime, Vol. 1* (Tribune Publishing Company, 2012), 214–215.

24. David Hunter and Montgomery Blair would testify before a congressional committee during the winter of 1862. Their sworn testimonies were distinctly different regarding who called Gen. Hunter to St. Louis to consult with Frémont. See *Report of the Joint Committee on the Conduct of the War, Part 3* (Washington, DC: Government Printing Office, 1863), 154–156 (Blair); 234–245 (Hunter). In addition, it is doubtful that Hunter was unprepared to join the meeting yet agreed with the proposition that Frémont should abandon plans for his campaign against Springfield. This was the gist of Montgomery Blair's testimony.

25. Abraham Lincoln Papers: General Correspondence, 1833–1916, Series 1. Letter, Simon Cameron to Abraham Lincoln, October 14, 1861. Library of Congress, Washington, DC.

CHAPTER 9

*"He seems to be here, there,
and everywhere all at once."*

—Israel Gibbons

Israel Gibbons was born in Chester, Pennsylvania, and raised in Louisville, Kentucky. He was hired in 1855 to report for the *New Orleans Daily Crescent*. Before the Civil War, he'd earned a reputation as one of that city's best reporters. While at Columbus in 1861, Gibbons was a soldier in the 11th Louisiana Infantry regiment of the Confederate army. Later, he was promoted to major in the Quartermaster Corps and continued to file stories with his hometown paper. Gibbons's date of birth and place of burial is unknown, but he died in New Orleans in 1866, still a young man. It is thought that his death was caused by a disease contracted during his war service, but it may have been hastened by a serious chest wound he suffered in a duel in 1858.

Fort DeRussy

Columbus, Kentucky, October 30, 1861

As the month of November approached, war correspondent Israel Gibbons of the *New Orleans Daily Crescent* visited Columbus, Kentucky. He was there, in no small part, to take stock of Missouri phenom M. Jefferson Thompson. Thompson was just coming off an extraordinary two weeks of fighting in Missouri. His first engagement during this period, at Big River Bridge, scared the daylights out of the populace of St. Louis; the second, a pitched battle in Fredericktown, Missouri (which both sides claimed as a victory), represented a rare reversal of fortune for Gen. Ulysses Grant.

Thompson was in Columbus to confer with Confederate general Gideon Pillow about what punishment they could next dole out to unionists in southeast Missouri. At the time, Gen. Frémont was more than just preoccupied with affairs in central and southwest Missouri—he was gone from his seat of command in St. Louis. He was instead 200 miles away from there, at Springfield, after draining the energy of thousands of men in his mighty yet unsuccessful effort to smite Sterling Price.

Gibbons's autumn trip to Columbus would produce a story for the *Crescent* that introduced Thompson, Missouri's "Swamp Fox," to the people of the South. Obviously enamored by the cocky man from Missouri, Gibbons described Gen. Thompson for his readers in exquisite detail, including this portrait:

> Let me picture this man to you. Imagine a tall, lean, lank, wiry-looking customer, at least six feet high and slender as a pair of tongs; a thin, long head, with a very long nose; what you would call a hatchet face; thick yellow hair, combed back of his ears and bobbed off short, displaying a very long and thin neck; face healthy and ruddy....[1]

Since the beginning of September, Jeff Thompson, brigadier general of the Missouri State Guard, had been relatively quiet. On September 2, 1861, he had issued his manifesto against Frémont's August 30 proclamation. Although Gen. Thompson had made a lot of noise with a small band of troops in August, as September turned to October, Thompson was taking the time he needed to recruit and train infantry and cavalry for service in his 1st District of the Missouri State Guard. He also found time for a few personal diversions. In the process, he moved his headquarters away from Camp Hunter to a more defensible location a few miles northeast of Bloomfield, in a remote area on Crowley's Ridge he called Camp Spring Hill. Thompson was joined there by Col. Adin B. Lowe of Doniphan, Missouri, a native of Tennessee and a Mexican-American War veteran. Lowe had risen from corporal to colonel in the short history of the Missouri State Guard, and he would take charge of Thompson's infantry at the camp.

View from the Bluffs, Columbus, Ky. Drawing by Henri Lovie, March 1862. The Becker Collection, Boston College Libraries.

During the first week of September, Thompson took his men to Columbus, Kentucky, where he could consult personally with Gens. Polk and Pillow. At that time, Thompson reported his strength at 1,400 infantry and 500 mounted rifles. On September 15, Gen. Thompson's status changed dramatically, as Missouri's governor-in-exile ordered that he and his force should report directly and only to Maj. Gen. Leonidas Polk, who was commanding Confederate forces from Memphis, Tennessee.[2] In the last week of September, Thompson wrangled a four-day furlough from his new boss, which he spent in Memphis. Perhaps one of Thompson's objectives was to rest and recreate, but the general, ever on the make, decided to use the occasion to enhance his growing reputation. And that he did.

Thompson attended the theater at least one night he was in Memphis, maybe more, and brought with him an orderly who called himself Ajax.[3] A Canadian subject with Mohawk ancestry, Ajax was dressed in Native garb, described by one witness as a "suit of black velvet, a headdress of eagle feathers, and a belt with imitation scalp locks dangling from it."[4] One night, in the middle of the play, Ajax rushed down the aisle with a paper in hand and showed it to Gen. Thompson, as though it were a dispatch from the front, causing Thompson to abruptly exit the theater. Of course, it was all an act. But to a throng of theatergoers—and to citizens of Memphis who later read the account in the paper—the "Swamp Fox" from Missouri had achieved his omnipresent aim: *Look at me.* Ajax's legal name was Simon Martin, and he along with his siblings co-owned a showboat that normally docked in Cincinnati. Martin was one of the actors who presented the family's most popular show, *Tableaus of American History.*[5]

By September 29, 1861, Thompson had returned from Memphis to his camp at Belmont. Confederate general Albert Sidney Johnston, who was on an inspection tour of his defenses across the width of Kentucky, was across the river at Columbus. Johnston suggested that Thompson and his Missouri men create a diversion in Missouri, in part to distract Frémont from his pursuit of Gen. Price. An order was issued to Gen. Thompson that he was to take his army to the vicinity of Farmington, Missouri, and "if possible to embarrass their [Union defenders'] movements by cutting their Ironton Railroad."[6] Thompson sprang into action, first alerting two of his three regiments of cavalry. These regiments were keeping tabs on Union activities between Belmont and Bloomfield, and they were now ordered to consolidate with Lowe's infantry at Camp Spring Hill.

Ulysses Grant, commanding Union troops in southeast Missouri from his headquarters in Cairo, had an excellent intelligence operation. Already on October 2, sources had informed him of Thompson's movements away from Belmont. By October 7, Gen. Grant had enough information to assume that Thompson *and* Lowe had reoccupied Sikeston, and perhaps even Benton, but he was unconcerned. According to Grant, they could "easily be driven out" if he had cavalry in the area, which he did not. Gen. Grant thought it useless to devote anything but cavalry to the task of containing Thompson. What Grant did not know was that Thompson was already well west of Sikeston, where he had access to a good road leading into the heart of the southeast Missouri highlands. Thompson was not going to test the Benton–to–Cape Girardeau route again, as he had in August.

The Jeff Thompson who cavorted in Memphis was no more. He was again the Thompson of the saddle, the fox of the swamp, who was "here, there, and everywhere all at once." In the first place, he took the contingent part of Gen. Johnston's order—that he should cut the St. Louis and Iron Mountain Railroad "if possible"—and made it his guiding star. Second, Thompson took a good look at a Missouri map. Farmington was nowhere near where he needed to be to cut the railroad and isolate Ironton, so he tacked on 30 miles above Farmington and decided he would strike first with cavalry.[7] Those in Thompson's circle who were familiar with this section of Missouri knew exactly where the St. Louis and Iron Mountain Railroad was most vulnerable. Just south of De Soto in Jefferson County, a substantial three-span timber structure bridged the Big River. Thompson sensed that this structure was the weak link in the Union's supply system, and he was right.

This bridge was Jeff Thompson's objective when he set off with 500 cavalry from Camp Spring Hill, early in the morning of October 12. His northerly movement—which traversed 110 miles—was not detected by Union authorities while it was in progress.

A brand-new regiment arrived at the East St. Louis rail yards on October 13, 1861. It was 10pm, and the regiment's soldiers went to sleep in the train cars. It had been an exhausting but exhilarating trip from Madison, where the men of the 8th Regiment Wisconsin Volunteer Infantry had taken their basic training. It was pure coincidence that the regiment arrived on the same evening that Simon Cameron and Adjutant General Thomas had returned to the city from their journey to Tipton. These 1,000 men were torn from their slumber in the early morning of October 14; the secretary of war needed an audience for remarks he planned to give outside the Planter's House Hotel. The Wisconsin men grumbled like veterans, then filed onto the ferries and entered the war zone for the first time.

It was a time of wonder for these mostly rural soldiers. Many felt like celebrities—and they were—because they carried with them a young bald eagle mascot called Old Abe. The regiment was cheered in Chicago, where it changed trains on October 12, because the bird's remarkable fame had already spread from Madison. Wisconsin's governor even traveled to Chicago with the 8th Regiment.

Old Abe, the "War Eagle." Stereograph by W. M. Chase, 1861–1881. Library of Congress, Prints and Photographs Division.

Old Abe's story is legendary in Wisconsin and among Civil War historians: A member of the Chippewa Tribe captured a newly hatched eaglet in northern Wisconsin, which he traded for a bushel of corn. The man who acquired the eaglet took it to Eau Claire, where he kept it as a pet, but he found the bird too expensive to maintain. Men who gathered in Eau Claire to form loyal regiments for the Union paid the man $2.50 for the eaglet. When fully organized, this group became part of Company C of the 8th Wisconsin Volunteer Infantry. They traveled to Camp Randall in Madison, where men from many places throughout Wisconsin went for basic training. There, the men of Company C fashioned a perch on a pole, thought to be suitable for parades and such. Before they left Camp Randall, the bald eagle had a name—Old Abe—and the regiment had been dubbed the Eagle Regiment.[8]

The men's first impressions of St. Louis on October 14, 1861, must have reinforced their experiences in Madison and Chicago, as they were hustled across the river to hear a politician's speech. When the speech concluded, the regiment formed in line of march, ready to move to their temporary camp at Benton Barracks in north St. Louis. One civilian was so impressed by the spectacle that he offered $500 for the eagle but was told emphatically, "No price can buy him."[9]

It was not uncommon for raw Union regiments to march into war sporting a rather triumphal attitude, only to be shocked when actually facing off in battle. No regiment saw the transition from hype to horror quite the way that the 8th Wisconsin and its famous eagle did. First, the 8th Wisconsin had been issued gray uniforms—traditionally, the color of the Confederacy—and on their 4-mile march to Benton Barracks, they suffered insults and jeers and a barrage of brickbats from crowds of Union sympathizers lining the route. Then, Old Abe escaped his handler for a brief time, soaring above the rooftops of north St. Louis before returning to his perch.[10] When the Wisconsin men finally bedded down at Benton Barracks, they surely felt a collective sense of relief.

Brigadier General M. Jeff Thompson. Carte de visite by E. and H. Anthony, New York, 1862. Missouri Historical Society Collections.

During the night of October 14, Gen. Jeff Thompson's cavalry, still undetected, was pounding north through St. Francois County. Thompson divided his force as he approached the Big River Bridge in the dark. The 3rd Regiment cavalry, commanded by Lt. Col. James White and accompanied by Gen. Thompson, waded into the Big River on their mounts, reaching the rails on the south side of the bridge at Blackwell. Col. John J. Smith's 2nd Regiment ranged off to the right, following the high ground that commanded the north side of the river. Smith's cavalry initiated the attack, which came at dawn on October 15. Thompson's forces, reaching their objective from the north and south at about the same time, made short work of the Big River Bridge. They burned the structure to the ground, successfully halting rail traffic between St. Louis and Ironton.

The psychological damage inflicted by Thompson's strike on the Big River Bridge far outweighed the physical consequences. Gen. Frémont's actions—his August 30 proclamation, his decision to throw Frank Blair in jail, his cumbersome move to Jefferson City—constantly made news in St. Louis and Washington. The war along the Mississippi River, thought to be a problem mostly for Kentucky and Tennessee, had suddenly reared its head just 50 train-miles from Frémont's Chouteau headquarters. The Brant Mansion was now near empty. Most of Frémont's army was west of Tipton; not more than a handful of Union combat troops were available in St. Louis, and 1,000 of them were the men and boys of the Eagle Regiment who had just arrived.

It's not clear what time news of Thompson's strike reached St. Louis, but the telegraph line was still intact in and north of De Soto. Five companies of the 8th Wisconsin boarded trains in St. Louis the afternoon of October 15. On their second night in the war zone, the men slept in De Soto, in the rain without shelter.[11] Soon, the whole regiment found its way to Ironton, as Gens. Frémont and Grant contemplated their next moves.

Thompson's plan was an elaborate one. His infantry—by most estimates in the range of 2,000 men—was to join him in the interior, a march that would take much longer than the time it took the cavalry to reach the area of their attack. According to the plan Thompson unveiled the night before he set off, Lowe's infantry and artillery would meet the cavalry at Fredericktown, Missouri, as the cavalry retired from the Big River Bridge. Fredericktown was 50 miles closer to Camp Spring Hill than the bridge. Hewing close to the plan, the two forces met in Fredericktown on October 17. Having the place to themselves, at least for a time, Thompson's men confiscated 10,000 pounds of lead from Mine La Motte, on the outskirts of Fredericktown.[12] They put their booty in wagons and put the wagons on the road south.

On October 16, Gen. Frémont ordered Gen. Grant to "send as large a force as you can from Cape Girardeau, in the direction of Ironton or Pilot Knob, to cut off [Thompson's] retreat into Arkansas."[13] Grant had perhaps 3,000 available troops spread between Cape Girardeau and Ironton. His reaction was swift. Grant's initial communications to Col. Joseph B. Plummer, commanding the post at Cape Girardeau, were uncharacteristically indecisive.

On October 18, for example, Grant wired instructions to Plummer that included this passage:

> I feel but little confidence in your even seeing [Thompson's forces], but information just received from Saint Louis reports Thompson as fortifying Fredericktown. You will, therefore, march upon that place unless you should receive such information on your march as to indicate a different locality of the ubiquitous individual.[14]

This and other correspondence demonstrates that Gen. Grant held Thompson's army in low regard. It's also flavored with another one of Grant's legendary traits: his coolness under fire, which he displayed during the first opportunity that presented itself. As John A. Rawlins, Grant's chief of staff, would later note in a postwar address to the Society of the Army of the Tennessee, "[Fredericktown] was the first affair, dignified by the name of battle, in which any of the troops under Gen. Grant had been engaged."[15]

Grant was nevertheless confident as he first directed Col. Plummer from Cape Girardeau—and a few days later, Col. William Carlin at Ironton—to consolidate at Fredericktown. The three regiments that Carlin could spare for this mission included the greenest of the green, the Eagle Regiment of Wisconsin.

The lead-up to the confrontation at Fredericktown saw an all-too-common incident in the early months of the Civil War: a lost dispatch. Jeff Thompson's troops captured a courier who was carrying a message from Col. Plummer intended for Col. Carlin. The message revealed that the two forces were rapidly converging on Thompson's position in Fredericktown. Thompson pulled his troops, his artillery, and his cavalry out of town and paused them a few miles south. Carlin's force arrived in Fredericktown around 9am on October 21; the soldiers roamed around the deserted town for several hours, waiting for Plummer to arrive from Cape Girardeau. Carlin established headquarters in a private home on Main Street and promptly went to sleep.

South of town, Thompson took stock of the situation. He wanted to impress the senior Confederate command, particularly Maj. Gen. Albert Sidney Johnston. It was Johnston's order on September 29 that launched Thompson's raid on the Big River Bridge. In addition to Johnston's request that the Missouri general disrupt the Iron Mountain line if he could, the orders expressed that "[t]he general desires you to remain in the field so long as you can do so in safety."[16] Thompson had exceeded all of Johnston's expectations and then some.

While it is unclear why Thompson waited until after Plummer's troops had reached Fredericktown to commence the battle, Thompson's decision to fight was probably foregone. The concept of "blooding" an untrained military force—which maintained that an inexperienced force retreating without doing battle could prove disastrous for morale—was an age-old one. So Thompson turned his men around and moved them into a valley a mile south of Fredericktown's courthouse square. He posted a few artillery pieces in the heights at the south side of the valley, creating the impression that he was prepared to fight a rear-guard action to cover his withdrawal. The Union forces, somewhat in disarray, were set in motion on the southbound road.[17] Halfway across the valley, they found Lowe when his infantry fired on them in flank. The fight raged for more than two hours, a full battle that engaged artillery, cavalry, and infantry on both sides. Gen. Thompson then disengaged and retreated to Spring Hill.

October 21, 1861, is a date that looms large in American history. Back in Washington, the Army of the Potomac's first foray out of the city since September's embarrassment at Munson's Hill ended in an unmitigated disaster known as the Battle of Ball's Bluff. There, a Union reconnaissance mission near Leesburg, Virginia, was bungled, resulting in a clash of arms that left 550 Union troops dead or wounded and as many captured. Among the dead was Col. Edward T. Baker, a popular US senator from Oregon and one of Abraham Lincoln's closest friends.[18] Meanwhile, out in central Missouri, Gen. Frémont passed the day in camp at Warsaw without suffering a disaster. For Frémont, this counted as good news. Arguably, though, the most significant event of October 21, 1861, was one that neither Grant nor Thompson nor Frémont could have imagined.

The 8th Wisconsin Infantry arrived in Fredericktown that morning, part of Carlin's force from Ironton. It had been precisely seven days since the Eagle Regiment had crossed into Missouri at St. Louis. In light of the regiment's inexperience, it was ordered to the center of town to guard the Union army's wagons. No doubt remembering Old Abe's escapade in St. Louis, the eagle's handlers gave him a sturdier line when they tethered him to the courthouse roof. One chronicler of Wisconsin history, writing in 1885, described the scene at the courthouse while the battle raged south of town: "[A]s the rattle of musketry, the hastening of ambulances, the shouting of officers, the screams of projectiles and the shrieks of the wounded burst upon [Old Abe's] senses in the full tide of battle, he became wild with excitement, leaping and screeching."[19]

Old Abe saw action in 37 battles during the Civil War. In 1862, Sterling Price watched the eagle at the Battle of Corinth, Mississippi, as he left his perch and soared high above Price's lines. Price is said to have exclaimed, "I would rather get that eagle than capture a whole brigade or a dozen battle flags."[20]

To this day, a bronze replica of Old Abe occupies a perch that oversees the workings of the Wisconsin State Assembly. In 1918 the US Army created a 101st Infantry Division, but World War I ended before it could fill its ranks with soldiers. It was disbanded, only to be reconstituted as a division of the Organized Reserve in 1921. Reserve units were assigned to individual states; the 101st Infantry was assigned to Wisconsin. In 1923, the division adopted a shoulder patch with the head of a bald eagle in profile in honor of Old Abe. When the US Army converted the 101st to airborne operations in 1942, the division inherited both the numerical designation and the shoulder patch of the Screaming Eagle. Old Abe was that eagle, and he first screamed at Fredericktown on October 21, 1861.

October 21, 1861, also marked the end of the journey to St. Louis for Secretary of War Simon Cameron and Adjutant General Lorenzo Thomas. The two headed south to visit William Sherman, the new commander at Louisville, who had taken over the Department of the Cumberland from the exhausted Gen. Robert Anderson. Cameron and Thomas collected a retinue of followers who accompanied them to Louisville, including "six or seven gentlemen who turned out to be reporters," Sherman wrote in his memoirs in 1875.[21] The men repaired to the Galt House hotel, where Sherman was lodging. By the time he penned his memoirs, Sherman had reason to be defensive, which is apparent in the words he chose. At the time of Cameron's visit, though, he evidently did not know the identities of the men in the room. He claimed that the federal cause in Kentucky was a disaster in waiting, leading many to declare that Sherman was "crazy."

The day after Cameron's return to Washington City, October 22, President Lincoln convened a meeting of his cabinet. Most of those present argued for Frémont's immediate replacement, siding with the opinions of the man they proposed to install in Frémont's place, David Hunter.[22] Lincoln put the plan in motion.

ENDNOTES

1. Israel Gibbons, *Crescent-Shine: Or, Gleams of Light on All Sorts of Subjects from the Columns of the "New Orleans Crescent"* (J. O. Nixon, 1866), 106.

2. *Official Records of the Union and Confederate Armies, Ser. 1, Vol. 3, Ch. 10* (Government Printing Office, 1881), 701–702.

3. Basil W. Duke, *The Civil War Reminiscences of General Basil W. Duke, C. S. A.* (Doubleday, Page & Co., 1911), 82. Kentuckian Basil Duke was the brother-in-law of Confederate general John Hunt Morgan. Duke was living in St. Louis at the time of the Camp Jackson affair and was instrumental in organizing a pro-secession group called the Minute Men. After returning to Kentucky, Duke rode with Morgan until the ill-fated Great Raid of 1863, when Duke was captured in Ohio.

4. Duke, 82.

5. Duke, 82. Duke referred to Ajax as a "Canadian Indian," without further context or explanation. The full story of the Martin family was explored by Lyle Randolph of Cape Girardeau, in "Dunklin County during the Civil War," *Delta Dunklin Democrat*, September 25, 2011.

6. *Official Records*, 709. The proper name of the railroad in 1861 was the St. Louis and Iron Mountain Railroad Company.

7. Thompson moved north with two mounted regiments, the 2nd and 3rd Missouri Dragoons. By 1861 the historic distinction between cavalry and dragoons—the latter a type of mounted infantry—was no longer operative.

8. James A. Page, "The Story of 'Old Abe,' Famous Wisconsin War Eagle on 101st Airborne Division Patch," November 15, 2012, US Army website, https://www.army.mil/article/91178/the_story_of_old_abe_famous_wisconsin_war_eagle_on_101st_airborne_division_patch.

9. Frank A. Flower, *Old Abe, the Eighth Wisconsin War Eagle* (Curran and Bowen, 1885), 21.

10. Flower, 20. See also John Melvin Williams, *The Eagle Regiment, 8th Wisconsin Infantry Volunteers* (The Recorder Printing, 1890).

11. Williams, 4.

12. Fredericktown was founded as St. Michael in 1802 by French families in the lead-mining trade. The famous Mine La Motte, 5 miles north of the present town, was discovered by Native peoples sometime before 1700. Frenchman Antoine de la Mothe Cadillac began exploiting the find around 1715. By the 1860s it was thought that the mine held an inexhaustible supply of lead. The mine was reason enough for Thompson to covet Fredericktown.

13. *Official Records*, 203.

14. *Official Records*, 204–205.

15. James Harrison Wilson, *The Life of John A. Rawlins* (Neale Publishing Company, 1916), 438.

16. *Official Records*, 709.

17. The Union effort at Fredericktown was hampered by a lost dispatch, as has been mentioned, and it also suffered from a conflict of rank. Col. Carlin, who claimed he was sick when he arrived in Fredericktown the morning of October 21, contested Col. Plummer's authority when the latter arrived about noon. *Official Records*, 208.

18. Edward D. Baker was a fellow lawyer in Lincoln's Springfield in the 1840s. He was a member of the US House of Representatives before moving to Oregon in 1860, where he was elected to the US Senate that same year. Baker was killed in the Battle of Ball's Bluff, the only person to die in battle while serving in the Senate. Lincoln named his second son after Baker. "Edward Dickinson Baker: A Featured Biography," www.senate.gov/senators/FeaturedBios/Featured_Bio_BakerEdwardDickinson.htm.

19. Flower, 22.

20. Page, "Old Abe."

21. William T. Sherman, *Memoirs of General William T. Sherman* (D. Appleton & Company, 1891), 219.

22. Howard K. Beale, ed. *The Diary of Edward Bates, 1859–1866* (Government Printing Office, 1933), 197–199.

CHAPTER 10

*"Down this narrow lane, leading into the
very jaws of death, came the three hundred."*

—Maj. William Dorsheimer

Figure 9

William Dorsheimer was born in New York in 1832, the son of German immigrants. He was appointed to John Frémont's staff in September 1861 with the rank of major. After Frémont was relieved of command in Missouri, Dorsheimer left the service and returned to Buffalo to resume practicing law. He immediately set upon the task of defending his former chief by writing a history of Frémont's 1861 campaign. His work, "Frémont's Hundred Days in Missouri," was published in *The Atlantic Monthly* in three successive issues, from January to March 1862. Dorsheimer was a patron of the arts and architecture, as well as a lecturer and author. After the war, he served as US Attorney for the Northern District of New York, the lieutenant governor of New York, and a member of Congress. He died in 1888.

Dorsheimer Law Offices

Buffalo, New York, January 30, 1862

HE HAD BECOME ACCUSTOMED to the title "Major" and to the crisp salutes of the soldiers and officers who surrounded him on the march. Nevertheless, William Dorsheimer was no soldier. First and foremost, he was a newspaperman. He and his father had been ardent supporters of John Frémont during his 1856 campaign for president, so when the general asked him to come to St. Louis and be his aide-de-camp, he felt obligated to do so. What Frémont needed was someone to deal with the press—after all, the general was addicted to media attention.

For Dorsheimer, Frémont's great campaign of October 1861 proved to be the adventure of a lifetime. The campaign ended for all practical purposes at Springfield, Missouri, on October 25, 1861, with a magnificent Union cavalry charge against an overwhelming force of Sterling Price's Missouri State Guard. It was vindication for the oft-maligned Frémont Body-Guard. Within a week, however, the campaign ended in personal tragedies for Gen. Frémont and for the brave men who made the charge. The general was "cashiered," while the legitimacy and the loyalty of his cavalry came under question.

Dorsheimer had just penned the last paragraph of his second installment of articles for *The Atlantic Monthly* magazine. It was the general's wife, Jessie, who had organized a public relations campaign to boost Frémont's standing in the public eye. The series of articles in the *Atlantic*, which took the form of a day-by-day catalog of events on the march from Jefferson City to Springfield, was having the desired impact, judging by public reception to the first installment.

We left John Frémont in Tipton on October 13, 1861, after he'd persuaded Simon Cameron to withhold the order dismissing him. Frémont asked Cameron for one more chance to bring Price's army to battle. On that day, according to Lorenzo Thomas, Frémont had already put two of his divisions in motion heading south.[1] Gen. Sigel was first off the line, moving rapidly with his 3rd Division from Sedalia toward Warsaw. David Hunter, at the head of his 9,500-man division, also seems to have set out on October 13, although his was a halting start. Hunter's troops, coming from Tipton, would form the left wing of Frémont's southbound force. Frémont ordered Hunter to take the Versailles Road, with an intermediate objective of securing a ferry crossing on the Osage River via the Duroc Ferry. As of October 13, Frémont directed that Pope follow Sigel on the right flank as soon as Sigel's route of march had cleared, and that Gen. Asboth's division would depart on October 14, taking the center route. McKinstry, from Syracuse, was to follow Asboth down the center.

From Frémont's vantage point at Tipton, the Osage River was the only formidable natural obstacle between the Pacific Railroad and Springfield. Flowing from west to east from its source near Topeka, Kansas, the Osage runs 500 miles before it joins the Missouri River east of Jefferson City. In all, the river drains an area of more than 15,000 square miles. It courses through western Missouri about 25 miles south of, and roughly parallel to, the Pacific Railroad. To Frémont's right was the town of Osceola in St. Clair County, 50 miles east of the Kansas border. Osceola, which was served by a ferry, was where the Missouri State Guard had crossed during its northbound trek to Lexington. Twenty miles north and east of Osceola (but twice that figure in river miles) was Warsaw, the crossing point for the road that carried the Butterfield Overland Mail route across the Osage River on its first leg from Tipton. In 1861 the town had both a ferry and a ford. Lastly, the Duroc Ferry—Hunter's immediate objective—was about 12 miles east of Warsaw, near the Benton/Morgan county line. These three points were the means available first to Price, then to Frémont, to get south across the Osage River. Price's choice was an easy one, as the State Guard's retreat from Lexington was along a straight and unfettered line south from Lexington, through Warrensburg to Osceola.[2]

Simon Cameron had established strict conditions when he agreed to withhold the order dismissing Frémont from command, writing in a letter to President Lincoln on October 14, "I told [Frémont] that I would withhold the order until my return to Washington, giving him the interim to prove the reality of his hopes as to reaching and capturing the enemy, giving him to understand that should he fail, he must give [his] place to some other officer."[3]

March from Tipton—General Frémont at the Head of His Column. Drawing by Henri Lovie, October 1861. The Becker Collection, Boston College Libraries.

As planned, Asboth's division left Tipton on October 14. Frémont, with his staff and Body-Guard, moved with Asboth through Syracuse and then southwest along the Butterfield Road. That night, Asboth's division made camp 9 miles south of Syracuse at a place dubbed Camp Zagonyi.[4] From this camp, on the morning of October 15, Frémont addressed a letter to his wife. Though fresh on the heels of the awful news Cameron delivered at Tipton, his letter to Jessie was oddly optimistic, particularly for a man who—as Cameron reported him—was mortified and humiliated:

Our force is in splendid condition. I intend to unite together all my scattered forces, and make my army such that it can go anywhere—that is, if we are not interrupted, and of that I suppose we shall learn within a week.

[...]

Keep your health good, and don't get agitated.... You say well that we are contending for honor and honorably; our opponents for base ends and basely.[5]

With his cavalry escort, Frémont arrived just north of Warsaw on the evening of October 16 and went into camp there. He rode into town the next morning, passing the camps of Sigel's men who had just arrived from their position in Sedalia. It was time to face the Osage River.

Despite the optimism and resolve Frémont expressed in his letter to Jessie, the fact was, for every day that passed and for every mile of distance that Gen. Price put between the Union army and the Missouri State Guard, Gen. Frémont was one step closer to his demise. If there was the slightest chance that he could have closed the gap with Price in the short amount of time Cameron had allotted him, even Frémont must have understood the stark reality within a few days of setting off from Tipton. It's possible that the elements simply conspired against Frémont to hinder his passage over the Osage, but—far more troubling—it's also possible that Frémont determined he would slog on in pursuit of Price, no matter the odds against him. The case of the bridge over the Osage suggests that it was the latter.

By midday on October 17, 1861, Gen. Sigel was well on his way transporting his division, 8,000 strong, across the Osage River via the ferry.[6] Although there had been a downpour in the area just before Frémont's arrival, there is evidence that the Warsaw ford was still usable that day.[7] Based on historic weather patterns, even if an autumn storm temporarily put the ford and the ferry out of commission, in mid-October the Osage was not at all likely to leave its banks. Nevertheless, Gen. Frémont brought forward his engineers to Warsaw to do what no one had ever found necessary to do before: bridge the Osage River.

The record is replete with inconsistent and puzzling references to the Osage River Bridge. For example, on October 17, an officer in Frémont's command reported that he heard the army engineer in charge of construction tell Frémont that the bridge would be finished by 2pm on October 18.[8] But the next day, Frémont reported to Jessie that the army had just then commenced building the bridge, and it would be ready on October 19 to provide passage to the divisions of Hunter, Pope, and McKinstry "as they come up."[9] Then, astonishingly, Frémont wrote to Jessie from the "Banks of the Osage" at 8am on October 19:

> I crossed the river yesterday afternoon, with part of the Guard, and sent them forward.... They may do a little something to put a white mark on the day. *Hunter's, Pope's and McKinstry's divisions are still alongside the railroad, transportation bound.*[10] (emphasis added)

Frémont's bridge was not completed until October 22, and even then, Asboth's was the only division present in Warsaw to cross it. Questions abound: Was October 19 the first Frémont had learned that three of his divisions had never left the safety of their camps on the Pacific Railroad? How could it be that McKinstry's division, which Secretary Cameron had found six days earlier to be "well equipped and supplied," had not yet completed a two-day march from Syracuse to Warsaw?

October 22 also marked the bohemian brigade's arrival in Warsaw. The reporters had been detained in Syracuse with McKinstry's division. If an order from on high had kept them in place, it was not stringently enforced. Franc Wilkie of the *New York Times* would report that on October 20, he and the men from the *Herald*, the *Tribune*, and the *Missouri Republican* met and decided they would like to "cross over" to Warsaw. Gen. McKinstry not only approved of their plan but also provided them with a mounted escort to their destination.[11] The reporters completed the trip in less than two days. Perhaps it was no coincidence that the Osage River Bridge was ready when the press arrived on the scene. Whatever the case, Frémont lost four days at the Osage when he had not a single one to spare.

To put John Frémont's activities in southwest Missouri in starker relief, consider this: From October 14 to October 21, while Frémont's army was allegedly stymied by a swollen river, Jeff Thompson of the Missouri State Guard raided and burned a bridge within 50 miles of St. Louis; Union troops under the command of Ulysses Grant fought and won a battle at Fredericktown; and George McClellan's Army of the Potomac committed the disaster at Ball's Bluff, Virginia.

Frank J. White was the son of a New York lawyer and judge with whom Gen. Frémont had been well acquainted before the Civil War. In April 1861 the younger White mustered in as a company commander of Company A, 10th New York Volunteers. He was just 21 when he joined the unit and fought at the First Battle of Bull Run. Later, White joined Gen. Frémont's staff in the west with the rank of major. While the general and the major were in Jefferson City awaiting the outcome of the siege at Lexington, young White persuaded his chief to let him organize a battalion of horsemen to act as scouts for the army. Close at hand in Jefferson City was a company of cavalry who had been recruited to join Col. Mulligan at Lexington, but they'd arrived too late. Combining these men with some troopers from the 1st Missouri Cavalry, White soon assembled about 160 men for his Prairie Scouts.

Despite his youth and inexperience, on October 16, 1861, White led his new battalion on a spectacular raid into Lexington. Sterling Price had left a small force there to guard the Union officers who'd been taken prisoner in battle.[12] While patrolling near Sedalia, Maj. White learned from an infantry colonel that two wounded and captured Union officers were under threat of execution in Lexington; White immediately volunteered his small force to rescue them. Riding nearly 60 miles without a break, the Prairie Scouts and an additional 70 troopers of a cavalry unit who joined them near Sedalia drove in the State Guard pickets at Lexington. They rid the town of remaining enemy occupiers and freed all the Union men held prisoner there. White was next directed to join Frémont's force at Warsaw. On October 24, 1861, after passing through Warsaw, he and his scouts reached Quincy, Missouri, 20 miles south of the Osage River on the Butterfield Road.[13] The Prairie Scouts would soon be called on again to help Frémont take the strategically significant city of Springfield. In eight days, the Prairie Scouts rode close to 170 miles.

When October 24 dawned, Sigel's division was camped on the prairie just north of Elkton, the most forward position of the infantry divisions. The two companies of the Body-Guard that crossed the Osage with Frémont were 3 to 4 miles south of Sigel's division, at Yoast's Station, an abandoned relay station on the Butterfield route. Gen. Frémont was with this battalion of his Body-Guard. Camp Haskell, as the camp at Yoast's Station was called, was 50 miles from Springfield. Asboth's 5th Division was the next closest to Sigel's. On October 24, Asboth was probably near Quincy, some 10 to 12 miles behind Sigel. McKinstry, Pope, and Hunter remained far in the rear.[14]

At 11pm on October 24, 150 troopers of the Body-Guard galloped out of Camp Haskell on a wild ride to reach Springfield. Zagonyi, their leader, had about the same distance to go—and similar circumstances to overcome—as White's Prairie Scouts did during their raid on Lexington. Like White, Zagonyi would ride all night to reach his destination. This was the last card the desperate Frémont could play, assuming that his only objective was to prove he could catch and fight the Missouri State Guard and meet the conditions Cameron had set forth when he gave Frémont a second chance. There was no way that Zagonyi and his few hundred men could capture and hold the city of Springfield. There is also this detail to consider: October 25, 1861, the day that Zagonyi would arrive in Springfield, was also the seventh anniversary of the Charge of the Light Brigade at Balaklava.[15]

According to Frank White's account, he had 154 men south of the Osage River on October 24, when he reported to Gen. Sigel near Elkton. White and his Prairie Scouts proceeded under orders from Sigel, joining Maj. Zagonyi that evening en route to Springfield. Zagonyi, by virtue of rank, took command of the entire force. At daybreak, the troopers stopped for an hour's rest and fed their horses. White, exhausted from his Lexington foray and the all-night ride he'd just completed, was too ill to mount his horse. Zagonyi suggested that he rest at a farmhouse and catch up later in the day. White agreed, keeping a small escort with him.

After resting briefly and appropriating a carriage from a local farmer, White moved on. In the meantime, Zagonyi clashed with a small Missouri State Guard foraging party north of Springfield. Most of the foragers were captured and detained, but one man escaped. Fearful that his movement would be reported to Springfield's defenders, Maj. Zagonyi found a loyal inhabitant of the area who agreed to guide the 300 horsemen along an alternate route. Zagonyi left the direct road about 8 miles north of Springfield, but he forgot to post a detail at that point to inform Frank White about the change in plans. White and his escort were captured when they unwittingly rode into the State Guard's lines.[16]

Zagonyi, meanwhile, found his way to the west side of Springfield. With his guide, he moved in a wide arc in a southwesterly direction until he reached the Mount Vernon Road. He consolidated his forces, including the leaderless Prairie Scouts, at a point 4 miles west of the town square. The city fairground was along the Mount Vernon Road, about halfway to the town center from Zagonyi's position to the west. This was a 10-acre plot largely surrounded by a tall board fence. East of the fairground, a broad field sloped gradually to the east and ended at a small brook. A patch of woods lay between the fairground and the field.

The Missouri State Guard infantry soldiers had just arrived in Springfield. For the most part, these were new recruits who had enrolled in Laclede and Wright counties, north and northeast of Springfield. Price's army was now well to the south as the infantry recruits were in transit. These estimated 300 infantrymen were poorly armed with personal weapons, if they were armed at all. As the infantry recruits of the State Guard arrived, they pitched tents on the crown of the slope, just east of the woods, hoping to eventually catch up to Price.

Two cavalry regiments attached to the 7th District of the Missouri State Guard were also in Springfield. The largest of these was the 1st Cavalry Regiment commanded by Col. John "Miscal" Johnson, reported to have an effective force of 500. Johnson's unit was an experienced one. Twelve days earlier, his men fought a fierce battle in Camden County, the Battle of Monday Hollow, and evidently left 90 troopers dead on the field there. Another contingent of cavalry at Springfield on October 25, 1861, was that of Col. Julian Frazier, which arrived that morning. Frazier carried the highest seniority and took command of the entire force of infantry and cavalry. Frazier's cavalry camped east of the woods and the infantry camp, on a slight rise along the south side of the Mount Vernon Road. The Southerners had no artillery.

The question of how many State Guardsmen were engaged that day in the First Battle of Springfield has long been disputed. Naturally, Union commanders exaggerated on the high side—estimating 1,800 to 2,000 of the enemy—while estimates from Missouri State Guard sources went in the opposite direction. What counts as "official" today is the number accepted by the National Park Service: 1,500 men of all arms. Sources also differ on whether the State Guard defenders were prepared to take the attack from the direction Zagonyi chose to make it. In retrospect, it appears they were not. Zagonyi was coming straight on from the west. When the Union cavalry arrived, the Southern forces were east of the fairground and east of the woods, the fenced-in fairground at their backs. There is no evidence that any part of Frazier's command was deployed west of the fairground to receive Zagonyi's attack from that direction.

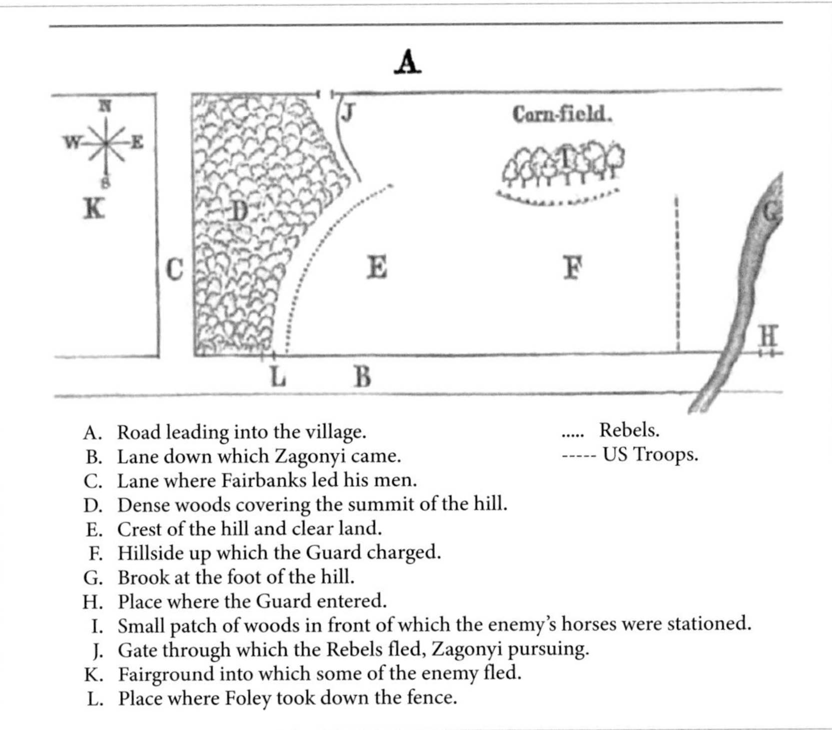

A. Road leading into the village.
B. Lane down which Zagonyi came.
C. Lane where Fairbanks led his men.
D. Dense woods covering the summit of the hill.
E. Crest of the hill and clear land.
F. Hillside up which the Guard charged.
G. Brook at the foot of the hill.
H. Place where the Guard entered.
I. Small patch of woods in front of which the enemy's horses were stationed.
J. Gate through which the Rebels fled, Zagonyi pursuing.
K. Fairground into which some of the enemy fled.
L. Place where Foley took down the fence.

..... Rebels.
----- US Troops.

Map of the battlefield of Zagonyi's charge in Springfield. Unknown creator, *The Atlantic Monthly*, 1862. Public domain.

Maj. Zagonyi's scouts reported that the main route into town, the Mount Vernon Road, was too confining around the State Guard camps, bordered as it was by fencing on both sides. Plus, the camps and the fairground opened onto the Mount Vernon Road. Zagonyi decided on a different tack, one available to him because there was no opposition west of the fairground. A few hundred yards west of the broad sloping field, the head of Zagonyi's column veered south to a small road that ran parallel to the Mount Vernon Road for a short distance. This was the celebrated "narrow lane." At the head of the column, with Maj. Zagonyi in the lead, was Company A of the Body-Guard, commanded by Lt. Walter Newhall of Pennsylvania. The column accelerated to a gallop as it passed the shelter of the board fence on the south side of the fairground. The battle began when Company A broke into the open at the patch of woods. The State Guard infantry posted there fired on the column in flank, resulting in a reported 50 casualties.

The next force to drive down the lane was Company C of the Body-Guard, commanded by Capt. James L. Foley. Then came the Irish cavalry who had joined Frank White in the raid on Lexington, commanded by Capt. Patrick Naughton. Fifty of Naughton's troopers—who had become separated from the remainder of White's Prairie Scouts—entered the narrow lane behind Foley's men.[17]

White's men from companies C and L of the 1st Missouri Cavalry were last in line if they were to follow the Body-Guard down the narrow lane. Capt. Charles Fairbanks, commanding Company L, later contended that as he emerged from behind the fairground fence, an officer of the Body-Guard directed him to take his company north of the Mount Vernon Road. According to this officer, whose name Fairbanks did not know, the State Guard camp was breaking up, and companies C and L needed to stand in the way of their retreat. In the wake of the battle, Maj. Zagonyi made shocking allegations that the Prairie Scouts had left the field, abandoning the Body-Guard. Their absence was attributed to cowardice, but in truth the Prairie Scouts had performed admirably in attacking the flank of the Missouri State Guard troops.

The Charge of Fremont's Body Guard, Springfield, Missouri. Drawing by Henri Lovie, October 25, 1861. The Becker Collection, Boston College Libraries.

Zagonyi's rush down the narrow lane seems to get most of the attention—even today, some chroniclers of Hungarian history refer to it as Zagonyi's Death Ride. Still, the most significant part of the battle at Springfield was Zagonyi's west-facing charge up the broad field and the rout of the State Guard that followed. Zagonyi's entry onto the field of battle from the narrow lane might have been the best option, but topography did not permit a direct attack from there, either. To mount a frontal attack, Zagonyi had to get his men through the lane so he could turn around and form a line of battle near the base of the field. The Union troopers, facing west, would charge uphill across a grassy slope littered with tree stumps.[18]

The men of the Body-Guard were armed with revolvers, but they would have been ineffective in the charge Zagonyi contemplated. Instead, the men drew their sabers. From Dorsheimer's colorful rendition that ran in *The Atlantic Monthly*, "The line opens out to give play to their sword-arm." From there, 30 men of the Body-Guard attack the rebel cavalry to the right, sending Miscal Johnson's men flying. Zagonyi holds the remainder of his force until he sees the outcome of this first charge, then orders a charge upon the Missouri State Guard's infantry near the woods. The infantry doesn't wait to receive the blow but begins its flight as the Body-Guard pounds up the slope. As they flee, the Body-Guard chops and stabs its way into their midst. Maj. Zagonyi—more self-interested than even Dorsheimer—would say in his first report to Gen. Frémont: "I have seen charges, but such brilliant unanimity and bravery I have never seen, and did not expect it."[19]

Even though the charge against State Guard was masterful, Zagonyi did not have the numbers to hold the town, and the Springfield campaign failed. This would not have been a surprise to Frémont: He knew he was about to be fired—and that the Union had no real chance of holding Springfield. That evening the Body-Guard, trailed by the Prairie Scouts and Naughton's Irishmen, moved away from Springfield until they reached Sigel's infantry at its camp 30 miles north.

Frank White's story did not end with his capture on the outskirts of Springfield on the morning of October 25. He had been ill on the road. He and the members of his cavalry escort were taken to Springfield, where they remained under guard until Zagonyi made his appearance west of town. The State

Guard defenders took White to the field of battle and placed him in the line of fire as a shield. He survived unharmed.

The Southern men retreated, taking Maj. White with them, but he escaped his captors the next morning. White returned to Springfield, where he was then the senior Union officer on the scene. There were wounded troopers to care for. Some others had been separated from their commands and did not depart with Zagonyi. White took command of Springfield's meager garrison, said to consist of just 24 men fit for duty.[20] Later that day, an officer of the Missouri State Guard approached under a flag of truce, requesting permission for a party to enter the field of battle to collect and bury the State Guard's dead. Sick and exhausted himself, White managed to fool the Southern emissary into believing that Zagonyi's entire force occupied the city. This was quite an exclamation point at the end of Frank White's astonishing 10 days in the saddle.

Zagonyi was not yet done with Maj. White and his Prairie Scouts, and he continued to slander their performance. After Frémont's army reoccupied Springfield, the prickly Zagonyi went so far as to refuse the offer of a hand-sewn flag to honor his troopers because the same offer had been extended to Frank White's Prairie Scouts.[21]

The charge of Zagonyi's Body-Guard at Springfield was a wholly unnecessary affair fueled by Frémont's hubris. Had Fremont waited a few more days, until Sigel's infantry division could join the cavalry when it entered Springfield, the State Guard's force would have been easily overwhelmed. In that sense, the charge on October 25 was a tragic waste of 17 lives. Nevertheless, in the wake of Bull Run and Ball's Bluff, it offered a news-hungry public in the North some sense that not all was lost for the Union cause. Seemingly, the charge was carefully engineered and publicized expressly for this purpose. It's possible that the date was *chosen* to coincide with the anniversary of the futile cavalry charge at Balaklava in Crimea, immortalized by Alfred, Lord Tennyson's 1855 poem "The Charge of the Light Brigade." William Dorsheimer thought so: "Down this narrow lane, leading into the very jaws of death...."

Whatever the outcome of Zagonyi's attack on Springfield, it did nothing to bolster John Frémont's future military career. Sure enough, on October 24, 1861, as Majs. Zagonyi and White were riding all day toward Springfield, Frémont's fate was being sealed in Washington.

ENDNOTES

1. *Official Records of the Union and Confederate Armies, Ser. 1, Vol. 3, Ch. 10* (Government Printing Office, 1881), 540–543.

2. See discussion of Price's advance in Chapter 5.

3. Abraham Lincoln Papers: General Correspondence, 1833–1916, Series 1. Letter, Simon Cameron to Abraham Lincoln, October 14, 1861. Library of Congress, Washington, DC.

4. This camp on the Missouri prairie was named for Maj. Charles Zagonyi, who is described in Chapter 6.

5. Jessie Benton Frémont, *The Story of the Guard: A Chronicle of the War* (Ticknor and Fields, 1863), 87–88. This book is replete with letters from Gen. Frémont and other officers who were on the road to Springfield; however, it is not suggested that Jessie's knowledge of what is reflected in these letters was contemporaneous. By all indications, these letters were routed through the normal army post, which could have taken days or weeks to reach St. Louis.

6. Frémont, 95.

7. An officer—described only as "H" in Jessie Frémont's *Story of the Guard*—reported in an October 17, 1861, letter that Sigel "was putting his brigade across on one small ferry-boat."

8. That same letter says Officer H overheard Capt. Pike telling Frémont that if he had enough men, "you shall cross by 2:00 o'clock tomorrow." See also William Dorsheimer, "Frémont's Hundred Days in Missouri, Part 1," *Atlantic Monthly* 9, no. 51 (January 1862): 124.

9. Frémont, 91.

10. Frémont, 93–94.

11. Michael E. Banasik, ed., *Missouri in 1861: The Civil War Letters of Franc B. Wilkie, Newspaper Correspondent* (Press of the Camp Pope Bookshop, 2001), 213–214.

12. See discussion of the battle at Lexington in Chapter 7.

13. Franc Wilkie, in his "Letter Eleventh," compiled by Banasik in *Missouri in 1861*, provides an excellent description of Frémont's army as it moved south along the old Butterfield route to Springfield. It is noteworthy that McKinstry's division had left Tipton, and, by October 23, was approaching Warsaw.

14. Dorsheimer reported that on October 28, 1861, McKinstry was 70 miles from Springfield; Pope was about the same distance away. Pope supposed that Hunter was south of the Osage. William Dorsheimer, "Frémont's Hundred Days in Missouri, Part 3," *Atlantic Monthly* 9, no. 53 (March 1862): 372–384.

15. Gen. Frémont was certainly aware of the date's significance, writing to Jessie on October 26, 1861, that "it was really a Balaklava charge." See Frémont, 151. This author would take it several steps further. Given the importance Frémont placed on public opinion, it is possible that he sent Zagonyi and White on their 50-mile ride so that he *could* compare their charge to the ill-fated charge of the Light Brigade at Balaklava.

16. Banasik, 215; Joseph Powers Hazelton, *Scouts, Spies, and Heroes of the Great Civil War* (N. G. Hamilton & Co., 1892), 212.

17. Just after the charge, Zagonyi began to distance his troopers from the men of White's Prairie Scouts, falsely stating in an October 26, 1861, report that "Major White's men did not participate in the charge." *Official Records*, 250.

18. William Dorsheimer, "Frémont's Hundred Days in Missouri, Part 2," *Atlantic Monthly* 9, no. 52 (February 1862): 247–258; 256.

19. *Official Records*, 250.

20. Dorsheimer, "Frémont's Hundred Days in Missouri, Part 2," 247–258.

21. R. I. Holcomb, ed., *History of Greene County, Missouri* (Western Historical Co., 1883), 393. This source reproduces Zagonyi's November 2, 1861, letter to "Mrs. Worrell and other Ladies of Springfield." Maj. Zagonyi states (among other things) that the Prairie Scouts "deserted me at the very moment of conflict," which "forbids the Body Guard to share the rewards of a victory with those who refused to participate in its hazards."

CHAPTER 11

*"Upon the facts, pure and simple,
I rest my vindication."*

—Brig. Gen. Justus McKinstry

Figure 10

Justus McKinstry was born in New York in 1814 and grew up in Detroit. After his release from the St. Louis Arsenal in February 1862, he started a publicity campaign and self-published a book he titled *The Vindication of Brigadier General Justus McKinstry*. Nevertheless, after his court-martial trial in October 1862, he was convicted on 26 of the 61 charges he faced, including neglect and violation of duty to the prejudice of good order and discipline, and he was dismissed from the army. He is said to be the only general officer in either army in the Civil War who was dismissed on account of fraud. Later in life, McKinstry worked as a stockbroker in New York. He died in St. Louis in 1897.

The St. Louis Arsenal

St. Louis, February 22, 1862

No ceremony. No warning. The guard stationed at Justus McKinstry's cell at the St. Louis Arsenal opened the cell door and matter-of-factly announced that McKinstry would be released on his own recognizance. He would have his liberty, so long as he exercised it within the city limits. Not long ago a major general in Frémont's army, McKinstry had returned to St. Louis from Springfield in an unorthodox way. On November 13, he traveled east on the Pacific Railroad with a cashier from the division he commanded. Twenty-five miles east of Jefferson City, an army officer—Capt. Philip H. Sheridan, 13th US Infantry—boarded the train. Sheridan arrested McKinstry and the cashier, then escorted them the rest of the way to St. Louis. Under orders of Brig. Gen. Samuel R. Curtis, McKinstry was locked up at the arsenal, without charges, where he had languished for three months.

Before McKinstry led Frémont's 5th Division in October, he'd spent nearly his entire career in the Regular Army as a quartermaster and procurement specialist. A West Point graduate (class of 1838) and a captain in the Mexican-American War, McKinstry was breveted for the gallantry he exhibited at the battles of Contreras and Churubusco. Before the Civil War broke out, he'd been assigned to St. Louis as chief quartermaster of the Army's Department of the West. McKinstry witnessed everything that happened after the city went on a war footing in May 1861.

McKinstry saw the handwriting on the wall. He was a professional soldier with his hands in the financial affairs of Frémont's administration in St. Louis. Surely, army investigators would dredge up the court-martial in Mexico in 1848, where he was acquitted of charges of bribery and corruption. It's the army. No indiscretion, no scurrilous rumor, ever dies.

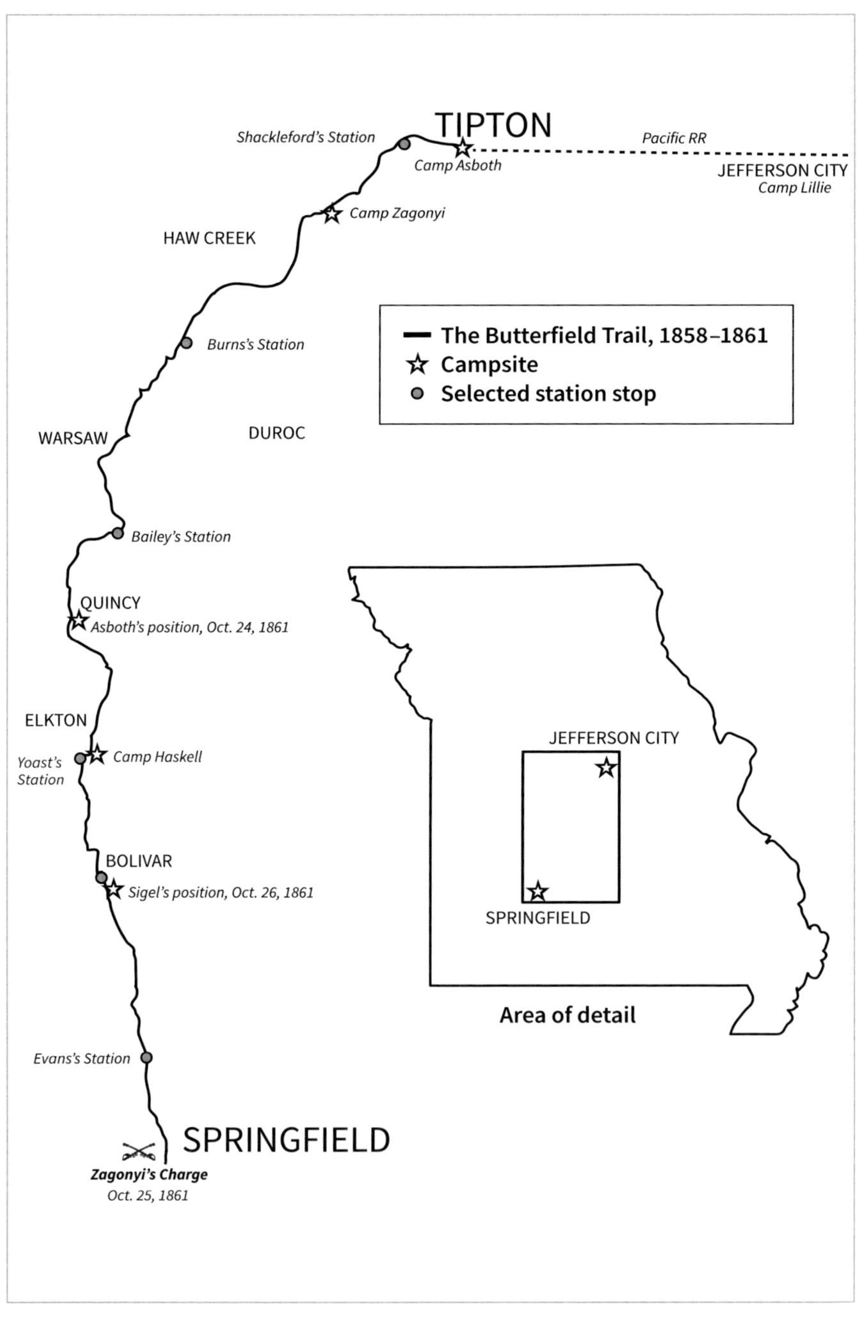

Frémont's campaign against Springfield, October 14–28, 1861.
Map prepared by Insite Advice, St. Louis, Missouri, 2025.

The town of Bolivar, seat of Polk County, prospered when it became a stop on the Butterfield Overland Mail route before the Civil War. Traveling south from Yoast's Station, it was the next stop on the trail. While Zagonyi and White raided Springfield on October 25, Franz Sigel's infantry division moved the 20 miles that separated these two places. Sigel was now 40 miles south of the Osage River crossing at Warsaw and 30 miles north of the Springfield square. Sigel's division retained its position in Frémont's advance.

Gen. Frémont was at Bolivar, along with Sigel, on October 26, and they greeted Maj. Zagonyi upon his arrival from Springfield. Asboth's division, which had been south of the Osage River for four days, probably occupied Sigel's former camp at Yoast's Station. The time had come to take Springfield in force, but the infantry of Sigel's division were the only troops Frémont had who were up to the task. In the wee hours of October 27, Sigel set out from Bolivar. Gen. Frémont, with his Body-Guard and the leaderless men of the Prairie Scouts, departed Bolivar some hours later.[1] This impressive mounted column, with a major general in the lead, rode 30 miles in 12 hours, overtaking Sigel's stragglers in the course of the day.[2]

According to Maj. William Dorsheimer, Pope's and McKinstry's divisions were still 70 miles away when Frémont entered Springfield, which would place them only 15 or 20 miles south of Warsaw. Per Dorsheimer, Gen. David Hunter and his division were still unaccounted for.[3] Frémont, who had to maintain the impression that he was actively pursuing Sterling Price, nevertheless paused in Springfield on October 28 to orchestrate and oversee an elaborate ceremony to honor the men killed in action in Zagonyi's charge. Henri Lovie sketched the scene, and an engraved version appeared on the front page of Frank Leslie's popular magazine.[4]

★ ★ ★

As Frémont labored from October 14 to 27 to get his army from Tipton to Springfield, the powerful forces arrayed against him steadily increased their intensity. The Lincoln administration, thrown into shock by Simon Cameron's refusal to dismiss Frémont at Tipton, was now playing catch-up. President Lincoln turned to an old friend and ally, a man from Keokuk, Iowa, by the name of Samuel Ryan Curtis. Curtis was a US congressman elected on the Republican ticket in 1856. A West Point graduate and Mexican-American War veteran, Curtis resigned his seat in Congress in June 1861 to accept the colonelcy of the 2nd Iowa Infantry. He brought his men into north Missouri and was soon promoted to the rank of brigadier general. Curtis—also an accomplished civil engineer—was assigned to St. Louis, where Gen. Frémont tasked him with superintending the "Camp of Instruction, Benton Barracks." This was Frémont's vision for a modern training facility capable of housing 20,000 recruits. He named it after Thomas Hart Benton.

Lincoln had leaned on Gen. Curtis earlier. At Lincoln's urging, on October 7, 1861, General in Chief Winfield Scott signed an order of removal to discharge Gen. Frémont. Lincoln passed the order to Secretary Cameron for delivery to Curtis in St. Louis, including a private note addressed to Gen. Curtis:

> Without prejudice, and looking to nothing but justice, and the public interest, I am greatly perplexed about Gen. Frémont: In your position, you can not [sic] but have a correct judgment in the case; and I beseech you to answer Gen. Cameron, when he hands you this, "Ought Gen. Frémont to be relieved from, or retained in his present command?" It shall be entirely confidential; but you can perceive how indispensable it is to justice & the public service, that I should have, an intelligent unprejudiced, and judicious opinion from some professional Military man on the spot, to assist me in the case.[5]

Gen. Curtis responded on October 11, 1861, to the president's very irregular inquiry, and he pilloried Frémont. Nevertheless, Curtis warned Lincoln that the public strongly supported Frémont, especially the St. Louis Germans. He stressed that the timing and manner of Frémont's removal "should be well considered"; he also (vaguely) warned that there could be repercussions from Frémont's men in the field.[6] This remark, though innocently made, set the stage for trumped-up concerns of mutiny that never came to pass.

When he returned to St. Louis without having delivered the removal order of October 7, Secretary Cameron penned a letter to the president that mentioned how mortified Frémont seemed to be. He lamely explained that Gen. Frémont promised he'd resign if he did not meet his promise to bring the secessionists to battle. Faced with this reality, Lincoln rather immediately put in motion the steps it would take to fire Frémont the right way.

By October 24, Lincoln had at the ready an updated version of Winfield Scott's original order, and it was odd. The date—October 7—had been crossed out and replaced with a new one, but it was otherwise the same order that Cameron had declined to deliver to Frémont.[7] The peculiarities might be explained by the fact that all through the second half of October 1861, George McClellan was locked in a battle to replace the aged Winfield Scott as the army's general in chief. Scott resigned on October 31, and McClellan succeeded him the next day. But as of October 24 President Lincoln made it clear to subordinates that he required absolute certainty and breakneck speed to bring about the end of Gen. Frémont's hold over the Western Department. Lincoln enlisted a close confidant of his named Leonard Swett to hand-carry a new message to Gen. Curtis in St. Louis. His message was emphatic: "you will take safe, certain, and suitable measures to have the inclosure [*sic*] addressed to Major-General Frémont delivered to him with all reasonable despatch [*sic*]."[8]

Swett left immediately for St. Louis. On October 27, in a meeting at Curtis's headquarters at Benton Barracks, Swett put the order in the hands of Curtis's aide-de-camp, Lt. Thomas McKenny. McKenny was also tasked with finding Gen. Hunter and delivering orders that would give him temporary command of Frémont's five divisions. McKenny then embarked on a dangerous mission that culminated on November 2, 1861. On that day, McKenny walked into Frémont's headquarters near Springfield and delivered the order relieving the second-ranking officer of the United States Army of his command. By then, Lt. Gen. Scott, who had signed the order at least 20 days earlier, was no longer on active duty.

For students of the Civil War in the Trans-Mississippi West, it's all but impossible to find nonpartisan information that sheds meaningful light on the end of Frémont's Springfield campaign. The Blair brothers had been actively engaged in engineering a case against Frémont since September 1. Lincoln himself was likely in full agreement by October 7, when he penned his first note to Gen. Curtis, even as he used covering language suggesting that he had *not* plotted out his course vis-à-vis Frémont: "looking to nothing but justice, and the public interest."

The story of Frémont's Springfield campaign might have ended here, except that Frémont's team included propagandists of a higher order, led by Jessie Benton Frémont. Take the case of Maj. William Dorsheimer, Frémont's aide-de-camp. Dorsheimer's series "Frémont's Hundred Days in Missouri" was published for three successive months in *The Atlantic Monthly*. Civil War memoirs are often unreliable, as they tend to promote the interests (and protect the legacy) of the author. Civil War diaries, on the other hand, are usually among the most reliable sources, but they're seldom accessible to the public at large.

Dorsheimer's *Atlantic Monthly* articles were neither memoir nor diary, but elements of both are present in his text. The first installment appeared in the January 1862 edition of the magazine—it had to be rushed into print. It's an invaluable resource for following Frémont's trek across southwest Missouri day by day, but as the months passed into March, Dorsheimer increasingly relied upon his talents as a creative writer. By the time the third installment of his work was packed up for the publisher, the public relations aspect of the Frémont saga had reached full flower in Washington.[9]

In his final article for *The Atlantic Monthly*, Dorsheimer relayed a fantastic account that cast Gen. David Hunter as the villain of the last chapter of "Frémont's Hundred Days in Missouri." Hunter was late. Frémont didn't know where he was with his 10,000 men. After he was relieved on November 2, Frémont received intelligence that Sterling Price was marching on Springfield with at least 30,000 men, and Frémont heroically organized what army he had to resist Price's onslaught. Then, on November 3, in Dorsheimer's words:

> We are perfectly prepared. Hunter's delay leaves us with only twenty-two thousand men, seventy pieces of artillery, and about four thousand cavalry. In view of our superiority as respects armament, discipline, and ordnance, we are more than a match for our opponent. We sleep to-night in constant expectation of an attack....[10]

There is no respectable source that confirms Dorsheimer's fanciful account. Nevins repeated a version of this story in *Pathmarker of the West*, stating that Price, along with Gen. McCulloch and his Confederate regulars, was just below Springfield, and on November 2 their advance guard was but 9 miles away, occupying the field of battle at Wilson's Creek.[11] In nearly the same breath, Nevins noted that Price had determined to turn and give battle if Frémont continued his advance—but the place where he would make his stand was fully 70 miles southwest of the battlefield at Wilson's Creek. In the same vein, Jay Monaghan posits in his landmark study of the Civil War in the West that Frémont had readied his men to march on Price's position on the morning of November 4, between the time that Frémont had received the order dismissing him and the time that Hunter arrived. In Monaghan's view, it was only when Hunter arrived the night of November 3 that Frémont stood down.[12]

The real story is not nearly as gripping as Dorsheimer described it, but it's fascinating nonetheless. According to the recorded remarks of Curtis's messenger, Lt. McKenny, there was a general fear in St. Louis, as well as in Washington, that Frémont would evade the order's delivery. McKenny prepared to leave St. Louis on the first train to Rolla, but first he visited a secondhand store in St. Louis to get a disguise. When he reached Rolla, fellow Iowan Col. Grenville Dodge, commander of the Rolla garrison, provided McKenny with a guide to take him through the tortuous 120 miles to Springfield. McKenny recalled that to start the journey, he first had to remove his guide from a Rolla saloon at 2am. Still, with the guide's help, McKenny located Frémont's headquarters south of Springfield. Posing in his disguise as a Missouri farmer, he told the camp guard that he had important information to relay about enemy movements. After some negotiations with the guard—with McKenny professing that his information could only be shared with the commanding general—he was admitted to Frémont's tent. With a flourish, as McKenny described it, he produced the order from inside the lining of his coat.[13]

Lt. McKenny also claimed that he was refused assistance in locating Gen. Hunter, to whom he had to deliver the order of command, but he'd heard a rumor that Hunter was near the town of Buffalo. McKenny found him there on November 3, still 40 miles short of Springfield.

Neither the administration in Washington nor the US Army's high command would be satisfied with the professional humiliation of John C. Frémont. There were trumped-up concerns, pushed by Frank and Montgomery Blair especially, of serious failings in the procurement and financial processes in the Western Department. It would seem that the Republicans in power—who routinely blamed Frémont for what they considered operational failures, such as failing to reinforce Lexington and Wilson's Creek—drew a line at accusing the first man of their party to be nominated for president of financial crimes. Besides, objectively speaking, this man, famously inept at managing his own affairs, hardly fit the profile of a financial mastermind. Justus McKinstry, on the other hand, was a likely suspect. Here is part of the physical description that Franc Wilkie conveyed to *New York Times* readers near the end of Frémont's reign in Missouri:

> [McKinstry] is a man of 38 or 40 years, over six feet in height and of massive build, has black hair, black eyes and a heavy black moustache, looking very much, as he travels around town, like a high tragedian or the Big Villain in a melodrama. This last aspect is somewhat ameliorated from the wearing of glasses, but even these do not hide from the observer the glitter of an eye whose blackness is unequaled save by the darkest of midnights.[14]

Putting aside McKinstry's innocence or guilt, as well as judgments of character based upon physical appearance, financial investigations of the Western Department were but one part of a dark campaign seemingly designed to destroy the image of John Charles Frémont in the public eye. For example, in October 1861, Illinois congressman Elihu Washburne headed up the Van Wyck Committee (formally, the Select Committee on Government Contracts of the House of Representatives), which had commenced its operations in July. On October 15, Washburne and members of the committee arrived in St. Louis. He had literally rushed to the scene while Gen. Frémont began his campaign from Tipton. Days later, on October 21, Washburne wrote a scathing "report" to Abraham Lincoln about the proceedings the committee members had conducted in the previous four days, claiming that they had interviewed between 30 and 40 people.

It shocks modern senses to see what he shared with the president, including his view that Gen. Frémont was utterly incompetent. He was most bitter in his reproach of Justus McKinstry: "[Y]ou will be lost in amazement...that such a man now wears the insignia of a Brig. General." Washburne's most memorable bit of hyperbole, though, must be: "[T]he history of the world affords no parallel to the state of things that has existed here." In reality, the message boiled down to the same one Montgomery Blair brought back to Washington in mid-September: A certain group of high-minded St. Louis citizens—including some who avidly supported Abraham Lincoln—were dissatisfied with Frémont's leadership.[15] The group's complaints about Frémont's tendency to isolate himself and his troops' supposed lack of discipline closely mimic the same complaints that Frank Blair enumerated in his letter to Montgomery. In fact, the language was so similar to Frank's, it hardly seems coincidental.

Some humor can be found in the events that surrounded Washburne's October trip to St. Louis, according to facts he disclosed in his October 21 letter to Lincoln. When Justus McKinstry resigned his position as quartermaster to the Western Department to accept Frémont's offer of a field command, McKinstry's detractors managed to bring in Maj. Robert Allen, a quartermaster with a solid record of accomplishment. McKinstry's assistant quartermaster, Parmenas T. Turnley, stayed on as Allen's assistant. Maj. Allen had provided a brief report to Adjutant General Lorenzo Thomas on October 11, as Thomas headed for Tipton. Although Allen had been in the role in St. Louis for only a few days, his report referred to "reckless expenditures," hinting that he could disclose revelations about the department's financial affairs.[16] Allen, it would seem, had postured himself to be the committee's star witness. Unfortunately, when Maj. Allen was called to testify before the committee in St. Louis (in the words of Congressman Washburne):

> [T]o our astonishment when [Allen] came he was apparently so drunk, either with opium or liquor, that we could not examine him as a witness and had to dismiss him.
>
> [...]
>
> In consideration of this, and of the horrible condition of the Department, the committee directed me to telegraph you to send some able and incorruptible quarter master General here instanter.[17]

The select committee would not hear from Assistant Quartermaster Turnley, either. On the day Maj. Allen provided his report to Adjutant General Thomas, Turnley went on a leave of absence, reporting to Thomas that his work for McKinstry "left his health so broken that he was no longer able to stand on his feet."[18]

Samuel Curtis provides the window through which to view the postclimactic period of Frémont's Springfield campaign. Soon after David Hunter officially took over command of the Western Department on November 4, he ordered Gen. Curtis to take control of military affairs in and around St. Louis, and to take possession of the telegraph lines emanating from the city. Within three days the new general in chief in Washington weighed in on the problem with Frémont via telegram. His communications showed how the situation in St. Louis would be complicated by George McClellan's promotion.

Reports of dissatisfaction among the men of Frémont's army began to waft through the Union command structure. For example, the men of Sigel's division marched 115 miles from Sedalia to Springfield. Always at the forefront of Frémont's campaign, they were the first foot soldiers to cross the Osage River at Warsaw. They were the first to reach Springfield, triumphantly entering the city in the wake of a masterful cavalry charge that even Frémont's detractors must have applauded.[19] But it could not have escaped the attention of these men that at least two of Frémont's divisions—Pope's and Hunter's—took no part in the campaign. The 8,000 men of Sigel's 3rd Division had bonded with their commander, so naturally, losing their leader under these circumstances brought more than the usual amount of grousing from the men on the line.

Nevertheless, the information reaching St. Louis in the first week of November was immediately overshadowed on November 7, after Gen. Hunter reported that Frémont's paymaster in Springfield "has deserted his post here carrying with him three hundred thousand...dollars & leaving the Army entirely without money." The rumor was that the paymaster, a Maj. Phinney, had left with Frémont for St. Louis. Gen. Curtis telegraphed this information to Gen. McClellan, and McClellan telegraphed back: "*Arrest the Pay Master.... And if you find it necessary to accomplish the object arrest Genl Frémont. Seize the funds.*"[20]

Recall, in early August, on the eve of the Battle of Wilson's Creek, a critical message from Frémont to Lyon had to be delivered by courier. Similarly, news of Lyon's defeat was brought into Rolla by courier, as no military telegraph connected Rolla to Springfield. Although some messages of a military nature were telegraphed from Springfield to St. Louis through Jefferson City, the connection south from Jefferson City was by way of a civilian wire. It appears this condition had not improved by November. When Curtis received word about the paymaster from his messenger, it was delivered in person.

The lack of military infrastructure and organization, relative to that of the national press corps, brought about this laughable situation: The news-consuming public in New York could often read about developments in southwest Missouri before Union headquarters in St. Louis knew what was happening. In one case, Thomas Knox reported on a cordial meeting between Frémont and Hunter on November 4; it was published in the *New York Herald* edition that hit newsstands on November 7. Knox's report went on to say that Frémont and most of his staff "left for Tipton today, at six A. M. The camps were not generally made aware of the departure," noting too that Frémont did this in order to forestall possible reaction by his soldiers.[21]

A clearly exasperated Gen. Curtis advised Washington via telegraph that false and extravagant dispatches were emanating from Springfield, and he was doing his best to suppress them. Curtis continued: "[M]y messenger returned. Hunter took command at Springfield on 4th. All quiet there. Enemy not offering battle. Frémont very indignant at my messenger and at me. Frémont will arrive at Sedalia to-night. All quiet in St. Louis."[22]

The New York Times was not too far behind the *Herald* in its reporting. Franc Wilkie filed a story published in its November 10, 1861, edition that summarized Springfield post-Frémont, and he commented upon some of the charges that swirled around Frémont's operations in St. Louis. He took a contrarian view on this subject, citing witnesses who disagreed with the allegations of purchasing fraud that Lorenzo Thomas and Elihu Washburne were pushing, including charges regarding the construction of the St. Louis fortifications. Wilkie reported that Maj. Franz Kappner, the engineer who designed the Cape Girardeau and St. Louis forts, called the allegation a lie. The next day, November 11, Gen. McClellan ordered Curtis to arrest Kappner and do the same "to any who give you trouble." Later that day, McClellan directed Hunter to arrest Justus McKinstry and confine him to the St. Louis Arsenal on unspecified charges.[23]

John Frémont lost his authority to command the Western Department on November 2, 1861, but at least two of his orders, both directed to affairs in southeast Missouri, seem to have had a life of their own. Ulysses Grant would soon move on to immortal fame, but first he would encounter Jeff "Swamp Fox" Thompson one more time.

After Fredericktown, the elusive Thompson brought his men south in good order. By November 1, 10 days after that battle, he was back in the swamps west of Sikeston. He was home. As usual, Union intelligence was spotty, but Frémont thought he knew where Thompson was. Frémont was in

Springfield, awaiting the fate that Lt. McKenny was about to deliver, when he sent a message off to his adjutant in St. Louis, who relayed it to Grant in Cairo:

> You are hereby directed to hold your whole command ready to march at an hour's notice, until further orders, and you will take particular care to be amply supplied with transportation and ammunition. You are also directed to make demonstrations with your troops along both sides of the river toward Charleston, Norfolk and Blandville, and to keep your columns constantly moving back and against these places, without, however, attacking the enemy.[24]

When McKenny pounced the very next day, Frémont's adjutant advised Grant by telegram from St. Louis that "Jeff. Thompson is at Indian's Ford of the St. Francois River, twenty-five miles below Greenville, with about 3,000 men."[25] Indian Ford was 40 miles west of Sikeston on a well-traveled road that passed through the town of Bloomfield, about halfway there. Grant's orders were reminiscent of those at the end of August that sent him chasing Thompson near Cape Girardeau, but in November the young Yankee general was not nearly so eager to give chase.

From his perch in Cairo, Grant was preoccupied by the position the Confederates held at Columbus, Kentucky, atop the Iron Banks, a mere 12 river-miles south of where he was. Grant therefore welcomed Frémont's invitation to make "demonstrations"—but not attacks—from near Charleston, Missouri, against the Confederate bulwark. Grant's point of attack was to be a village on the Missouri side of the river called Belmont. On November 3, Gen. Grant placed in motion a brigade of 2,200 men, directing that they pursue Thompson at Indian Ford. Another regiment departed Cape Girardeau the next day, on the same mission.

By the time these troops stepped off, it is likely Gen. Thompson and his Missouri State Guard had already arrived in Bloomfield, but he was gone by the time the first Union men arrived five days later. Meanwhile, most of Grant's column endured an epic slog through the sunken lands that separated Bloomfield from the heights around Cape Girardeau. Thompson's bluff had the impact of depriving Ulysses Grant of about 3,000 able-bodied infantrymen—a force that might have changed the course of the battle at Belmont.

Ironically, the last act of John Frémont's 100 days in command was authoring the telegram that warned Grant that Thompson had 3,000 men at Indian Ford. On November 7, at Belmont, Grant fought his first battle as the commander of troops in the field. It was a bold stroke on his part—probably contrary to orders—made possible by Frémont's loss of command.

By mid-November 1861, the immediate aftereffects of John Frémont's service in Missouri had ended, although long-term results would be felt for months and even generations to come. However, before moving on to the long view, there's a November 17 dispatch from Franc Wilkie to be considered. The sage from Dubuque aptly summarized the doomed march to Springfield: "It is scarcely a month since your correspondent left [St. Louis], and within that time he has witnessed the last acts of one of the most stupendous and remarkable farces ever exhibited to this or any other public."[26]

To illustrate Wilkie's point: After Gen. Hunter was firmly in command, President Lincoln ordered the Union army to abandon Springfield. The bulk of the infantry wintered in Rolla; many other units were scattered to the winds. The fact of the matter is that the purely symbolic charge of Zagonyi's cavalry succeeded—and magnificently so—largely because the State Guard troops Zagonyi encountered there were heading south as rapidly as they could. Winter was coming on. In a real sense, the State Guard troops who remained in Springfield late in October were Price's stragglers.

As a consequence of the Union withdrawal to Rolla, the offensive to come still had to contend with the difficult terrain that dominated the landscape between Rolla and Springfield. Now it would wait until the dead of winter. One stroke of luck, in the face of all this bumbling, was that on Christmas Day 1861, Samuel Curtis was appointed to replace David Hunter. Curtis proved to be not only an excellent engineer and proficient administrator but also a top-notch field commander. His Pea Ridge campaign kicked off from Lebanon, Missouri, on February 9, 1862. His army swept through Springfield on February 13 and 14, and by the next day, his advance elements skirmished with Missouri State Guard troops about 50 miles southwest of there. The ease with which Curtis moved is proof positive that the level of danger Hunter faced in Springfield, if he had stayed put for the winter, was zero.

ENDNOTES

1. R. I. Holcombe, ed., *History of Greene County, Missouri* (Western Historical Company, 1883), 386–387.

2. William Dorsheimer, "Frémont's Hundred Days in Missouri, Part 3," *Atlantic Monthly* 9, no. 53 (March 1862): 372–375.

3. Dorsheimer, 376.

4. Dorsheimer. Seventeen men of the Body-Guard were killed in Zagonyi's charge, as were two troopers from the Prairie Scouts.

5. Roy P. Basler, ed., *The Collected Works of Abraham Lincoln* (Rutgers University Press, 1953), 549.

6. Kenneth E. Colton, ed., "With Frémont in Missouri in 1861: Letters of Samuel Ryan Curtis," *Annals of Iowa* 24 (1942): 139–142.

7. John P. C. Shanks, "Vindication of Major General John C. Frémont, Against the Attacks of the Slave Power and Its Allies," speech delivered to the US House of Representatives, March 4, 1862; https://www.loc.gov/item/10029591.

8. Basler, 562.

9. By mid-March 1862, a joint committee of the US Senate and House of Representatives had completed hearings on Frémont's performance in Missouri. See *Report of the Joint Committee on the Conduct of the War, Part 3* (Government Printing Office, 1863).

10. Dorsheimer.

11. Allan Nevins, *Frémont: Pathmarker of the West* (University of Nebraska Press, 1939), 540.

12. Jay Monaghan, *Civil War on the Western Border, 1854–1865* (Bonanza Books, 1955), 204.

13. Ida M. Tarbell Collection. Letter, T. I. McKenny to J. McCan Davis, November 16, 1898. The details of McKenny's journey are set forth in this letter, which has been heavily edited, apparently by Davis. Allegheny College, Meadville, PA.

14. Galway, "Our Syracuse Correspondence," *New York Times*, October 25, 1861. "Galway" was a nom de plume Franc Wilkie used when editorializing for the *Times*.

15. The St. Louisans who, along with the Blairs, complained about Frémont's performance included Samuel Glover, James Broadhead, Robert Campbell, and Giles F. Filley.

16. *Official Records of the Union and Confederate Armies, Ser. 1, Vol. 3, Ch. 10* (Government Printing Office, 1881), 549.

17. Abraham Lincoln Papers: General Correspondence, 1833–1916, Series 1. Letter, Elihu B. Washburne to Abraham Lincoln, October 21, 1861.

18. *Official Records*, 550.

19. Zagonyi mounted his charge just days after the Union's loss at Ball's Bluff, Virginia.

20. Colton, 153.

21. Thomas Knox, "Important from Missouri…Departure of Gen. Frémont from Springfield," *New York Herald*, November 7, 1861.

22. Colton, 155–156.

23. Colton, 159.

24. *Official Records*, 267.

25. *Official Records*, 268. Note there is no historical record to indicate whether Thompson was at Indian Ford as reported.

26. Michael E. Banasik, ed., *Confederate Tales of the War in the Trans-Mississippi, Part 1: 1861* (Press of the Camp Pope Bookshop, 2010), 238.

CHAPTER 12

"General Frémont was unfitted for the command of that department."

—Maj. Gen. Frank Blair

Figure 11

Francis Preston Blair Jr., known as Frank, was born in Lexington, Kentucky, in 1821. His father, the senior Francis P. Blair, was a newspaperman in Kentucky until he moved his family to Washington City in 1828 to serve the interests of President Andrew Jackson. The young Blair graduated from Princeton University in 1842, then studied law. Originally a Free Soil Democrat, he joined the Republican Party in 1856. Frank Blair intermittently served in Congress in the 1850s and '60s as a Republican. In 1868 he ran unsuccessfully for vice president on the Democratic ticket, and ultimately he became a US senator.

Blair House

Washington City, March 7, 1862

Frank Blair stayed at his brother's house in Washington whenever business brought him to the capital. Frank's business in Washington in March 1862 required a lengthy stay—Congressman Blair was there to attend the second session of the 37th Congress. Not known as a sentimental man, Frank nevertheless could feel the history that pulsed through that great house on Pennsylvania Avenue, which his father had bought in 1836. From 1845 to 1852, while Preston Blair pursued his interest in politics from his suburban estate, Silver Spring, the house was rented out to a variety of government luminaries. Then, in 1852, Montgomery Blair left St. Louis to practice law in Washington. Montgomery had occupied Blair House since that time.

Except for a few of his teenage years, young Frank had never really lived in the house, and when he did, he was successively attending three universities in search of a diploma. Princeton University conferred a degree in 1842, a year after Frank finished his coursework—the result of a barroom brawl on the eve of his intended commencement in 1841. After studying law in Kentucky, he went to St. Louis to practice law with Montgomery in the office of Thomas Hart Benton. Montgomery, eight years his senior, was the city's mayor when Frank arrived.

As the carriage clopped its way to the main entrance of Blair House, Frank gathered the sheaf of papers that he would use as his notes. The speech he was to give to the House of Representatives, already typeset and ready for release in the *Washington Globe*, would be the vindication due the Blairs for their part in the affairs in Missouri in 1861.

n March 1862, as Frank Blair prepared to make remarks to his fellow congressmen, he was seething. Much had transpired in the weeks and months since John Frémont was relieved at Springfield, most notably the creation of the so-called Joint Committee on the Conduct of the War. Formed in December 1861, this committee of three US senators and four members of the House was charged with exploring the Union disaster at Ball's Bluff, Virginia. Even before the committee's work got underway, proponents added to the mission by agreeing to examine the case of John Frémont's firing. The committee's tasks expanded and evolved over the years, but in the last analysis it was a battleground for an increasingly radical Congress to critique the war policies of the Lincoln administration. To an astute politician like Frank Blair, the makeup of the joint committee—five Republicans and two Democrats—seemed to dictate that Frémont had the upper hand. The Radical Republicans in Congress would paint the picture that Lincoln had cashiered Frémont because of his August 30, 1861, order of emancipation. Lincoln's closest allies in Congress would raise issues of Frémont's competence and improprieties.

John Frémont was called to testify before the joint committee beginning on January 10, 1862, and continued, with intermittent recesses, for the rest of the month.[1] He presented a written statement, along with rafts of orders and correspondence to support his positions. It was a masterful point-by-point refutation of all the charges and innuendos his many detractors lodged against him. Adding to Blair's ire, someone on the committee leaked Frémont's testimony to the press.[2]

In early February, Frank and Montgomery Blair gave their testimonies. Montgomery's was remarkable in that he freely—in fact, proudly—admitted his role in torpedoing the career of Gen. Harney in favor of Capt. Lyon. He went on to state that he recommended John Frémont for the post Lyon was to occupy because authorities in Washington would not promote Lyon. He admitted as well that he did not want George McClellan ruling the roost in Missouri from Cincinnati.[3]

The joint committee took a recess on March 7, 1862, when Frank Blair would address his fellow congressmen in a last-ditch effort to gain support. By then, Dorsheimer had published his first two articles about Frémont in *The Atlantic Monthly*—and they were having the desired effect on public opinion.

Blair, of course, was not without his own weapons in this war of propaganda. His father controlled the official Capitol press organ, and he laid out Frank's whole speech for publication in the *Washington Globe* before he even delivered it. Then too, Frank Blair was an orator of legendary power and persuasiveness. His speech was powerful, but surely he already saw the writing on the wall—and it had been scrawled there by the Radical Republican majority of the Joint Committee on the Conduct of the War.

The Members of President Lincoln's Cabinet. Unknown creator, ca. 1861. The men in Lincoln's cabinet who were also in John Frémont's orbit include Simon Cameron (at top left) and Montgomery Blair (at bottom center). Library of Congress, Rare Book and Special Collections Division.

The most memorable passage from Blair's oration mocked Frémont's imperial airs while ridiculing the theme coined by Dorsheimer in the title of his work, "Frémont's Hundred Days in Missouri":

> Is there anything in this campaign, as portrayed by the general himself, and by his several aids-de-camp [*sic*], that resembles, except in the number of days, the historic campaign of the first Napoleon? Can imagination conceive of Bonaparte returning to Paris, and announcing that he had lost two armies, liberated two negroes, and published a bombastic proclamation?[4]

The testimony and documents considered by the committee are too involved, too complex, and too self-serving on both sides to recommend for further study, but it's worth pointing out that congressional investigations then and now share the same peculiarities. The hearing's outcome was dictated not by the testimony of witnesses but by the objectives of the investigators. Predictably, at the end of it all, John Frémont was exonerated in an April 1863 report that stated:

> Whatever opinion may be entertained in reference to the time when the policy of emancipation should have been inaugurated, or by whose authority it should have been promulgated, there can be no doubt that General Frémont at that early day rightly judged in regard to the most effective means of subduing this rebellion. In proof of that it is only necessary to refer to the fact that his successor, when transferred to another department, issued a proclamation embodying the same principle. And the President, as commander-in-chief of the army and navy, has applied the same principle to all the rebellious States, and few will deny that it must be adhered to until the last vestige of treason and rebellion is destroyed.[5]

Another predictable point: The conclusions of the joint committee had absolutely no impact on the outcome of the Civil War or on the course of future history.

Most commentators consider Frank Blair to be one of the best, if not *the* best, of the US Army's political generals. Ulysses Grant singled out Blair in these words from his 1885 memoir: "There was no man braver than he, nor was there any who obeyed all orders of his superior in rank with more unquestioning alacrity. He was one man as a soldier, another as a politician."[6]

No one can criticize the zeal and commitment of the young Frank Blair to the cause of freedom for the enslaved population. Just like Thomas Hart Benton, the Blairs were Free Soil Democrats before the Civil War, a popular stance among border-state politicians. During the debates of the 1850s, Frank Blair argued eloquently and often for gradual, compensated emancipation, combined with voluntary "resettlement" of those who were freed in this process. This was not an unreasonable position for the times: Border states like Maryland, Kentucky, and Missouri had smaller proportions of soon-to-be-freed persons in relation to the already free, so the formerly enslaved could more easily integrate into their societies and economies. Concerns about the impacts of immediate emancipation in the Deep South motivated Lincoln's cautious approach in 1861–1862 and held back other people of good faith as well. In those years, Frank Blair's perspective was much closer to Lincoln's view than it was to the views of John and Jessie Frémont.

The infant Republican Party was an amalgam of former Whigs, abolitionists, and Free Soilers. It is perhaps incidental that the Blairs and the Frémonts were instrumental in creating it. But built into the party's structure were the seeds of future strife. Blair gradually moved toward a sympathy for the South, over what he viewed as excesses in President Grant's Reconstruction policies. He returned to the Democratic Party. A tool for emancipation that he had once espoused—voluntary resettlement to South America or Africa—became his sole objective. Blair's political transformation was complete by 1868, when he was the vice-presidential candidate on the Democratic ticket headed by New York governor Horatio Seymour; they faced off against Ulysses Grant and Schuler Colfax. Seymour and Blair ran on this mortifying slogan: "This Is a White Man's Country. Let White Men Rule." Grant won the election with more than 72 percent of the vote.

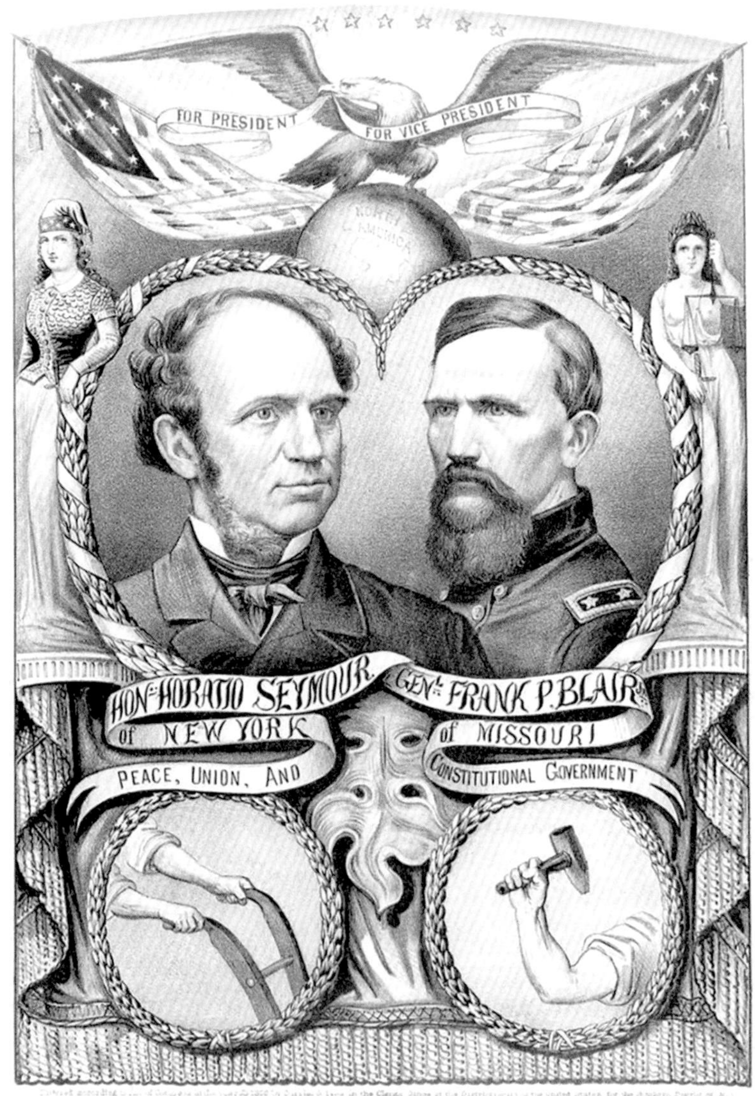

National Democratic Banner of Victory, 1868. Lithograph by Currier & Ives, 1868. Library of Congress, Prints and Photographs Division.

What remains to conclude is the root cause or causes of the breakdown between members of the greater Preston family—embodied in Frank Blair and Jessie Benton Frémont. John Frémont seems for the most part like an outside observer to the battle between the families. The peculiarities of his personality sometimes played a role in the interfamily strife that began in earnest in 1861, but his impact must be interpreted through a lens provided by Jessie. That is to say, his interests were generally defined *by her*, and dictated by her to others, from a vantage point that never swayed from her devotion to him. It seems that for most of their marriage, through his long absences and even infidelities, she stayed in love with this most unworthy of men. The cost: Her first important male relationship—the one she had enjoyed with her father, Thomas Hart Benton—soured in 1856. He would not abandon the Democratic Party to vote for her husband for president of the United States. In 1861, Jessie lost her oldest and best friend, Lizzie Lee, because of John. Undaunted devotion to John Frémont was the tragedy in Jessie Frémont's life.

It's possible that issues existed between Jessie Benton and Frank Blair from childhood.[7] For one thing, their fathers, as old men who are old friends tend to do, spun the idea that Jessie and Frank would be a perfect wedding match. It's been theorized that Frank courted Jessie before she met John Frémont.[8] Jessie, then a 13- or 14-year-old young lady, must have found the wedding musings appalling. It must be noted that Jessie and Frank hardly had an opportunity to interact once Frank headed off to school. Having said that, all of the circumstances suggest that Jessie, cultured and educated from a young age and knowing Frank's brutish character and past escapades, thoroughly detested him from the time she was a child.

Many historians who have speculated about the explosive end of Frémont's reign in Missouri—and many have—suggest that it was a result of Jessie Frémont disrespecting the president when she appeared at the White House. It is true: Jessie Frémont disrespected President Lincoln on September 10, 1861. However, Montgomery Blair was already on a westbound train, armed with the means and motive to replace Gen. Frémont with his brother-in-law, Gen. Meigs. Whatever anger motivated Jessie to board the train to Washington, her trip was *not* fueled by knowledge that Frank Blair was engaged in a plot to remove her husband from his command. She did not even know of the existence of Frank's letter of September 1 until Preston Blair revealed it on September 11.

If none of these reasons persuade, the question is still an open one: Why did the Blairs withdraw their support for the generalship of John Frémont? After Frémont arrived in St. Louis on July 25, 1861, the following events unfolded in quick succession: First, the session of Congress that Frank Blair attended in Washington ended on August 6. Second, Frank Blair's return to St. Louis was delayed while he visited his family in Connecticut.[9] Third, the military disaster and family tragedy happened at Wilson's Creek on August 10. And finally, on August 13—probably because Frank was still detained in the East—Frank's father proposed on Frank's behalf that his family join the Frémonts in establishing a "co-partnership in the West" for the price of a major-generalship in the Missouri militia.[10]

Mere days after Preston Blair sent his letter to Jessie Frémont proposing this trade-off, Gen. Frémont did request of provisional governor Hamilton Gamble a commission as a brigadier general in the state militia for Frank Blair.[11] But before that request was submitted, on August 18, 1861, Gamble had advised Frémont in writing that it was not legal for him to do such a thing.[12] It is likely that Frémont made the request knowing it would be rejected. In other words, this was an effort by Frémont to pass blame away from himself. Another point not to be disregarded: Frémont asked Gamble for a brigadier's commission, not the major-general post that the Blairs demanded. In any case, soon thereafter the Blairs intensified their campaign to rid the Western Department of John Frémont. Frank Blair's September 1 letter to his brother Montgomery that urged the firing of Gen. Frémont "the sooner the better" followed.[13]

We will never know who started the arguments that turned the Blair clan against John Frémont. Frank Blair was fueled by arrogance, misunderstanding, and perhaps deep-seated hatred, and the animosity spiraled out of control until John Frémont was of no use to the government. The rest of the saga—why it was so difficult for Lincoln to fire him—can be accounted for by politics, plain and simple. Frémont was the previous Republican candidate for president, and Lincoln faced the risk that Frémont would run for the office again. Sure enough, Frémont began a new campaign for president in 1864. With a sense of poetic justice, Frémont withdrew his name from consideration when Lincoln agreed to oust Montgomery Blair from his cabinet.

The Benton-Blair feud may have uttered its last gasp on September 29, 2022. Since 1899, Missouri had been represented in the US Capitol's National Statuary Hall by two men: Thomas Hart Benton and Francis Preston Blair Jr. When the time came to honor former President Harry Truman, one of these statues had to go. Frank Blair remained in his honored place in the Capitol at the expense of Thomas Benton. Blair, it should be clear, was the least consequential of the two during the country's long battle for equal rights. Blair is honored still as the man who saved Missouri for the Union, for no reason this writer can discern except his support for Nathaniel Lyon in 1861. His marble image in the US Capitol stands further diminished by the company it keeps. Harry Truman, a man of Southern heritage who by executive fiat integrated the armed services and the federal civil service, must stand near one who ultimately espoused the principle "Let White Men Rule."

ENDNOTES

1. *Report of the Joint Committee on the Conduct of the War, Part 3* (Government Printing Office, 1863), 32, 43–379.

2. The *New York Tribune* printed Frémont's entire testimony in early March, claiming it had the committee's permission to do so. William E. Parrish, *Frank Blair: Lincoln's Conservative* (University of Missouri Press, 1998), 134–135.

3. *Report of the Joint Committee*, 154.

4. "Speech of Hon. F. P. Blair, Jr. of Missouri on Frémont's Defense," *The Washington Globe*, 1862. Blair's reference is to Napoleon's *Les Cent-Jours*, the 100 days between Napoleon's return to Paris on March 20, 1815, after his exile on Elba, and the second restoration of King Louis XVIII on July 8, 1815, following Napoleon's defeat at Waterloo.

5. *Report of the Joint Committee*, 6. The committee's reference to Frémont's successor is a reference to Gen. David Hunter. In May 1862, after Hunter was assigned to a command in South Carolina, he issued an order purporting to free all enslaved peoples in the states of Georgia, South Carolina, and Florida. Lincoln swiftly countermanded the order.

6. Ulysses S. Grant, *Personal Memoirs of U. S. Grant* (New York: Charles L. Webster & Company, 1885), 385.

7. Sally Denton, *Passion and Principle: John and Jessie Frémont, the Couple Whose Power, Politics, and Love Shaped Nineteenth-Century America* (Bloomsbury, 2007), 233.

8. Denton, 305.

9. Parrish, 115.

10. Abraham Lincoln Papers: General Correspondence, 1833–1916, Series 1. Letter, Francis P. Blair Sr. to Jessie Benton Frémont, August 13, 1861. Library of Congress, Washington, DC.

11. Marguerite Potter, "Hamilton R. Gamble, Missouri's War Governor," *Missouri Historical Review* 35, no. 1 (October 1940): 25–71.

12. Allan Nevins, *Frémont: Pathmarker of the West* (University of Nebraska Press, 1939), 510.

13. Abraham Lincoln Papers. Letter, Francis P. Blair Jr. to Montgomery Blair, September 1, 1861.

EPILOGUE

*"I have a comfortable home on
Pleasant Street where I expect to spend
the remaining years of my life."*

—Pvt. Hiram W. Reed

John Charles Frémont went into the railroad-building business after the Civil War, where he made—and lost—another fortune. From 1878 to 1881, he was the territorial governor of Arizona. In the circumstances of his poverty, his last, great quest was to secure a military pension, one that had been denied him because of the controversy surrounding his service. It is a fitting coda to this impactful, epic life story—which ultimately played out as a tragedy—that in March 1890 Congress restored him to the rank of major general and awarded him a monthly pension of $500. But by the time the first payment arrived, Frémont was dead and buried.

John Frémont died in New York City on July 13, 1890, at the age of 77, after a brief and acute bout of peritonitis. Fortunately, his son John C. Frémont Jr., a navy lieutenant, was stationed nearby and was able to reach his father's deathbed. It fell upon John Jr. to notify his mother, at home in Los Angeles, of John's passing and make the burial arrangements.

Jessie Benton Frémont's final quest was to recover compensation for the loss of her beloved home at Black Point on San Francisco Bay. Thirty years had gone by since she last saw the cottage she treasured, when she packed up a few belongings and her three children to join the general in New York. She'd rented the house out while John served in the Civil War, and in 1863 the US government took possession of Black Point. The Frémont cottage was demolished to make way for a battery of coastal guns. Not surprisingly, perhaps, there were problems with the original land titles. The Frémonts sued, as did many of their neighbors, but they lost their case before the US Supreme Court. In July 1893 the Senate's Committee on Military Affairs issued a report recommending that the government fairly compensate Jessie for Black Point. This effort produced yet another lawsuit, but it too came to naught.[1]

Jessie lived out the remaining years of her life in Los Angeles in a modest home she shared with daughter, Lily. Jessie finally received a widow's pension from the army and died in 1902. She's buried in LA, the width of a continent away from the grave of her husband.

She penned John's lasting epitaph: "From the ashes of his campfires have sprung cities."

Frank Blair served as a US senator from Missouri (1871–1873), filling the unexpired term of his predecessor. Although he suffered a debilitating stroke in November 1872, he refused to drop out of the race for a full term in the US Senate, which was to be decided by the Missouri legislature. In January 1873 the legislators elected another candidate to serve in the US Senate.[2] Frank Blair died in St. Louis in July 1875 at age 54. As St. Louis author and historian Carol Shepley wrote in 2008: "He wore himself out with hard living, deep drinking, and smoking thirty cigars a day."[3]

Joseph C. Palmer, the tarnished financial wizard from Nantucket, maintained an off-and-on friendship with John Frémont for most of the rest of his life. Signs suggest that Frémont's patience for Palmer had cooled considerably by the time the Frémonts moved to Arizona in 1878. Looking for one last bonanza, Palmer arrived in Arizona Territory in 1879. Palmer left a footnote in Arizona history, as he was the man who laid out the original town of Tombstone. He visited Governor Frémont in Prescott, but it seems the visit was primarily a social one. Palmer died in 1882 in Oakland, California.

★ ★ ★

Hiram Reed, the first man freed by Gen. Frémont's orders of September 12, 1861, did not know Jessie Benton Frémont or the part she had played in his manumission. We are left to speculate that Reed and his crewmate Frank Lewis were freed because of John Frémont's fit of pique after the reception his wife had received at the White House on September 10. The timing suggests it was not the cause: Montgomery Blair and Gen. Meigs were well on their way to St. Louis to confront Frémont. But it is no matter why Reed and Lewis gained their freedom. What matters is that they did.

Veterans of integrated Thomas M. Gardner GAR Post 207, Nantucket, Massachusetts, including Private Hiram W. Reed of 5th Massachusetts Cavalry Regiment and Company E, 138th US Colored Troops Regiment, second row, third from right. Photograph by Henry S. Wager[?], 1894. Library of Congress, Prints and Photographs Division.

Hiram Reed carried away with him the order that John Frémont signed on September 12. His whereabouts over the next days or weeks is not known, but he could not stay in a slave state, which Missouri was in 1861. He could not move through any state that wasn't controlled by the Union army. In the eyes of the law, his order of manumission amounted to nothing but a pass through Union lines. Of all people, Joseph Palmer stepped into the gap in 1861, shepherding Reed to the safety of Palmer's former home of Nantucket island.

Over the course of the next 50 years, Reed made a life for himself on the island. First, though, he volunteered and served in the 5th Massachusetts Cavalry, which was intended to be the cavalry complement to the 54th and 55th Massachusetts regiments of Black infantrymen. Reed was present when Richmond fell in 1865. After the war, he joined the local post of the Grand Army of the Republic and occasionally served as one of its officers. He bought a house on Pleasant Street, 200 yards above Nantucket Harbor, and made a living as a teamster.

In 1865, Reed married Isabela Draper, who descended from the native Wampanoag Tribe of Nantucket. It's likely that Isabela was the last Wampanoag descendant to live on Nantucket island.[4] The couple were childless, and when Isabela died in 1882, 12,000 years of Wampanoag habitation on Nantucket came to an end.[5]

In 1910, a reporter from the *Boston Daily Globe* visited Nantucket to interview Reed. His Civil War story was generally known among his Nantucket neighbors, but many of the details were first revealed in the newspaper.

Hiram Reed passed away on June 19, 1911, three months shy of the 50th anniversary of the day John Frémont acknowledged his natural-born freedom.

ENDNOTES

1. The history of Jessie's loss of the Black Point property is laid out in full in an 1892 *Report of the US Senate Committee on Military Affairs.* "Report to accompany S. 3311, a bill to refer the claim of Jessie Benton Frémont to certain lands and the improvements thereon at Point San Jose...." (Government Printing Office, 1892).

2. William E. Parrish, *Frank Blair: Lincoln's Conservative* (University of Missouri Press, 1998), 284–285.

3. Carol Ferring Shepley, *Movers and Shakers, Scalawags and Suffragettes: Tales from Bellefontaine Cemetery* (Missouri History Museum Press, 2008), 29.

4. Frances Ruley Karttunen, "Nantucket's Last Indian?" *Yesterday's Island* magazine, May 23, 2013, https://yesterdaysisland.com/nantuckets-last-indian. See also Frances Ruley Karttunen, *The Other Islanders: People Who Pulled Nantucket's Oars* (Spinner Publications, 2005), 56.

5. Nantucket Historical Association, https://nha.org/research/nantucket-history/history-topic/native-peoples.

APPENDIX

First Confiscation Act

An Act to confiscate Property used for Insurrectionary Purposes.

Be it enacted by the Senate and House of Representatives of the United States of America in Congress assembled, That if, during the present or any future insurrection against the Government of the United States, after the President of the United States shall have declared, by proclamation, that the laws of the United States are opposed, and the execution thereof obstructed, by combinations too powerful to be suppressed by the ordinary course of judicial proceedings, or by the power vested in the marshals by law, any person or persons, his, her, or their agent, attorney, or employée, shall purchase or acquire, sell or give, any property of whatsoever kind or description, with intent to use or employ the same, or suffer the same to be used or employed, in aiding, abetting, or promoting such insurrection or resistance to the laws, or any person or persons engaged therein; or if any person or persons, being the owner or owners of any such property, shall knowingly use or employ, or consent to the use or employment of the same as aforesaid, all such property is hereby declared to be lawful subject of prize and capture wherever found; and it shall be the duty of the President of the United States to cause the same to be seized, confiscated, and condemned.

SEC. 2. And be it further enacted, That such prizes and capture shall be condemned in the district or circuit court of the United States having jurisdiction of the amount, or in admiralty in any district in which the same may be seized, or into which they may be taken and proceedings first instituted.

SEC. 3. And be it further enacted, That the Attorney-General, or any district attorney of the United States in which said property may at the time be, may institute the proceedings of condemnation, and in such case they shall be wholly for the benefit of the United States; or any person may file an information with such attorney, in which case the proceedings shall be for the use of such informer and the United States in equal parts.

SEC. 4. And be it further enacted, That whenever hereafter, during the present insurrection against the Government of the United States, any person claimed to be held to labor or service under the law of any State, shall be required or permitted by the person to whom such labor or service is claimed to be due, or by the lawful agent of such person, to take up arms against the United States, or shall be required or permitted by the person to whom such labor or service is claimed to be due, or his lawful agent, to work or to be employed in or upon any fort, navy yard, dock, armory, ship, entrenchment, or in any military or naval service whatsoever, against the Government and lawful authority of the United States, then, and in every such case, the person to whom such labor or service is claimed to be due shall forfeit his claim to such labor, any law of the State or of the United States to the contrary notwithstanding. And whenever thereafter the person claiming such labor or service shall seek to enforce his claim, it shall be a full and sufficient answer to such claim that the person whose service or labor is claimed had been employed in hostile service against the Government of the United States, contrary to the provisions of this act.

Approved August 6, 1861

John Frémont's Proclamation

St. Louis, August 30, 1861

Circumstances, in my judgment of sufficient urgency, render it necessary that the Commanding General of this Department should assume the administrative powers of the State. Its disorganized condition, the helplessness of the civil authority, the total insecurity of life, and the devastation of property by bands of murderers and marauders who infest nearly every county in the State and avail themselves of the public misfortunes and the vicinity of a hostile force to gratify private and neighborhood vengeance, and who find an enemy wherever they find plunder, finally demand the severest measure to repress the daily increasing crimes and outrages which are driving off the inhabitants and ruining the State. In this condition the public safety and the success of our arms require unity of purpose, without let or hindrance, to the prompt administration of affairs.

In order, therefore, to suppress disorders, to maintain as far as now practicable the public peace, and to give security and protection to the persons and property of loyal citizens, I do hereby extend, and declare established, martial law throughout the State of Missouri. The lines of the army of occupation in this State are for the present declared to extend from Leavenworth by way of the posts of Jefferson City, Rolla, and Ironton, to Cape Girardeau on the Mississippi River.

All persons who shall be taken with arms in their hands within these lines shall be tried by court-martial, and, if found guilty, will be shot. The property, real and personal, of all persons in the State of Missouri who shall take up arms against the United States, and who shall be directly proven to have taken active part with their enemies in the field, is declared to be confiscated to the public use; and their slaves, if any they have, are hereby declared free.

All persons who shall be proven to have destroyed, after the publication of this order, railroad tracks, bridges, or telegraphs, shall suffer the extreme penalty of the law.

All persons engaged in treasonable correspondence, in giving or procuring aid to the enemies of the United States, in disturbing the public tranquility by creating and circulating false reports or incendiary documents, are in their own interest warned that they are exposing themselves.

All persons who have been led away from their allegiance are required to return to their homes forthwith; any such absence without sufficient cause will be held to be presumptive evidence against them.

The object of this declaration is to place in the hands of the military authorities the power to give instantaneous effect to existing laws, and to supply such deficiencies as the conditions of war demand. But it is not intended to suspend the ordinary tribunals of the country, where the law will be administered by the civil officers in the usual manner and with their customary authority, while the same can be peaceably exercised.

The Commanding General will labor vigilantly for the public welfare, and in his efforts for their safety hopes to obtain not only the acquiescence, but the active support of the people of the country.

J. C. Frémont
United States Army, Western Department
Major-General Commanding

Frank Blair's Letter to Montgomery Blair

September 1, 1861

[Note: Typographical errors are original to the letter.]

DEAR JUDGE—I wrote you quite fully about our affairs here by Judge GAMBLE, and I am more and more convinced of the views I stated to you in that letter. Affairs are becoming quite alarming in the northern part of the State, as well as in the South. Men coming here to give information are not allowed to approach FRÉMONT, and go away in disgust.

I have felt it my duty to tell him what they say, and he throws himself behind the reports of his officers, who are trying to prevaricate and shield themselves for neglect of duty, and he still clings to them, and refuses to see for himself. I told him he would not escape responsibility in that way, and he would very soon find an army of rebels 10,000 strong on his hands in North Missouri, threatening St. Louis, and diverting his attention and occupying the forces he desired to use against McCULLOCH and PILLOW. He talks of the vigor he is going to use, but I can see none of it, and fear it will turn out to be some rash and inconsiderate move adopted in haste, to make head against a formidable force which could not have accumulated except through gross and inexcusable negligence. Oh, for one hour of our dead LYON. Many have been disposed to blame FRÉMONT for not sending reinforcements to LYON, and thus averting the calamities brought on by his death, and the abandonment of Springfield by his command. It is very certain that if he had sent the reinforcements to LYON that he took to Cairo, when it was supposed that place was threatened, LYON would have driven McCULLOCH from the State. I cannot say whether the attack was seriously contemplated on Cairo that time or not; but I am disposed to believe that the movement by McCULLOCH and PILLOW were intended to be simultaneous and cooperate, but LYON should have had some part of the reinforcements at any rate; and if he had received two regiments his victory would have been complete. I undertake to say, if FRÉMONT acted then as he does now, (I was away, and cannot speak on that head,) he could not have informed himself very accurately of the necessities of his position. The event shows that no attack was made on Cairo, and it was probably averted by the reinforcements sent. If the same, or one-half of the regiments, had been sent to LYON, we should have had equally satisfactory results.

The views I have given of this matter are fast becoming public opinion here, and I think the Government should know it. Probably you have information which will satisfy you that FRÉMONT was to blame. If so, the public here should know it also, in order that the confidence of the people should not be withheld from the Commanding General. I could not think, when I first returned here, that any part of the blame could rest with him, but my observations since have shaken my faith to the very foundation.

There is one point which I did not refer to in my letter, and which I intended to remark on, and that is the utter want of discipline in the camps round and about St. Louis. It is a rehersal of the state of affairs in Washington before the fight at Manassas, and will, I am apprehensive, conduce to similar results. I brought these matters to FRÉMONT's attention, but he put it aside by saying that it would not do to be too exacting at once. Our enemies at the door, and yet too early to impart discipline to our troops and keep them out of the whisky shops!! I know that you and I are both in some sort responsible for FRÉMONT's appointment, and for his being placed in command of this Department, and, therefore, I feel another and additional motive to speak out openly about these matters. My decided opinion is that he should be relieved of his command, and a man of ability put in his place—the sooner it is done the better.

I have given you my opinion and the ground for it. If the Government knows more of his plans than I know—if you are satisfied with them—then you can burn this paper, and say that I am an alarmist; you know, however, that I am not. No man has been more hopeful and confident than I have been up to within a few days past. I felt satisfied on my return that affairs were critical, but that the success and elation of the enemy could be turned to good account, if the proper steps were promptly taken. They have not been taken, and either the Government has failed to support FRÉMONT as he should have been, or he has failed to apply the means at his disposal. Affairs are worse than they were two weeks ago, and are getting worse every day. Secession increasing, Union men driven out, and the General, I fear, incapable of comprehending his position. His recent proclamation is the best thing of the kind that has been issued, but should have been issued when he first came, when he had the power to enforce, and the enemy no power to retaliate. Now they are substantially enforcing against us the substance of his proclamation outside of St. Louis and our garrisons. I want you to lay these things to your heart, and get ready to apply the remedy before it is too late.

I will write you again very soon. I hope I may have better news to give you. I shall be but too happy if any thing comes to restore my confidence in FRÉMONT. I am well—better than I have been for eight months.

Yours, affectionately,
Frank P. Blair

M. Jeff. Thompson's Proclamation

Camp Hunter, September 2, 1861

To all whom it may Concern:

Whereas, Major-General John C. Frémont, commanding the minions of Abraham Lincoln in the State of Missouri, has seen fit to declare martial law throughout the whole State, and has threatened to shoot any citizen-soldier found in arms within certain limits; also, to confiscate the property and free the negroes belonging to members of the Missouri State Guard:

Therefore, know ye, that I, M. Jeff. Thompson, Brigadier General of the first military district of Missouri, having not only the military authority of Brigadier General, but certain police powers, granted by acting Governor Thomas C. Reynolds, and confirmed afterward by Governor Jackson, do most solemnly promise that for every member of the Missouri State Guard, or soldier of our allies, the armies of the Confederate States, who shall be put to death in pursuance of the said order of General Frémont, that I will "hang, draw and quarter" a minion of said Abraham Lincoln.

While I am anxious that this unfortunate war should be conducted, as far as possible upon the most liberal principles of civilized warfare, and every order that I have issued has been with that object, yet, if this rule be abandoned (and it must first be done by our enemies,) I intend to exceed General Frémont in his excesses, and will make all tories that come within my power rue the day that a different policy was adopted by their leaders.

Already mills, barns, warehouses and other private property has been wastefully destroyed by the enemy in this district, while we have taken nothing except articles strictly contraband, or absolutely necessary. Should these things be repeated, I will retaliate tenfold, so help me God.

M. Jeff. Thompson,
Brigadier-General Commanding

Deed of Manumission of Hiram Reed

St. Louis, September 12, 1861

Whereas, Thomas L. Snead, of the city and county of St. Louis, State of Missouri, has been taking an active part with the enemies of the United States, in the present insurrectionary movement against the Government of the United States; now, therefore, I, John Charles Frémont, Major General commanding the Western Department of the Army of the United States, by authority of law, and the power vested in me as such Commanding General, declare Hiram Reed, heretofore held to service or labor by Thomas L. Snead, to be free, and forever discharged from the bonds of servitude, giving him full right and authority to have, use, and control his own labor or service as to him may seem proper, without any accountability whatever to said Thomas L. Snead, or any one to claim by, through, or under him.

And this deed of manumission shall be respected and treated by all persons, and in all courts of justice, as the full and complete evidence of the freedom of said Hiram Reed.

In testimony whereof, this act is done at Headquarters of the Western Department of the Army of the United States, in the city of St. Louis, State of Missouri, on this twelfth day of September, A.D. eighteen hundred and sixty-one, as is evidenced by the Departmental Seal, hereto affixed by my order.

John C. Frémont
United States Army, Western Department
Major-General Commanding

Telegram from Montgomery Blair
to President Abraham Lincoln,

September 14, 1861

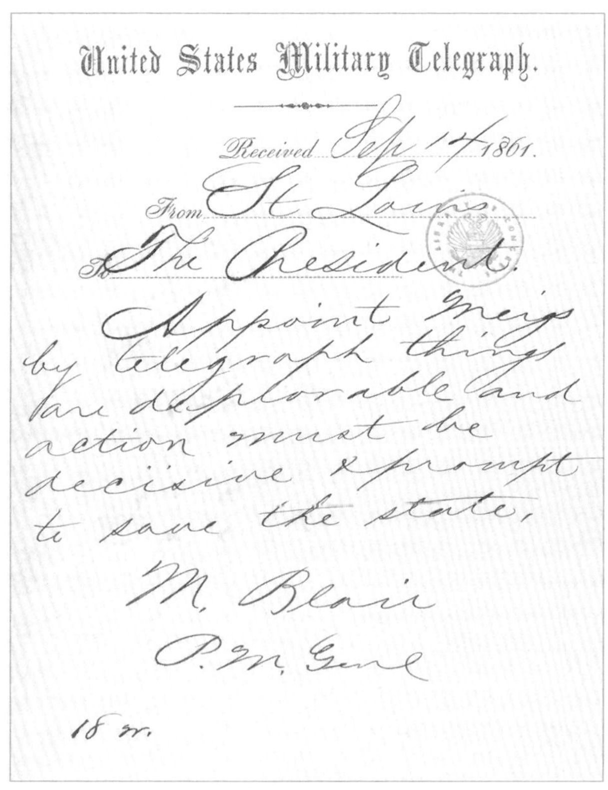

Library of Congress, Manuscript Division, Abraham Lincoln Papers.

Timeline of Fremont's 100 Days

July 25	▸ Gen. Frémont arrives in St. Louis	DAY 1
	▸ Thompson elected brigadier general of the Missouri State Guard	
	▸ McClellan promoted to command the Army of the Potomac	
July 28	▸ Confederate troops land at New Madrid	DAY 4
August 10	▸ Battle of Wilson's Creek; Gen. Lyon killed	DAY 17
August 18	▸ Thompson fires on ships plying the Mississippi River	DAY 24
August 30	▸ Frémont declares martial law throughout Missouri	DAY 36
	▸ Gen. Grant takes command in Cape Girardeau	
September 3	▸ Gen. Pillow invades Kentucky	DAY 40
	▸ Grant arrives in Cairo, Illinois	
September 4	▸ Prince Napoleon arrives in East St. Louis, Illinois	DAY 41
	▸ Gen. Sherman departs for Louisville, Kentucky	
September 10	▸ Jessie Frémont arrives at the White House	DAY 47
	▸ Blair and Meigs travel to St. Louis	
September 12	▸ Frémont issues orders freeing Reed and Lewis	DAY 49
September 20	▸ Col. Mulligan surrenders Lexington to Gen. Price	DAY 57
September 27	▸ Frémont departs St. Louis for Jefferson City	DAY 64
October 8	▸ Frémont departs Jefferson City for southwest Missouri	DAY 75
October 14	▸ Sec. Cameron arrives in St. Louis from Tipton	DAY 81
	▸ Wisconsin's Eagle Regiment lands in Missouri	
October 21	▸ Battle of Fredericktown	DAY 88
	▸ Battle of Ball's Bluff (Virginia)	
	▸ Frémont is delayed at Warsaw	
October 25	▸ Zagonyi's charge in Springfield	DAY 92
November 1	▸ McClellan promoted to army general in chief	DAY 99
November 2	▸ Frémont relieved of command	DAY 100

PORTRAIT CREDITS

Figure 1: Major General John C. Frémont. Photograph by J. A. Scholten, 1861. Missouri Historical Society Collections.

Figure 2: Chester Harding Jr. Unknown artist and date. Wikimedia Commons.

Figure 3: Lieutenant Colonel Camille Ferri-Pisani. Hand-colored daguerreotype by Mathew Brady, 1861. Digital image courtesy of Getty's Open Content Program.

Figure 4: Jessie Benton Frémont. Carte de visite by E. and H. Anthony, New York, ca. 1863. Missouri Historical Society Collections.

Figure 5: Elizabeth "Lizzie" Blair Lee and her son Blair. Unknown photographer, 1861. Courtesy of Princeton University Library.

Figure 6: Major General William Tecumseh Sherman. Unknown photographer, 1861–1865. Missouri Historical Society Collections.

Figure 7: Journalist Franc Bangs Wilkie. Photograph by Charles D. Mosher, unknown date. Chicago History Museum.

Figure 8: Simon Cameron. Photograph by Anthony Edward and Matthew Brady, New York, 1861. Library of Congress, Prints and Photographs Division.

Figure 9: William Dorsheimer. From *Geschichte der Deutschen in Buffalo und Erie County, N.Y.*, 1898. Wikimedia Commons.

Figure 10: Major Justus McKinstry. Unknown photographer, 1861–1865. Library of Congress, Prints and Photographs Division.

Figure 11: Frank Blair Jr. Photograph by J. Gurney and Son, New York, 1861–1865. Missouri Historical Society Collections.

ACKNOWLEDGMENTS

I decided years ago to lay down my thoughts about John and Jessie Frémont and their days in Civil War Missouri. Even more daunting than the task I faced in 2018 is the task before me now: to give thanks, in this limited space, to the legions of people and organizations that have assisted me in this endeavor. I cannot thank everyone, and those whom I acknowledge here I cannot thank enough. At the top: the professional team of editors, designers, archivists, and others at the Missouri Historical Society who shepherded my rough-hewn manuscript through the process of publication.

Thanks to my colleagues at the National US Grant Trail Association, many of whom are authors themselves: Whit McCoskrie of Fulton, Missouri; Jim Erwin of Crestwood, Missouri; Curt Fields of Collierville, Tennessee; and Michael E. Banasik of Johnston, Iowa. As first among these equals, I acknowledge Mike Banasik for his *The Civil War Letters of Franc B. Wilkie.* For me, Wilkie "wrote the script" for the military aspects in this book, and his dark but delightful humor allowed me to avoid using my own sense of humor to tell what is a deadly serious story. Thanks, Mike.

To my wife of 49 years, the former Debra Dorsey of Brooklyn, New York, and to my sons, Alex Wolk and Adam Wolk: Thanks for giving me the time and occasional periods of solitude to carry this book to fruition.

The following repositories of knowledge, and their able staff members, contributed greatly to this endeavor: The archives of the Missouri Historical Society, the Nantucket (MA) Historical Association, and the Ulysses S. Grant National Historic Site in St. Louis County. For online resources, the images that are made available to the public by the Becker Collection are extraordinary and have inspired a major theme of the book. Lastly, and of course, I owe a debt to the online resources of the US National Archives.

Thanks also to the Missouri Humanities Council and the Soldiers Memorial Military Museum in St. Louis for their decade-long support for the annual US Grant Symposium—an obsession of mine that Missouri's Civil War Heritage Foundation launched in 2014.

BIBLIOGRAPHY

Anderson, Galusha. *The Story of a Border City during the Civil War.* Little, Brown and Company, 1908.

Banasik, Michael E., ed. *Confederate Tales of the War in the Trans-Mississippi, Part 1: 1861.* Press of the Camp Pope Bookshop, 2010.

Banasik, Michael E., ed. *Missouri in 1861: The Civil War Letters of Franc B. Wilkie, Newspaper Correspondent.* Press of the Camp Pope Bookshop, 2001.

Bancroft, Hubert H. *History of California: Vol. 24, 1860–1890.* The History Company, 1890.

Basler, Roy P., ed. *The Collected Works of Abraham Lincoln.* Rutgers University Press, 1953.

Beale, Howard K., ed. *The Diary of Edward Bates, 1859–1866.* Government Printing Office, 1933.

Bearss, Edwin C. *The Battle of Wilson's Creek.* Wilson's Creek National Battlefield Foundation, 1992.

Browne, Junius Henri. *Four Years in Secessia: Adventures within and beyond the Union Lines.* O. D. Case and Company, 1865.

Carroll, Thomas F. "Freedom of Speech and of the Press during the Civil War." *Virginia Law Review* 9, no. 7 (May 1923).

Castel, Albert. *General Sterling Price and the Civil War in the West.* Louisiana State University Press, 1968.

Catton, Bruce. *The Coming Fury.* Doubleday & Company, 1961.

Catton, Bruce. *Grant Moves South.* Little, Brown and Company, 1960.

Christensen, Lawrence O., William Foley, Gary Kremer, eds. *Dictionary of Missouri Biography.* University of Missouri Press, 1999.

Colton, Kenneth E., ed. "With Frémont in Missouri in 1861: Letters of Samuel Ryan Curtis." *Annals of Iowa* 24 (1942).

Cozzens, Peter. *General John Pope: A Life for the Nation.* University of Illinois Press, 2000.

Craig, Berry. *Kentucky Confederates: Secession, Civil War, and the Jackson Purchase.* The University Press of Kentucky, 2014.

Crane, James L. "Grant as a Colonel, Conversations between Grant and His Chaplain." *McClure's Magazine* 7 (June 1896).

Denton, Sally. *Passion and Principle: John and Jessie Frémont, the Couple Whose Power, Politics, and Love Shaped Nineteenth-Century America.* Bloomsbury Publishing, 2007.

Diary of the Paymaster of Frémont's Body Guard, dated November 29, 1861. Including transcription by J. Kaufman and D. Northcott, Missouri Historical Society Collections.

Dinges, Bruce J. and Shirley A. Leckie, eds. *A Just and Righteous Cause: Benjamin H. Grierson's Civil War Memoir.* Southern Illinois University Press, 2016.

Dorsey, Florence L. *Master of the Mississippi.* Houghton Mifflin Co., 1941.

Dorsheimer, William. "Frémont's Hundred Days in Missouri, Part 1." *Atlantic Monthly* 9, no. 51 (January 1862).

Dorsheimer, William. "Frémont's Hundred Days in Missouri, Part 2." *Atlantic Monthly* 9, no. 52 (February 1862).

Dorsheimer, William. "Frémont's Hundred Days in Missouri, Part 3." *Atlantic Monthly* 9, no. 53 (March 1862).

Duhse, R. J. "Last Cruise of the SS *Central America.*" *Naval History* 4, no. 1 (January 1990).

Duke, Basil W. *The Civil War Reminiscences of General Basil W. Duke, C.S.A.* Doubleday, Page & Co., 1911.

Encyclopedia Dubuque. "Wilkie, Franc." Last modified October 1, 2024. https://www.encyclopediadubuque. org/index.php/WILKIE,_Franc.

Erwin, James W. *Guerrillas in Civil War Missouri.* The History Press, 2012.

Flower, Frank A. *Old Abe, the Eighth Wisconsin War Eagle.* Curran and Bowen, 1885.

Fracchia, Charles A. "Melville in San Francisco." *The Book Club of California Quarterly News-Letter* 42 (Spring 1977).

Frémont, Jessie Benton. *The Story of the Guard: A Chronicle of the War.* Ticknor and Fields, 1863.

Gibbons, Israel. *Crescent-Shine: Or, Gleams of Light on All Sorts of Subjects from the Columns of the* New Orleans Crescent. J. O. Nixon, 1866.

Gibson, Campbell. *American Demographic History Chartbook: 1790 to 2010.* http://demographicchartbook. com.

Goodsell, Leo J. "Leonidas Polk." In *Tennessee Encyclopedia.* University of Tennessee Press, 1998.

Grant, Ulysses S. *Personal Memoirs of Ulysses S. Grant.* Charles L. Webster & Company, 1885.

Grant, Ulysses S. *Selected Letters, 1839–1865.* Literary Classics of the United States, 1990.

Harris, Brayton. *Blue & Gray in Black & White: Newspapers in the Civil War.* Potomac Books, 1999.

Harrison, Lowell H. *The Civil War in Kentucky.* The University Press of Kentucky, 2009.

Hazelton, Joseph Powers. *Scouts, Spies, and Heroes of the Great Civil War.* N. G. Hamilton & Co., 1892.

Herr, Pamela. "Permutations of a Marriage: John Charles and Jessie Benton Frémont's Civil War Alliance." In *Intimate Strategies of the Civil War: Military Commanders and Their Wives,* edited by Carol K. Bleser and Lesley J. Gordon. Oxford University Press, 2001.

Herr, Pamela and Mary Lee Spence, eds. *The Letters of Jessie Benton Frémont.* University of Illinois Press, 1993.

History of St. Charles, Montgomery and Warren Counties, Missouri. National Historical Company, 1885.

Holcomb, R. I., ed. *History of Greene County, Missouri.* Western Historical Co., 1883.

Hollingsworth, John Hampton. *The Battle of Blackwell.* Two Trails Publishing, 2007.

Hughes, Nathaniel Cheairs, Jr. *The Battle of Belmont: Grant Strikes South.* University of North Carolina Press, 1991.

Hughes, Nathaniel Cheairs, Jr. *General William J. Hardee: Old Reliable.* Louisiana State University Press, 1992.

Inskeep, Steve. *Imperfect Union: How Jessie and John Frémont Mapped the West, Invented Celebrity, and Helped Cause the Civil War.* Penguin Press, 2020.

Karamanski, Theodore J., Eileen M. McMahon, eds. *Civil War Chicago: Eyewitness to History.* Ohio University Press, 2014.

Karttunen, Frances Ruley. "Nantucket's Last Indian?" *Yesterday's Island,* May 23, 2013.

Keller, Rudi. *Life During Wartime, Vol. 1.* Tribune Publishing Company, 2012.

Knox, Thomas W. *Boy's Life of General Grant.* The Werner Co., 1899.

Laas, Virginia Jeans, ed. *Wartime Washington: The Civil War Letters of Elizabeth Blair Lee.* University of Illinois Press, 1991.

Library of Congress. Biographic summary for Leonidas Polk. Accessed October 14, 2024. https://www.loc.gov/item/2021669718.

"Martial Law Proclaimed in St. Louis." *New York Times,* August 15, 1861.

McCoskrie, Joseph W. *The War for Missouri: 1861–1862.* The History Press, 2020.

McKenney, T. I. Letter to J. McCan Davis dated November 16, 1898. Ida M. Tarbell Collection of Allegheny College. Accessed November 9, 2022. https://dspace.allegheny.edu/handle/10456/30250.

Melcher, S. H. Letter to Martin J. Hubble dated August 17, 1910. In *Personal Reminiscences and Fragments of the Early History of Springfield and Greene County, Missouri.* Inland Printing Co., 1914. Accessed October 10, 2024. https://thelibrary.org/lochist/history/reminis/lyon.html.

Mero, Bill. "The Looting of California: Bankers, Corruption and Theft." Contra Costa County Historical Society. https://www.cocohistory.org/essays/the-looting-of-california-bankers-corruption-and-theft.

Miller, Edward A. "VMI Men Who Wore Yankee Blue, 1861–1865." *VMI Alumni Review* (Spring 1996).

Missouri State Archinves. Introduction to Benjamin Gratz Brown Papers. Accessed October 10, 2024. https://www.sos.mo.gov/archives/mdh_splash/default.asp?coll=brown.

Monaghan, Jay. *Civil War on the Western Border, 1854–1865.* Bonanza Books, 1955.

Mudd, Joseph A. *With Porter in North Missouri.* The National Publishing Company, 1909.

Mueller, Doris Land. *M. Jeff Thompson: Missouri's Swamp Fox of the Confederacy.* University of Missouri Press, 2007.

National Park Service. "Civil War Defenses of Washington: The Civil War Years." Last updated October 29, 2004. https://npshistory.com/publications/cwdw/hrs/chap4-1.htm.

National Register of Historic Places. "Fort D, Cape Girardeau, Missouri, National Register #100004219." Accessed October 10, 2024. https://npgallery.nps.gov/AssetDetail/NRIS/100004219.

National Register of Historic Places. "Maclay Mansion, Tipton, Missouri, National Register #79001383." Accessed November 6, 2024. https://mostateparks.com/sites/mostateparks/files/Maclay%20Mansion.pdf.

Nevins, Allan. *Frémont: Pathmarker of the West.* University of Nebraska Press, 1939.

Nevins, Allan. *The War for the Union, Vol. 1: The Improvised War, 1861–1862.* Charles Scribner's Sons, 1959.

Official Records of the Union and Confederate Armies, Ser. 1, Vol. 3, Ch. 10. "Operations in Missouri, Arkansas, Kansas, and the Indian Territory, May 10–November 19, 1861." Government Printing Office, 1881.

Official Records of the Union and Confederate Armies, Ser. 1, Vol. 7, Ch. 17. "Operations in Kentucky, Tennessee, North Alabama, and Southwest Virginia. November 19, 1861–March 4, 1862." Government Printing Office, 1881.

Page, James A. "The Story of 'Old Abe,' Famous Wisconsin War Eagle on 101st Airborne Division Patch." November 15, 2012. article/91178/the_story_of_old_abe_famous_wisconsin_war_eagle_on_101st_airborne_division_patch.

Parrish, William E. *Frank Blair: Lincoln's Conservative.* University of Missouri Press, 1998.

Peckham, James. *Gen. Nathaniel Lyon and Missouri in 1861.* American News Company, 1866.

Phillips, Christopher. *Damned Yankee: The Life of General Nathaniel Lyon.* University of Missouri Press, 1990.

Plum, William R. *The Military Telegraph during the Civil War in the United States.* McClurg & Company, 1882.

Potter, Marguerite. "Hamilton R. Gamble, Missouri's War Governor." *Missouri Historical Review* 35, no. 1 (October 1940).

Primm, James Neal. *Lion of the Valley.* Missouri Historical Society Press, 1998.

Randolph, Lyle. "Dunklin County during the Civil War." *Delta Dunklin Democrat,* September 25, 2011.

Rather, Lois. *Jessie Frémont at Black Point.* Rather Press, 1974.

Report of the Joint Committee on the Conduct of the War, Part 3. Government Printing Office, 1863.

Richardson, Albert D. *The Secret Service, the Field, the Dungeon, and the Escape.* American Publishing Company, 1865.

Rolle, Andrew. *John Charles Frémont: Character as Destiny.* University of Oklahoma Press, 1991.

Rombauer, Robert J. *The Union Cause in St. Louis in 1861.* Nixon-Jones Printing Co., 1909.

Scharf, John Thomas. *History of Saint Louis City and County, From the Earliest Periods to the Present Day: Including Biographical Sketches of Representative Men.* L. H. Everts and Co., 1883.

Shanks, John P. C. "Vindication of Major General John C. Frémont, Against the Attacks of the Slave Power and its Allies." Speech, Washington, DC, March 4, 1862. Library of Congress. https://www.loc.gov/item/10029591.

Shepley, Carol Ferring. *Movers and Shakers, Scalawags and Suffragettes: Tales from Bellefontaine Cemetery.* Missouri History Museum Press, 2008.

Sherman, William T. *Memoirs of General William T. Sherman.* D. Appleton & Company, 1891.

Shillingberg, Wm. B. *Tombstone, A. T.: A History of Early Mining, Milling, and Mayhem.* University of Oklahoma Press, 2016.

Shumate, Albert. *The Notorious I. C. Woods.* Arthur H. Clark Co., 1986.

Simon, John Y., ed. *The Papers of Ulysses S. Grant, Vol. 2: April–September 1861.* Southern Illinois University Press, 1969.

Snead, Thomas L. *The Fight for Missouri: From the Election of Lincoln to the Death of Lyon.* J. J. Little & Co., 1886.

Spence, Mary Lee. "George W. Wright: Politician, Lobbyist, Entrepreneur." *Pacific Historical Review* 58 (August 1989).

Straight, David. "The Iowa Boys Winter in St. Louis, 1861–1862." *The Confluence* 2, no. 2 (Spring/Summer 2011).

Tap, Bruce. "Amateurs at War: Abraham Lincoln and the Committee on the Conduct of the War." *Journal of the Abraham Lincoln Association* 23, no. 2 Summer (2002).

Tarbell, Ida M. *The Life of Abraham Lincoln, Vol. 2.* Doubleday, Page & Co., 1909.

Trollope, Anthony. *North America.* Chapman & Hall, 1862.

Tucher, Andie. "Reporting for Duty: The Bohemian Brigade, the Civil War, and the Social Construction of the Reporter." *Book History* 9 (2006).

United States Congress. *The Statutes at Large and Treaties of the United States of America, from December 5, 1859, to March 3, 1863. With References to the Matter of Each Act and to the Subsequent Acts on the Same Subject, Vol. 12.* Little, Brown and Company, 1863.

Vasvary, Edmund. *Lincoln's Hungarian Heroes: The Participation of Hungarians in the Civil War, 1861–1865.* The Hungarian Reformed Federation of America, 1939.

Victor, Orville J. *The History, Civil, Political and Military, of the Southern Rebellion.* James D. Torrey, 1861.

Wilkie, Franc B. *Pen and Powder.* Ticknor and Company, 1888.

Williams, John Melvin. *The Eagle Regiment, 8th Wisconsin Infantry Volunteers.* The Recorder Printing, 1890.

Wilson, James Harrison. *The Life of John A. Rawlins.* Neale Publishing Company, 1916.

Winks, Robin W. *Frederick Billings: A Life.* University of California Press, 1991.

Winslow, Helen L. "Nantucket Forty-Niners." *Historic Nantucket* 4, no. 3 (January 1956).

Wolk, Gregory. *A Tour Guide to Missouri's Civil War: Friend and Foe Alike.* Monograph Publishing, 2020.

Wurthman, Leonard B., Jr. "Frank Blair: Lincoln's Congressional Spokesman." *Missouri Historical Review* 64, no. 3 (April 1970).

INDEX

ABOUT THE AUTHOR

Gregory Wolk is a retired civil trial lawyer and a graduate of the New York University School of Law (JD 1975). During the time he practiced law, he also served as the executive director of Missouri's Civil War Heritage Foundation, an organization responsible for placing interpretive panels and producing travel maps that contributed to the state's commemoration of the 150th anniversary of the Civil War (2011–2015). In retirement, Greg was for a time a program coordinator for the Missouri Humanities Council, and he currently serves on the board of directors of the National US Grant Trail Association. Greg is the author of numerous articles about personalities and events of the Civil War in Missouri, and most notably is a regular contributor to *Missouri Humanities* magazine. His first book-length history of the Civil War, *Friend and Foe Alike: A Tour Guide to Missouri's Civil War*, tells the stories of 237 Civil War sites across the state. It was published in 2010, and a revised edition was reissued in 2012. Greg has been a public speaker since 2006. His passion is fueled in part by family history: Greg's great-great-grandfather was a private in Ulysses Grant's own 21st Illinois Infantry when Grant entered Missouri in July 1861.